Study Guide

for

Jurmain/Nelson/Kilgore/Trevathan's

Essentials of Physical Anthropology

Fourth Edition

Study Guide

for

Jurmain/Nelson/Kilgore/Trevathan's

Essentials of Physical Anthropology

Fourth Edition

Marcus Young Owl
California State University, Long Beach

Denise Cucurny
California State University, Long Beach

WADSWORTH

THOMSON LEARNING

Australia • Canada • Mexico • Singapore • Spain • United Kingdom • United States

ISBN 0-534-57818-7

For more information, contact
Wadsworth/Thomson Learning
10 Davis Drive
Belmont, CA 94002-3098
USA

For more information about our products, contact us:
Thomson Learning Academic Resource Center
1-800-423-0563
http://www.wadsworth.com

International Headquarters
Thomson Learning
International Division
290 Harbor Drive, 2nd Floor
Stamford, CT 06902-7477
USA

UK/Europe/Middle East/South Africa
Thomson Learning
Berkshire House
168-173 High Holborn
London WC1V 7AA
United Kingdom

Asia
Thomson Learning
60 Albert Complex, #15-01
Singapore 189969

Canada
Nelson Thomson Learning
1120 Birchmount Road
Toronto, Ontario M1K 5G4
Canada

ACKNOWLEDGEMENTS

The development and composition of this study guide not only entailed the work of the authors, but also the patience of our families. We would like to thank our families for their understanding while we secluded ourselves to produce this study guide.

Marcus Young Owl
Departments of Anthropology and Biological Sciences
California State University, Long Beach

Denise Cucurny
Department of Anthropology
California State University Long Beach

PREFACE

The subject matter of physical anthropology has always been fascinating to us. However, we would be the first to admit that it is not easy to study for. Students often see the word *anthropology* and think "social science." Physical anthropology's direct historical roots are from anatomy (indeed, the American Association of Physical Anthropologists was formed at the 1931 meetings of the American Anatomical Association.) Thus, you need to approach the study of physical anthropology as you would any other life science such as biology or anatomy and physiology. Like the textbooks in those disciplines, physical anthropology texts are information intensive.

A study guide is intended to guide you in your study so that you learn efficiently. This study guide is designed to make you become an interactive learner rather than a passive learner. This study guide will require you to write down key words as you proceed through a chapter. The act of writing down a word not only focuses you on the subject, but also reinforces the ideas being dealt with.

The chapters in this study guide correspond to the chapters in the textbook, *Essentials of Physical Anthropology, Fourth Edition*, by Jurmain, Nelson, Kilgore and Trevathan. The study guide begins with a list of **objectives**. You should look at these objectives and then read the corresponding chapter in the text.

After reading the chapter return to the study guide and go to the **fill-in outline**. The fill-in outline will walk you through the chapter systematically in the order that the material appears in the text chapter. Fill in the blanks as you proceed through this section. Upon completion of the fill-in outline look up the answers in the back of the study guide chapter. Note which questions you got correct without guessing and those answers that you missed. This will give you a good indication of the areas that you are weak in. Redo these sections.

The next section of the study guide is **key terms**. Your study of physical anthropology will introduce you to many new words. Studies have actually shown that science students learn as many new words in a course as a student taking a foreign language course. Many terms are defined in the margins of your text. There is also a glossary at the end of the textbook. Many of these key terms are also repeated in this study guide, many rephrased so that you get a different perspective. Some of the key terms in the study guide were not defined in the text, but it was felt it would be of value to elucidate them in the study guide.

The next two sections of the study guide, **fill-in questions** and **multiple-choice questions**, will provide you review and reinforcement. You should view these two sections as practice tests. There is a certain amount of repetition between the two types of tests and this will help to reinforce the content of the text. The multiple-choice questions will sometimes require you to apply the information you have learned to a new situation. This is entirely fair and your course instructor may expect the same of you. The answers are at the end of the study guide chapters. Answers for fill-ins and multiple-choice questions also include a page reference. If you did poorly on certain questions re-read the pages in the text that you are referred to.

Master the content. You should set a goal of learning 90% of the material before you go on to the next chapter. Review previous chapters weekly. If you do this you should be well prepared when the date of your course's exams comes. The study guide can direct you in your study, but ultimately you are responsible for learning the material. Do not wait until just before the test to study or you will be overwhelmed with the amount of material that you must assimilate.

TABLE OF CONTENTS

Study Guide

for

Jurmain/Nelson/Kilgore/Trevathan's

Essentials of Physical Anthropology

Fourth Edition

CHAPTER 1
INTRODUCTION TO PHYSICAL ANTHROPOLOGY

LEARNING OBJECTIVES

After reading this chapter you should be able to:
- Define the word hominid (p. 2)
- Define biocultural evolution (p. 6)
- Discuss what the subject matter of anthropology is (p. 6)
- Identify the four main subfields of anthropology (pp. 6-9)
- Identify the main research areas within physical anthropology (pp. 9-13)
- Describe the method by which scientists attempt to understand the world (pp. 13-14)
- Understand the steps involved in analyzing a situation scientifically (pp. 13-14)

Fill-in Outline

Introduction

Anthropology is the scientific discipline that has the human species as its subject matter. Anthropologists study all aspects of the human species including our biology (from an evolutionary perspective)

I. INTRODUCTION

A. Humans belong to the taxonomic family _hominidae_.
   1. A critical feature of hominids is that they are _bipedally_, by which we mean that hominids walk on two legs.
   2. Humans are also members of the Order _Primate_, the group of mammals that includes prosimians, monkeys and apes, as well as humans.

B. Physical anthropologists, also known as biological anthropologists, focus largely on the study of human _evolution_, _variation_ and _adaptation_.
   1. Physical anthropologists study human biology from an _____ perspective.
   2. Most human biologists approach the study of humans from a clinical perspective.

C. Human evolution must consider the influence of _____ on the development of our species.
   1. Culture is the strategy by which humans _adapt_ to the natural environment.
      a. It includes _technologies_ ranging from simple stone tools to computers.
      b. It also includes _Subsistence_ _patterns_ ranging from hunting and gathering to agribusiness.
   2. Other aspects of culture include religion, social values, social organization, language, kinship, marriage rules, and gender roles, among others.

3. An important property of culture is that it is ___learned___, not biologically inherited.
D. Humans, as biological organisms, are subject to the same ___evolutionary___ forces as all other species.
   1. Evolution is a ___change___ in genetic makeup of a population from one generation to the next.
   2. Evolution can be defined and studied at two different levels.
      a. At the ___species___ level (microevolution), there are genetic changes within the population. This type of evolution does not result in the formation of a new species.
      b. At the _____ level (macroevolution), the result is the appearance of a new species.
E. Biocultural Evolution
   1. Over the vast time of human evolution, the role of culture has increasingly assumed importance.
   2. Over time, biology and culture have interacted in such a way that we say that humans are the result of ___biocultural___ evolution.

II. WHAT IS ANTHROPOLOGY?
A. Anthropology is the scientific study of ___human___ .
B. Anthropology is a multidisciplinary field in that it _____ the findings of many disciplines, including sociology, economics, history, psychology, and biology.
C. In the United States anthropology consists of three main subfields:
   1. ___cultural___ or ___social___
   2. ___archaeology___
   3. ___physical___ or ___biological___
   4. Some universities include ___linguistic___ as a fourth area of anthropology.

III. CULTURAL ANTHROPOLOGY
A. Cultural anthropology is the study of all aspects of ___human behavior___.
B. The recorded description of traditional lifestyles is called an ___ethnography___
C. Ethnographic accounts formed the basis for ___comparative studies___ studies which broadened the context within which cultural anthropologists studied human behavior and enabled them to formulate theories about the fundamental aspects of human behavior.
D. The focus of cultural anthropology has shifted over the twentieth century. Some of the new subfields of cultural anthropology include
   1. ___urban___ anthropology which deals with issues of inner cities.
   2. ___medical___ anthropology explores the relationship between various cultural attributes and health and disease.
   3. ___economic___ anthropology is concerned with factors that influence the distribution of goods and resources within and between cultures.
E. Many of the subfields of anthropology have a practical application, this type of anthropology is called ___applied___ .

IV. ARCHEOLOGY

A. _archaeology_ is the discipline that studies and interprets material remains recovered from earlier cultures.

B. Archeologists are concerned with culture, but obtain their information from _artifacts_ and other _material_ _culture_, rather than from living people.

C. Archeology is aimed at answering specific questions.

   1. _excavation_ is conducted for the purpose of gaining information about human behavior, not simply for the artifacts present at a site.

   2. By identifying human behavior patterns on a larger scale, archeologists attempt to recognize behaviors shared by all human groups, or _commonalities_

V. LINGUISTIC ANTHROPOLOGY

A. The field that studies the origin of language, as well as specific languages, is _Linguistic_ _anthropology_.

B. Linguistic anthropologists also examine the relationship between culture and language. These include:

   1. how members of a society _perceive_ phenomena.

   2. how the use of language shapes perceptions in different _cultures_

C. The spontaneous _acquisition_ and _use_ of language is a unique human characteristic. Research in this area may have implications for the evolution of language skills in humans, making this area of research of interest for physical anthropologists.

VI. PHYSICAL ANTHROPOLOGY

A. _Physical_ _anthropology_ is the study of human biology within the framework of evolution. Many physical anthropologists emphasize the interaction between _biology_ and _culture_.

B. Physical anthropology is divided into a number of subfields. Some of these are:

   1. Paleoanthropology, which is the study of _human_ _evolution_

      a. Paleoanthropology focuses particularly on the _____ _____

      b. The ultimate goal of paleoanthropology is to identify and establish a time sequence among the early _hominid_ _species_.

   2. Human variation is a field which looks at observable physical variation in humans.

      a. This field was prominent in the nineteenth century

      b. Techniques used to measure human physical variation are still used today and are called _Anthropometry_.

   3. _Genetics_ is the field which studies gene structure and action as well as the patterns of inheritance.

      a. Genetics is crucial to the study of _physical_ _Anthropology_.

      b. Genetics can help anthropologists investigate the _evolutionary_ _distance_ between living primate species.

   4. _Primatology_ is the discipline that studies nonhuman primates.

a. The ___declining___ number of primates species in their natural environments has placed a greater urgency on the study of these animals.

b. Because primates are humanity's closest ___relatives___, anthropologists feel that the study of these animals can shed light on our own behavior and other aspects of our biology.

5. ___Primate___ ___paleontology___ is the study of the primate fossil record.

6. The field which studies skeletal biology and is central to physical anthropology is ___Osteology___.

a. The subdiscipline of osteology that studies disease and trauma in archeologically derived populations is ___Paleopathology___.

b. ___Forensic___ ___anthropology___ is a field directly related to osteology and paleopathology. It applies the techniques of anthropology to law.

7. Many physical anthropologists specialize in ___genetics___, the study of structure.

VII. PHYSICAL ANTHROPOLOGY AND THE SCIENTIFIC METHOD

A. Science is a process of understanding phenomena through ___observation___, ___generalization___ and ___verification___.

1. Scientists rely on experimentation and/or observation. This is referred to as an ___empirical___ approach, which is part of the scientific method.

2. As scientists, physical anthropologists must adhere to the ___scientific___ method, whereby a research problem is identified, and information is subsequently gathered in order to solve it.

B. The gathering of information is referred to as ___data___ collection.

1. An approach should be used in which the investigator can describe precisely their techniques and results in a manner that facilitates ___comparisons___ with the work of others.

2. In physical anthropology, data is usually expressed ___numerically___, or quantitatively.

C. Once facts have been established, scientists attempt to explain them.

1. A ___hypothesis___, a provisional explanation of phenomena, is developed.

a. Before a hypothesis can be accepted, it must be ___tested___ by means of data collection and analysis.

b. The testing of hypotheses with the possibility of proving them ___false___ is the very basis of the scientific method.

2. If a hypothesis cannot be demonstrated to be false, it is accepted as a ___theory___.

a. A theory is a statement of relationships that has a firm basis as demonstrated through testing and through the accumulation of evidence.

b. A theory should also ___predict___ how new facts may fit into the established pattern.

D. Bias
    1. Scientific method permits various types of _*bias*_ to be addressed and controlled.
    2. Bias occurs in _*ALL*_ studies due to many different factors.
    3. Science is an approach used to _*eliminate*_ bias.

KEY TERMS

adaptation: functional response of organisms or populations to the environment.

anthropology: the scientific discipline that studies all aspects of the human species.

anthropometry: the measurement of the human body.

archeology: the discipline of anthropology that interprets past cultures through their material remains which are recovered through excavation.

artifacts: objects that have been modified or, in some other way, used by ancient humans.

biocultural evolution: the interaction between biology and culture in human evolution.

bipedal: walking habitually on two legs as in humans and ground birds.

cultural anthropology: the area within anthropology that focuses on the study of human behavior.

culture: the behavior aspects of humans, including their technology and institutions, which is learned and transmitted between generations.

ethnography: the study of human societies.

forensic anthropology: the field that applies the techniques of anthropology to the law. This usually refers to the techniques used by osteologists and sometimes archeology: the discipline within anthropology which recovers, through excavation, the material culture of past populations of humans.

genetics: the study of gene structure and action, and the patterns of inheritance of traits.

hominidae: the taxonomic family that humans belong to.

hominid: a member of the family hominidae.

linguistic anthropology: the area within anthropology that studies the origins and cultural perceptions and uses of language.

material culture: the physical remains of human cultural activity.

osteology: the study of skeletal biology. Human osteology focuses on the interpretation of the skeletal remains of past populations.

paleoanthropology: the subdiscipline within physical anthropology which studies human evolution.

paleopathology: the branch of osteology that studies the evidence of disease and injury in human skeletal remains.

primate: a member of the mammalian Order Primates. Primates include lemurs, bushbabies, monkeys, apes, and humans.

primatology: the study of the mammalian Order Primates. Humans are members of this order.

species: a group of interbreeding organisms that produce fertile offspring and are reproductively isolated from other such groups.

Fill-In Questions

1. The taxonomic family to which humans belong to is the family ___Hominidae___ .

2. A critical trait to classifying a primate fossil as a hominid is that they walk on two legs. Walking on two legs is referred to as walking ___Bipedal___ .

3. A ___species___ is a group of interbreeding organisms that produce fertile offspring and are reproductively isolated from other such groups.

4. ___Physical___ ___antropology___ is the study of human biology from an evolutionary perspective.

5. The strategy by which humans adapt to their natural environment is ___biocultural___ .

6. ___Evolution___ is a change in the genetic makeup of a population from one generation to the next.

7. The human predisposition to assimilate a particular culture and to function within it is influenced by biological factors. Culture has assumed more and more importance over the course of human evolution. This interaction between biology and culture is referred to as ___Biocultural___ ___evolution___ .

8. The scientific discipline whose subject matter is the study of humankind is ___anthropology___ .

9. The discipline of anthropology that studies human societies, and produces ethnographies, is ___cultural anthropology___ anthropology.

10. Archeologists study ___material___ ___remains___ .

11. Remains left behind, and recovered by excavation, are called ___artefacts___ .

12. An area within archeology that evaluates archeological sites that are threatened by development is called ___cultural___ ___resource___ ___management___

13. An anthropologist who is interested in the origins of human language would be a(n) ___Linguistic___ anthropologist.

14. An anthropologist who studies human evolutionary biology is a(n) ___physical___ anthropologist.

15. The ultimate goal of paleoanthropology is to identify and establish the relationship of the various early ___human___ species and to gain insights into their adaptation and behavior.

16. Physical (biological) traits that characterize the different human populations throughout the world are seen by physical anthropologists as having evolved as biological ___adaptations___.

17. Modern physical anthropology would not exist as an evolutionary science if it were not for advances in understanding ___genetic___ principles.

6

18. The behavioral study of any animal species provides a wealth of data pertaining to that species' _____*adaptation*_____.

19. Many osteologists specialize in metric studies which emphasize skeletal _____*elements*_____.

20. A _____*hypothesis*_____ is a provisional statement about the relationships between observations.

21. A crucial feature of scientific statements is that they are _____*true*_____.

22. Ideally, a theory should _____*predict*_____ how new facts may fit into an established pattern.

23. All branches of anthropology attempt to broaden our viewpoints to better enable us to understand humanity. This is called the _____*anthropological perspective*_____.

24. Humans are a product of the same forces that produced life on earth. All life represents a single biological _____*continuum*_____.

MULTIPLE CHOICE QUESTIONS

1. Walking on two legs, as humans and chickens do, is referred to as
   A. bipedalism.
   B. quadrupedalism.
   C. cursorial.
   D. brachiation.

2. The mammalian group that humans belong to is the Order
   A. Carnivora.
   B. Rodentia.
   C. Primates.
   D. Chiroptera.

3. Culture is
   A. inherited by a simple genetic transmission.
   B. a biological trait of our species.
   C. learned.
   D. the strategy by which many mammals adapt to their environments.

4. The biological characteristics of humans enabled culture to develop and culture, in turn, influenced human biological development. This is called
   A. biocultural evolution.
   B. microevolution.
   C. quantum evolution.
   D. convergent evolution.

5. Anthropology differs from other disciplines which study humans in that anthropology
   A. studies humans exclusively.
   B. allows no biases from other disciplines to interfere in anthropological studies.
   C. never uses an evolutionary perspective.
   D. is integrative and interdisciplinary.

6. An anthropologist who is studying the subsistence strategy of the Mbuti pygmies in Zaire belongs to the anthropological subfield of
   A. archeology.
   B. cultural anthropology.
   C. linguistic anthropology.
   D. physical anthropology.

7. Anthropologists who conduct excavations in order to recover artifacts, and other aspects of material culture, are
   A. archeologists.
   B. cultural anthropologists.
   C. linguistic anthropologists.
   D. medical anthropologists.

8. The applied approach in archeology that has expanded greatly in recent years is
   A. magnetometry.
   B. climatic reconstruction.
   C. cultural resource management.
   D. dendrochronology.

9. Physical anthropology emphasizes the interaction between
   A. geology and genetics.
   B. genetics and anthropometry.
   C. anatomical observation of human physical variation.
   D. biology and culture.

10. Physical anthropologists became interested in human change over time (i.e. evolution) with the publication of
    A. Blumenbach's *On the Natural Varieties of Humankind*.
    B. Malthus' *An Essay on the Principle of Population*.
    C. Darwin's *Origin of Species*.
    D. Wood Jones' *Man's Place Among the Mammals*.

11. Anthropologists who specialize in the fossil remains and the physical evidence of early human
    behavior are called
    A. cultural anthropologists.
    B. linguists.
    C. paleoanthropologists.
    D. geneticists.

12. Contemporary physical anthropologists, whose main interest is in modern human variation, approach their subject matter from the perspective of
    A. racial typologies.
    B. adaptive significance.
    C. behavioral genetics.
    D. constitutional typology.

13. Physical anthropologists developed techniques for measuring the human body. Not only physical anthropologists employ these techniques. Such measurements are used at health clubs and include techniques for measuring body fat. These type of measurements are called
    A. calibration.
    B. dermatoglyphics.
    C. genetics.
    D. anthropometrics.

14. A researcher is studying the nutritional ecology of howler monkeys in Panama. Her area of expertise is
    A. primatology.
    B. paleoanthropology.
    C. osteology.
    D. genetics.

15. A family reports to the police that their dog has brought home a leg bone that appears to be human. The police also believe this bone is human. To find out vital information about the person this bone came from the police will consult a(n)
    A. forensic anthropologist.
    B. primatologist.
    C. paleoanthropologist.
    D. evolutionary geneticist.

16. A physical anthropologist who studies bones exclusively is called a(n)
    A. primatologist.
    B. paleoanthropologist.
    C. mammalogist.
    D. osteologist.

17. An important and basic discipline, for osteology, paleopathology, and paleoanthropology is
    A. ecology.
    B. anatomy.
    C. ethology.
    D. genetics.

18. A scientific hypothesis
    A. must always be a correct statement.
    B. is not a necessary part of the scientific method.
    C. is the same thing as a law.
    D. must be falsifiable.

19. If a researcher measures some biological variable and then uses the numbers obtained to arrive at conclusions we would say that this study is
    A. quantitative.
    B. qualitative.
    C. descriptive .
    D. natural history.

20. Scientific hypothesis are falsifiable. This means that they
    A. can provide proof.
    B. are testable.
    C. are subject to supernatural law.
    D. do not offer predictions.

21. To view a culture from the biased perspective of one's own culture is termed
    A. ethnocentric
    B. cultural relativism
    C. anthropological perspective
    D. naive realism

Answers to Fill-In Outline

I. INTRODUCTION
    A. Hominidae
        1. Bipedal
        2. Primates
    B. Evolution, variation, and adaptation
        1. Evolutionary
    C. Culture
        1. Adapt
            a. Technologies
            b. Subsistence patterns

10

3. Learned
D. Evolutionary
    1. Change
    2. a. Population
        b. Species
E. 1. Greater
    2. Biocultural

II. INTRODUCTION TO ANTHROPOLOGY
A. humankind
B. integrates
C. 1. cultural or social anthropology
    2. archeology
    3. physical or biological anthropology
    4. linguistics

III. CULTURAL ANTHROPOLOGY
A. human behavior
B. ethnography
C. cross-cultural
D. 1. urban
    2. medical
    3. economic
E. applied anthropology

IV. ARCHEOLOGY
A. archeology
B. artifacts, material culture
C. 1. excavation
    2. commonalities

V. LINGUISTIC ANTHROPOLOGY
A. linguistics
B 1. perceive
    2. cultures
C. acquisition, use

VI. PHYSICAL ANTHROPOLOGY
A. physical anthropology, biology, culture
B. 1. human evolution
        a. fossil record
        b. hominid species
    2. anthropometry
    3 genetics
        a. evolutionary processes
        b. evolutionary distances
    4. primatology
        a. Living relatives
        b. declining
    5. primate paleontology

6. osteology
   a. paleopathology
   b. Forensic anthropology
7. anatomical studies

VII. PHYSICAL ANTHROPOLOGY AND THE SCIENTIFIC METHOD

A. observation, generalization, verification
   1. empirical
   2. scientific
B. data
   1. comparisons
   2. numerically
C. 1. hypothesis
     a. tested
     b. false
   2. theory
     b. predict
D. 1. bias
   2. all
   3. minimize

Answers & References To Fill-In Questions

1. Hominidae, p. 2
2. Bipedal, p. 2
3. Species, p. 3
4. Physical anthropology, p. 4
5. Culture, p. 4
6. Evolution is, p. 4
7. Biocultural evolution, p. 6
8. Anthropology, p. 6
9. Culture, p. 6
10. Past societies, p. 8
11. Artifact and/or material culture, p. 8
12. Cultural resource management, p. 9
13. Linguistics, p. 9
14. Physical, p. 9
15. Hominid, p. 10
16. Adaptations, p. 11
17. Genetics, p. 11
18. Adaptation, p. 12
19. Measurements, p. 12
20. Hypothesis, p. 13
21. tested , p. 13
22. Predict, p. 14
23. anthropological perspective, p. 16
24. continuum, p. 15

Answers & Rererences To Multiple Choice Questions

1. A, p. 2
2. C, p. 4
3. C, p. 4
4. A, p. 6
5. D, p. 6
6. B, p. 6
7. A, p. 8
8. C, p. 9
9. D, p. 9
10. C, p. 10

11. C, p. 10
12. B, p. 11
13. D, p. 11
14. A, p. 11
15. A, p. 12
16. D, p. 12
17. B, p. 13
18. D, p. 13
19. A, p. 13
20. B, p. 13
21. A, p. 15

CHAPTER 2
THE DEVELOPMENT OF EVOLUTIONARY THEORY

LEARNING OBJECTIVES

After reading this chapter you should be able to
- Trace the development of evolutionary thought (pp. 24-30)
- Identify the major influences on the thought of Charles Darwin (pp. 24-31)
- Describe the processes of natural selection (p. 35)
- Describe a case of natural selection (pp. 36-37)
- Understand the short-comings of Nineteenth-Century evolutionary thought (p. 38)
- Distinguish between science and non-science. (pp. 38-40)

FILL-IN OUTLINE

Introduction

Evolution is a theory that has been increasingly supported by a large body of evidence.   Evolution is the single-most fundamental unifying force in biology. Evolution is particularly crucial to the discipline of physical anthropology because its subject matter deals with human evolution and the physiological adaptations we have made to our environment.   This chapter presents the development of evolutionary thought as well as the social and political context in which it developed.

I.   A BRIEF HISTORY OF EVOLUTIONARY THOUGHT

A.   The pre-scientific view

    1. the European world view throughout the middle ages was one of _____, the

       idea that the world was fixed and unchanging.

       a.   part of this world view was the _____ _____ ___ _____.

          This was a hierarchy in which life was arranged from the simplest to the most

          complex (i.e., humans).

       b.   it was believed that the world was "full" of species and there could not be any other

          species added, nor had any species disappeared.

       c.   the world was seen as the result of the "_____ _____," in which

          anatomical structures were viewed as planned to meet the purpose for which they

          were required - an argument from design.

    2. the creation of the world was believed to be recent, the earth being only about 5500 years

       old; this was a major obstacle to the idea of evolution, which requires immense time.

B.   The scientific revolution

    1. the discovery of the _____ _____ challenged the traditional ideas of Europe.

a. the world could not be perceived as flat.

b. exposures to new plants and animals increased the awareness of the biological diversity on the planet.

2. _____ challenged the old idea that the earth was the center of the universe.

3. Galileo's work further pushed the notion that the universe was a place of motion rather than of _____.

4. by the 16th and 17th centuries scholars began searching for natural laws rather than supernatural explanations. This approach viewed nature as a _____.

C. The Path to Natural Selection

1. John Ray, living in the 16th century, distinguished groups of plants and animals from other such groups.

a. organisms capable of reproducing and producing offspring were classified by Ray as

_____ .

b. Ray also recognized that species shared similarities with other species. He grouped similar species together in a _____.

2. Carolus Linnaeus developed a system of classification and laid the basis for

_____ .

a. Linnaeus standardized the use of the genus and the species to identify each organism, a procedure called _____ _____.

b. Linnaeus' most controversial act was to include _____ among the animals in his taxonomy.

3. Comte de Buffon

a. Buffon stressed the important of change in nature.

b. Buffon recognized that the _____ was an important agent of change.

4. Jean Baptiste Lamarck

a. _____ was the first scientist to produce a systematic explanation for the evolutionary process.

b. Lamarck postulated that the environment played a crucial role in the physical change an organism would go through.

1. as the environment changed, the organism would adjust to the environment by _____ also.

2. Lamarck believed that as an organism used certain body parts, or did not use

those regions, the structures would change in response to the environment.

    a. future _____ would inherit the modified condition.

    b. this idea of Lamarck was called _____ ___

      _____ _____ . It is also called use-

    disuse theory.

5. Georges Cuvier was the archenemy of Lamarck.

    a. despite founding vertebrate paleontology (as well as comparative anatomy and zoology), Cuvier believed strongly in the _____ ___ _____.

    b. Cuvier is strongly associated with the idea that animal and plant species disappeared because of local disasters.

      1. this theory was called _____.

      2. following a set of extinctions, new life forms migrated in from unaffected neighboring areas.

6. Charles Lyell is considered the founder of modern geology.

    a. Lyell emphasized that the earth had been molded by the same geological forces observable today. This theory is called _____.

    b. in order for uniformitarianism to be explanatory, the earth would have to be _____ than previously thought.

7. Thomas Malthus was a political economist.

    a. Malthus wrote about the relationship between food supplies and population increase. He stated that population size increases _____ while food supplies remained relatively stable.

    b. Malthus' ideas contributed to the thinking of both Darwin and Wallace, namely the idea of _____ for food and other resources.

8. Charles Darwin

    a. many of Darwin's ideas were formed from his observations while serving as a naturalist on *H. M. S. Beagle*'s surveying voyage around the world.

    b. in the late 1830's a number of ideas coalesced for Darwin.

      1. Darwin saw that biological variation within a species was _____ _____ .

      2. Darwin also recognized the importance of sexual reproduction in increasing _____ .

      3. Malthus' essay was a watershed event for Darwin and from Malthus Darwin got

        a. that in animals population size is continuously _____ by limits of food supply.

      b. that there is a constant "_____ _____ _____."

   4. by the year _____ Darwin essentially had completed the work that he would publish fifteen years later.

9. A. R. Wallace

    a. Wallace was a naturalist who worked in South America and Southeast Asia.

    b. Wallace published an article suggesting that

       1. species are descended from _____ _____

       2. the appearance of new species was influenced by the _____ _____ .

    c. the coincidental development of evolution by natural selection by both Darwin and Wallace was resolved by the joint presentation of their papers to the Linnean Society of London.

D. The processes of natural selection

   1. all species can produce offspring at a _____ rate than food supplies increase.

   2. there is biological _____ within all species.

   3. over-reproduction leads to _____ for limited resources.

   4. those individuals within a species that possess favorable traits favored are more likely to survive than other individuals and produce _____ .

   5. the _____ context determines whether a trait is favorable or not.

   6. traits are _____ .

    a. individuals with traits favored by the environment contribute _____ offspring to the next generation.

    b. over time such traits will become _____ _____ in the population.

   7. over _____ _____ ____ _____ _____ , successful variations accumulate in a population, so that later generations may be distinct from ancestral one; thus, in time, a new species may appear.

   8. geographical _____ may also lead to the formation of new species.

    a. when populations of a species inhabit different ecological zones they begin to _____ to the different environments.

    b. over time each population responds to the different _____ _____ and the end result, given sufficient time, may be two distinct species.

E. Natural selection operates on individuals, but it is the population that evolves.

    1. the unit of natural selection is the _____ .

    2. the unit of evolution is the _____ .

II. NATURAL SELECTION IN ACTION

A. Industrial melanism is one of the best documented cases of _____
_____ .

    1. two forms of peppered moth exist: a light gray mottled form and a dark form.

        a. prior to the industrial revolution the light morph predominated.

            1. when resting on lichen covered tree trunks the mottled moth was _____ from birds.

            2. in contrast the dark forms stood out on light, lichen covered trees.

            3. birds served as _____ _____ which resulted in few dark moths surviving to produce offspring.

        b. by the end of the nineteenth century the dark form was the more common.

            1. as the industrial revolution progressed coal dust settled on trees.

            2. the light moths stood out on the dark tree trunks and were _____ upon by birds; this resulted in dark forms leaving more offspring to the next generation and subsequently becoming the more common variety.

    2. the example of _____ _____ emphasizes several of the mechanisms of evolutionary change through natural selection.

        a. a _____ must be inherited to have importance in natural selection.

        b. natural selection cannot occur without _____ in inherited characteristics.

        c. selection can work only with variation that already _____ .

            1. _____ is a relative measure that changes as the environment changes.

            2. fitness is simply reproductive _____ .

B. _____ _____ _____ _____ refers to the number of offspring produced by an individual that survive to reproductive age.

III. CONSTRAINTS ON NINETEENTH-CENTURY EVOLUTIONARY THEORY

A. Variation

    1. the _____ of variation was a major gap in 19th century evolutionary theory.

    2. Darwin suggested that _____ - _____ might cause variation.

B. Transmission

    1. Darwin did not understand the mechanisms by which parents transmitted traits to

offspring.

2. the most popular contemporary idea was _____ _____ ;
    the idea that offspring expressed traits intermediate between the traits of their parents.

IV   OPPOSITION TO EVOLUTION

A.   When Darwin proposed evolution it was controversial mainly because it denied humanity
     its _____ and exalted place in the universe; to many it denied the existence of God.

B.   140 years later, debates still center around evolution.

1. for the majority of scientists evolution is _____.

2. nevertheless, almost _____ of all Americans believe that evolution has not occurred.

C.   Why evolution is not easily accepted.

1. evolutionary mechanisms are complex and cannot be explained _____.

2. most people want _____ answers to complex questions, rather than the
    tentative and uncertain answers that scientists work with.

3. while religions and belief systems deal with some natural phenomena, none propose
    biological change over time.

D.   The relationship between science and religion has never been easy.

1. scientific explanations are based on analysis and interpretation; they are _____
    and capable of being _____ .

2. religious beliefs are not falsifiable and are based on _____.

E.   Different religious groups deal with evolution differently.

1. Catholics and mainstream Protestants do not generally see a conflict between evolution
    and religion.

2. _____ are opposed to the teaching of evolution in public schools.

    a.   creation "science" propounds "_____ _____ _____."

    b.   creation "science" is not considered science because it doctrines are considered
         _____ and _____ , while scientific theory must be
    testable and falsifiable.

KEY TERMS

binomial nomenclature: identifying each organism by two names, the genus and the species.
biology: the study of life.
catastrophism: a view that the earth's geology is the result of a series of cataclysmic events.
creation "science": a view that explains the existence of the universe as a result of a sudden
    creation. Creation "science" asserts its views to be absolute and infallible.

differential net reproductive success: the number of offspring that are produced, survive, and reproduce themselves.

evolution: the change in the genetic structure of a population generationally.

fitness: a measure of the relative reproductive success of individuals and, hence their genetic contribution to the next generation.

fixity of species: the idea that species do not change, i.e., they do not evolve.

genus: the taxon (category) in biological classification that consists of similar and related species.

natural selection: the mechanism of evolutionary change in which certain traits from among existing variation are favored resulting in an increase in those traits in the next generation.

reproductive success: the number of offspring that an individual produces and the genetic contribution to the next generation that this implies.

selective pressures: forces in the environment that influence reproductive success in individuals.

species: a group of organisms capable of interbreeding under natural conditions and producing fertile and viable offspring; the second name in a binomen.

stasis: in biology, this was the view that nature and all of its organisms were unchanging.

taxonomy: the biological discipline that names and classifies organisms.

transmutation: the word that meant change in species that predated the word evolution.

uniformitarianism: the theory that the earth's geology is the result of long-term processes, still at work today, that requires immense geological time.

world view: general cultural orientation or perspective shared by members of a society.

FILL-IN QUESTIONS

1. The individual most responsible for the elucidation of the evolutionary process was

   _____ _____.

2. The belief that life forms cannot change is called _____ ___ _____.

3. A paradigm, dating back to Aristotle, in which a hierarchy of life forms were arranged from the simplest to the most complex was termed the _____ _____ __

   _____ .

4. Copernicus proposed that the sun was the center of the solar system. This idea is called the

   _____ solar system.

5. The idea of a mechanistic universe relied on natural explanations rather than

   _____ explanations.

6. The naturalist who developed the species concept was _____ _____.

7. In his work, *The Wisdom of God Manifested in the Works of Creation* , John Ray emphasized that nature was the deliberate outcome of a _____ _____.

8. The naturalist who developed a classification of plants and animals, the basis of the same system of taxonomy that we use today, was _____.

9. Linnaeus gave humans their binomen which is _____ _____.

10. A French naturalist, working in the mid-eighteenth century, who emphasized the importance of change in nature and the importance of the environment was _____ .

11. _____ _____ was an English physician who expressed evolutionary concepts in his book of poetry *Zoonomia.*

12. Lamarck went beyond the work of Buffon and Erasmus Darwin in that he attempted to _____ the evolutionary process.

13. Lamarck believed that if an animal was modified by the environment it could pass on the new trait to its offspring. This idea is called _____ __ _____ _____ .

14. _____ was a French anatomist strongly opposed to any idea of evolution. He proposed that new species appeared by occupying area vacated by extinct species that were destroyed by catastrophes.

15. _____ is considered the founder of modern geology.

16. Lyell contributed an important influence on Charles Darwin, namely that _____ processes have been uniform over a long period of time.

17. _____ influenced both Darwin and Wallace with his ideas about population increase and competition for limited food supplies.

18. The _____ _____ was a social movement that had members who supported Lamarck's evolutionary ideas. Their support actually hindered the acceptance of new revolutionary ideas like evolution.

19. A term predating evolution was _____ , which also meant the change of one species into another.

20. When Darwin set sail on the *Beagle* he believed in the _____ of species.

21. The *Beagle* 's stopover on the _____ Islands was an important event in Darwin's development. He noted the similarity of the flora and fauna of these islands with that of South America and particularly gained insight from the finches on these islands.

22. Darwin wrote that under certain circumstances "favourable variations would tend to be preserved, and unfavourable ones to be destroyed. The result of this would be the formation of a new species." This describes _____ _____ .

23. The naturalist _____ also developed a theory of evolution by natural selection at the same time as Darwin.

24. Those individuals within a species that produce more offspring, compared to other individuals, are said to have greater _____ _____ .

25. The individual member of a species is the unit of _____ ; the population is the unit of _____ .

26. One of the best documented cases of natural selection acting on modern populations involves the _____ _____ in Britain.

27. Natural selection _____ occur without variation in inherited characteristics.

28. Differential net reproductive success refers to the number of offspring produced by an individual that survive to _____ .

MULTIPLE CHOICE QUESTIONS

1. The idea that organisms never change is called
   A. catastrophism.
   B. fixity of species.
   C. transmutation of species.
   D. evolution.

2. The naturalist who developed the concepts of the genus and species was
   A. Charles Darwin.
   B. John Ray.
   C. Carolus Linnaeus.
   D. Jean-Baptiste Lamarck.

3. The discipline within biology that is concerned with the rules of classifying organisms on the basis of evolutionary relationships is
   A. anatomy.
   B. genetics.
   C. taxonomy.
   D. ethology.

4. Which of the following is an example of binomial nomenclature?
   A. vole.
   B. chimpanzee.
   C. human.
   D. *Homo sapiens* .

5. The system of biological classification, or taxonomy, that is still used today was devised by
   A. Charles Darwin.
   B. J. B. Lamarck.
   C. Georges Cuvier.
   D. Carolus Linnaeus.

6. The first person to class humans with another animal group, the primates, was
   A. Linnaeus.
   B. Aristotle.
   C. John Ray.
   D. Archbishop James Ussher.

7. The naturalist who believed that species could change by adapting to new environmental conditions, yet rejected the notion of one species evolving out of another, was
   A. Linnaeus.
   B. Buffon.
   C. Lamarck.
   D. Cuvier.

8. Lamarck believed that
   A. organisms do not change
   B. only genetically determined traits are passed from parent to offspring
   C. the environment plays a major role in evolution
   D. only populations evolve

9. A body builder works hard to build large muscles. He marries a beauty queen/life guard. The body builder expects his male offspring to be born muscle bound. His beliefs resemble those of
   A. catastrophism.
   B. uniformitarianism.
   C. the inheritance of acquired characteristics.
   D. evolution by natural selection.

10. The idea that species were fixed, but became extinct due to sudden, violent events and were replaced by neighboring new species is called
    A. evolution.
    B. phyletic gradualism.
    C. catastrophism .
    D. uniformitarianism.

11. Which scientist was most associated with the concept of catastrophism?
    A. Lamarck.
    B. Cuvier.
    C. Buffon.
    D. Lyell.

12. Uniformitarianism refers to the concept that
    A. the geological processes at work today are the same as those at work in the past.
    B. evolution is a universal fact.
    C. the basic biological processes of life are the same wherever life is found.
    D. the laws of heredity are universal.

13. Uniformitarianism implies which of the following
    A. new species are created by natural disasters.
    B. the earth is very old.
    C. the earth has a living history, short as it may be.
    D. biological species evolve.

14. Which of the following ideas of Charles Lyell contributed to Darwin's thinking?
    A. there is variation within any population of organisms.
    B. there is a "struggle for existence" between individuals.
    C. a trait must be inherited to have any importance in evolution.
    D. there is an immense geological time scale.

15. The concept of the "struggle for existence," the constant competition for food and other resources, was the idea of
    A. Charles Darwin.
    B. Charles Lyell.
    C. Thomas Malthus.
    D. A. R. Wallace.

16. Which of the following developed a theory of evolution by natural selection?
    A. Lamarck.
    B. A. R. Wallace.
    C. Erasmus Darwin.
    D. Lyell.

17. Which of the following is **not** a statement that Darwin would have made?
    A. there is biological variation within all species.
    B. the environment selects which traits are beneficial.
    C. geographical isolation may lead to a new species.
    D. traits acquired within an individual's lifetime are passed to the next generation.

18. Those individuals that produce more offspring, relative to other individuals in the population, are said to have greater
    A. reproductive success.
    B. selective pressure.
    C. variation.
    D. survival potential.

19. Forces in the environment which influence reproductive success are called
    A. k-selection.
    B. selective pressures.
    C. phyletic gradualism.
    D. differential reproduction.

20. Which of the following did **not** believe in the Fixity of Species?
    A. Lamarck.
    B. Linnaeus.
    C. Cuvier.
    D. Buffon.

21. The best documented case of natural selection acting on modern populations is
    A. starfish as keystone predators of mussels in the Pacific Northwest.
    B. mutualism involving sharks and remoras.
    C. industrial melanism involving peppered moths near Manchester, England.
    D. the symbiosis formed by cork sponges and hermit crabs.

22. What happened to the peppered moth population in England?
    A. there was a change in wing length due to the stability of the environment.
    B. there was a loss of functional wings due to a change in the environment.
    C. they became extinct because these moths could not adapt to the environment.
    D. there was a shift in body color from light to dark in this population.

23. Industrial melanism refers to
    A. a case of natural selection in Britain.
    B. Lamarck's example for the inheritance of acquired characters.
    C. Darwin's example for evolution by natural selection.
    D. A and C.

24. Differential net reproductive success refers to
    A. an individual leaving more offspring than another.
    B. the number of offspring that survive to reproduce relative to other individuals.
    C. an evolutionary shift in a trait.
    D. the development of new traits.

25. Darwin's explanation for evolution suffered from his ability to explain
    A. the role of variation in natural selection.
    B. the origins of variation.
    C. the effects of the environment.
    D. the immense time span that would be required.

26. Darwin believed that inheritance took place by
   A. particulate inheritance.
   B. blending inheritance.
   C. spontaneous generation.
   D. the principle of independent assortment.

27. Which of the following did **not** influence Charles Darwin?
   A. Lamarck.
   B. Malthus.
   C. Mendel.
   D. Lyell.

28. Which of the following statements is **true**?
   A. Creation Science is falsifiable.
   B. The term Creationism has been replaced by the term Intelligent Design Theory.
   C. Evolutionary science asserts that it theories are absolute and infallible.
   D. Creation Science is amenable to modification based on hypothesis testing.

ANSWERS TO OUTLINE

I.   A BRIEF HISTORY OF EVOLUTIONARY THOUGHT.
   A. 1. stasis
         a. Great Chain of Being
         c. Grand Design
   B. 1. New World (i. e., North and South America, new worlds that the Europeans did not know existed)
      2. Copernicus
      3. fixity
      4. mechanism
   C. 1. a. species
         b. genus
      2. taxonomy
         a. binomial nomenclature
         b. humans
      3. b. environment
      4. a. Lamarck
         b. 1. changing
            2. a. offspring
               b. inheritance of acquired characteristics
      5. a. fixity of species
         b. 1. catastrophism
      6. a. uniformitarianism
         b. ancient (or old)
      7. a. exponentially

26

        b. competition
    8. b. 1. critically important
            2. variation
            3. a. checked
                b. struggle for existence
            4. 1844
    9.   1. other species
            2. environment
  D. 1. faster
      2. variation
      3. competition
      4. offspring
      5. environmental
      6. inherited
          a. more
          b. more common
      7. long periods of geological time
      8. isolation
          a. adapt
          b. selective pressures
  E. 1. individual
      2. population

II. NATURAL SELECTION IN ACTION.
  A. Natural Selection
      1. a. 1. camouflaged
              3. selective agents
          b. 2. preyed
      2. industrial melanism
          a. trait
          b. variation
          c. exists
              1. fitness
              2. success
  B. Differential Net Reproductive Success

III. CONSTRAINTS ON NINETEENTH-CENTURY EVOLUTIONARY THEORY
  A. 1. source
      2. use, this idea was originally introduced in the section on Lamarck
  B. 2. blending inheritance

IV. OPPOSITION TO EVOLUTION
  A. unique
  B. 1. fact
      2. half
  C. 1. simply
      2. definitive

D. 1. faith
E. 2. Creationists
   a. intelligent design theory

ANSWERS & REFERENCES TO FILL-IN QUESTIONS

1. Charles Darwin, p. 24
2. fixity of species, p. 25
3. Great Chain of Being, p. 25
4. heliocentric, p. 26
5. supernatural, p. 26
6. John Ray, p. 26
7. Grand Design, p. 27
8. Carolus Linnaeus, p. 27
9. *Homo sapiens*, p. 27
10. Buffon, p. 27
11. Erasmus Darwin, p. 27
12. explain, p. 28
13. inheritance of acquired characteristics, p. 28
14. Georges Cuvier, p. 28
15. Charles Lyell, p. 30
16. geological, p. 30
17. Thomas Malthus, p. 30
18. Reform Movement, p. 31
19. transmutation, p. 31
20. fixity, p. 32
21. Galápagos, p. 32
22. natural selection, p. 33
23. Wallace, p. 34
24. reproductive success, p. 35
25. selection; evolution, p. 35
26. peppered moth, p. 36-37
27. cannot, p. 36
28. reproduce, p. 37

ANSWERS & REFERENCES TO MULTIPLE CHOICE QUESTIONS

1. B, p. 25
2. B, p. 27
3. C, p. 27
4. D, p. 27
5. D, p. 27
6. A, p. 27
7. B, p. 27
8. C, p. 28
9. C, p. 28
10. C, p. 29
11. B, pp. 28-29
12. A, p. 30
13. B, p. 30
14. C, p. 30
15. B, p. 33
16. B, p. 34
17. D, pp. 31-33
18. A, p. 35
19. B, p. 35
20. D, p. 27

21. C, pp. 36-37
22. D, pp. 36-37
23. A, p. 36
24. B, p. 37
25. B, p. 38
26. B, p. 38
27. C, p. 38
28. B, p. 40

CHAPTER 3
THE BIOLOGICAL BASIS OF LIFE

LEARNING OBJECTIVES

After reading this chapter you should be able to
- To describe the structure of a generalized cell (44-45).
- To describe the structure and function of DNA (pp. 46-47).
- Understand the process of protein synthesis (pp. 47-52).
- To define a gene and what it does (p. 52).
- Understand how a mutation occurs (p. 52).
- Know the difference between autosomes and sex cells (pp. 54-55).
- Understand the importance of mitosis and meiosis and what their differences are (pp. 53-59).
- Understand why genetics is important to the study of evolution (p. 59)

Fill-In Outline
Introduction

Human evolution and adaptation are intimately linked to life processes stemming from the genetic processes of cells, both in cell replication and in the decoding of genetic information into products usable by the organism and the transmission of this information to future generations.

I. **THE CELL**
A. The Cell is the Basic _unit_ of Life in All Living Organisms.
1. complex _multicellular_ life forms, such as plants and animals, are made up of billions of cells.
2. prokaryote cells are _single_ - _celled_ organisms.
   a. the earliest life on earth, appearing by at least 3.7 billion years ago, were such life forms.
   b. _prokaryotic_ cells lack a nucleus.
3. more complex cells with a nucleus first appeared around 1.2 billion years ago.
   a. these cells are called _Eukaryotic_ cells.
   b. multicellular organisms, which includes humans, are composed of eukaryotic cells.
B. General Structure of a Eukaryotic Cell
1. the type of cell studied in textbooks is a generalized or composite cell.
   a. a generalized cell contains structures known to exist in cells.
   b. on the other hand, no single cell has all the structures seen in a general cell.
2. the _cell_ _membrane_ is the outermost and functional boundary of the cell.
3. _Organelles_ are functional structures found within the cytoplasm.

30

4. the third major region of the eukaryotic cell is the _nucleus_ which is surrounded by the cytoplasm and contains chromosomes.
5. this section of the textbook discusses organelles important for the discussion of genetics (and ultimately variation and evolution).
    a. mitochondria
        1. these organelles produce _energy_ for the cell.
        2. mitochondria also contain their own _DNA_ which directs mitochondrial activities.
    b. ribosomes are structures that are essential to the production of _proteins_ .
C. There are two types of cells found in the animal body.
    1. _Somatic_ cells are the cells of the body with the exception of the sex cells.
    2. gametes are sex cells involved with _reproduction_ .
        a. ova are egg cells produced in _female_ ovaries.
        b. sperm are sex cells produced in _male_ testes.
        c. a _zygote_ is the union between a sperm and an ovum.

II. DNA STRUCTURE
A. Cellular Function and an Organism's Inheritance Depends on the Structure and Function of DNA.
B. DNA is composed of _two_ chains of nucleotides.
    1. a _nucleotide_ consists of a sugar, a phosphate, and one of four nitrogenous bases.
    2. nucleotides form long chains and the two chains are held together by bonds formed by the bases with their _____ on the other chain. This complementary phenomenon is what enables DNA to fulfill its functions. (This is sometimes called the "base pairing principle").
        a. adenine (A) is the complement of _thymine_ (T).
        b. guanine (G) is the complement of _cytosine_ (C).
        c. the complementary property of the DNA bases is what enables DNA to make _exact_ copies of itself.

III. DNA REPLICTION
A. A cell cannot function properly without the appropriate amount of _DNA_ .
B. The Replication Process
    1. specific enzymes break the bonds between the DNA molecule
    2. the two nucleotide chains serve as _models/templates_ for the formation of a new strand of nucleotides
    3. unattached nucleotides pair with the appropriate _complementary_ ~~parental~~ nucleotide
    4. the end result is _two_ newly formed strands of DNA. Each new strand is joined to one of the original strands of DNA.
C. See figure 3-3.

31

IV. PROTEIN SYNTHESIS

A. One of the most important functions of DNA is that it directs _Protein_ synthesis within the cell.

B. Proteins are the major _structural_ components of tissue.

C. Enzymes are proteins that serve as catalysts, i.e. they initiate and enhance _chemical_ reactions.

D. the building blocks of proteins are smaller molecules called _amino_ acids.

    1. there are _20_ important amino acids.

    2. what makes proteins different from one another is the number of amino acids involved and the _sequence_ in which they are arranged.

E. ribosomes are cytoplasmic organelles which help convert the genetic message from the DNA into _protein_ .

F. messenger RNA (mRNA) carries the genetic message from the cell nucleus to the _a ribosome_ .

    1. RNA differs from DNA in that it is _single_ - _stranded_ , has a different type of sugar and substitutes the base uracil (U) for thymine (T)

    2. mRNA has triplets (a series of three bases) called _codons_ which specify a particular amino acid

G. transfer RNA (tRNA) is another type of RNA that is usually found in the cytoplasm

    1. tRNA binds to one specific _amino_ acid

    2. each tRNA has an amino acid matching the _mRNA_ condon being translated.

H. transcription

    1. a portion of the DNA unwinds and serves as a _template_ for the formation of a mRNA strand.

    2. the process of coding a genetic message for proteins by formation of mRNA is called _transcription_ .

I. translation

    1. the mRNA travels through the nuclear membrane to the _ribosome_ .

    2. tRNAs arrive at the ribosome carrying their cargoes of specific _amino acids_ .

    3. the base triplets on the _tRNA_ match up with the codons on the mRNA.

    4. as each tRNA line up according to the sequence of mRNA codons their amino acids link together to form a _protein_ .

    5. the process in which the genetic message on the mRNA is "decoded" and implemented is called _translation_ .

J. The entire sequence of DNA bases that code for a specific sequence of amino acids is a _gene_ .

K. If the sequence of bases in a gene are altered a _mutation_ has occurred.

    1. this may interfere with the organisms ability to produce vital _proteins_ .

2. it may also lead to a new variety within the species and, hence, evolution.
L. The gene consists of exons and introns.
    1. DNA segments transcribed into mRNA that code for specific amino acids are called _exons_.
    2. DNA sequences not expressed during protein synthesis are called _introns_.
M. Not all genes produce structural proteins.
    1. some genes are _regulatory_ and produce enzymes and other proteins which switch on or turn off other segments of DNA.
    2. all somatic cells contain the same _genetic_ information, but only a small fraction of the DNA is used for the specialized functions of any particular cell.
        a. some genes are only active during particular periods of the life cycle
        b. alterations in the behavior of regulatory genes may be responsible for some of the _physical_ differences between closely related species.
N. The universality of the genetic code.
    1. the genetic code is _universal_ ; this means that the DNA of all life forms on earth is composed of the same molecules and carries on similar functions.
    2. the universality of the genetic code implies a _common_ ancestry for all of this planet's life forms; what makes organisms different is the arrangement of the DNA.

V. CELL DIVISION: MITOSIS AND MEIOSIS
A. Much of a cell's existence is spent in _uncoiled, threadlike substance_
    1. during this period the cell is involved with normal cellular and metabolic processes
    2. During cell division the cell's _DNA_ becomes tightly coiled.
B. Cell division is the process that results in the production of _new_ cells. It is during cell division that DNA becomes visible under a light microscope as _chromosomes_.
C. Chromosome Structure
    1. a chromosome is composed of a _DNA_ molecule and associated proteins.
    2. during normal cell function chromosomes exist as _single_-_stranded_ structures.

    3. during early cell replication chromosomes consists of _two_ strands of DNA.
        a. these two strands are joined together at a constricted region called the _centromere_ .
        b. the reason there are two strands of DNA is because _replication_ has occurred and one strand is an exact copy of the other.
D. Each Species is Characterized by a Specific Number of _chromosomes_ .
    1. humans have _46_ chromosomes.

2. chromosomes occur in pairs and humans have 23 _pair_ . The members of chromosomal pairs are called _homologous_ .
   a. homologous chromosomes carry genetic information influencing the same _traits_ .
   b. however, homologous chromosomes are not genetically _identical_ .

E. Types of Chromosomes
   1. ~~somatre~~ _autosomes_ carry genetic information that governs all physical characteristics except primary sex determination.
   2. the two _sex_ chromosomes are the X and Y chromosomes.
      a. genetically normal mammal females have two _X_ chromosomes.
      b. genetically normal mammal males have one X chromosome and one _Y_ chromosome.

F. In order to function properly a human cell must have both members of each chromosome _X_ .

G. Mitosis
   1. cell division in somatic cells is called _mitosis_ .
   2. mitosis occurs during _growth_ and repair/replacement of tissues
   3. steps in mitosis
      a. by the time that chromosomes can be seen they have already duplicated - hence, what we see represents two DNA molecules.
      b. the 46 chromosomes line up in the center of the cell (see fig. 3-8).
      c. the chromosomes are then pulled apart at the _centromere_ .
      d. the separated chromosomes are pulled towards opposite ends of the cell; each separated chromosome is composed of _one_ DNA molecule.
      e. the cell membrane pinches in and two new cells now exist.
   4. the result of mitosis is two identical _daughter_ cells that are genetically _identical_ to the original cell.

H. Meiosis
   1. meiosis is the production of sex cells, or _gametes_ . half the normal complement of chromosomes.
   2. meiosis is characterized by
      a. _two_ divisions
      b. _four_ daughter cells
      c. _recombination_ , or crossing over
   3. meiosis and sexual reproduction are highly important _evolutionary_ innovations.
      a. meiosis increases genetic variation at a faster rate than _mutation_ alone could.
      b. offspring in _sexually_ _reproducing_ species represent the combination of genetic information from two parents.

c. Darwin emphasized that natural selection acted on
    ___genetic___ variation in all populations.
    (1) ___mutation___ is the only source of new genetic
        variation.

I. Problems with Meiosis
    1. meiosis must be _exact_ to produce a viable gamete and
        a. must have exactly _23_ chromosomes.
        b. have only one member of each _chromosome_ pair
            present.
    2. errors in meiosis may lead to spontaneous abortions, or
        ___miscarriage___ .
    3. chromosomes may fail to separate during meiosis. This is called
        ___nondisjunction___
        a. nondisjunction may lead to an affected gamete fusing with a
            normal gamete.
        b. an affected gamete that contains one less chromosome and fuses
            with a normal gamete will produce a zygote containing _45_
            chromosomes.
        c. an affected gamete that contains an extra chromosome and fuses
            with a normal gamete will produce a zygote containing 47
            chromosomes.
    4. examples of abnormal numbers of chromosomes.
        a. Down's syndrome, or trisomy 21, occurs because of three copies of
            chromosome #_21_ .
            1. congenital problems associated with _Trisomy_
                _21_ include mental retardation, heart defects, and
                increased susceptibility to respiratory infections.
        b. nondisjunction may also occur in _____ chromosomes
            which frequently result in sterility.

KEY TERMS

amino acids: small molecules that are the basic building blocks of proteins.
autosomes: one of the pairs of chromosomes that determines traits other than sex.
cell (plasma) membrane: the living boundary of an animal cell.
chromosome: structures that are composed of DNA and protein, found in the nucleus of
    the cell, and are only visible during cell replication.
clone: an organism that is genetically identical to another organism.
codon: three nitrogeneous bases (i.e., a triplet) found on the mRNA which complements
    three bases on a tRNA carrying a specific amino acid.
complementarity (,principle of): the rule that certain bases in DNA and RNA always
    bind together. Cytosine always pairs with guanine and, in DNA, Adenine always
    pairs with Thymine. In RNA Uracil replaces Thymine and pairs with Adenine.
    Sometimes referred to as the "base-pairing principle."

cytoplasm: the region of a cell that is contained within the cell membrane, excluding the nucleus.

diploid: the full complement of chromosomes of a species.

DNA (deoxyribonucleic acid): a double-stranded molecule that contains the genetic information.

eukaryote cell: cells of organisms in which the DNA is enclosed by membranes forming a nucleus

gametes: sex cells, viz. ova (eggs) and sperm.

gene: a seqeuence of DNA nucleotides that code for a particular polypeptide chain.

generalized cell: a eukaryotic cell that has all of the structures known to exist in cells; also referred to as a composite cell. The generalized cell is a teaching device. Most cells are specialized and may not have some of the structures of a generalized cell. For example, mature red blood cells do not have a   nucleus.

genetics: the discipline within biology that studies the inheritance of biological characteristics.

genome: the complete genetic makeup of an individual or a species.

haploid: half the normal complement of chromosomes of a species. The haploid condition is characteristic of animal sex cells.

homologous: the pair of chromosomes that carry genes for the same traits.

Human Genome Project: an international effort aimed at sequencing and mapping the entire human genome.

karyotype: the chromosomal complement of an individual or that typical for a species. Usually displayed as a photomicrograph, often using special stains to highlight the bands or centromeres.

meiosis: specialized cell division in the reproductive organs which produce gametes. The gametes are haploid and are not identical.

messenger RNA (mRNA): a form of RNA, formed on one strand of the DNA, that carries the DNA code from the nucleus to the cytoplasm where protein synthesis takes place.

mitochondria: organelles found in the cytoplasm which produce cellular energy.

mitosis: cell division in somatic cells.

monosomy: the absence of a member of a chromosome pair.

mutation: a change in the sequence of bases coding for the production of a protein.

nondisjunction: the failure of homologous chromosomes to separate during meiosis.

nucleotide: the basic unit of DNA. A nucleotide consists of one of four nitrogeneous bases, plus a sugar and a phosphate.

nucleus: a structure found in eukaryotic cells which contains chromosomal DNA.

organelle: a structure found in the cytoplasm that performs some physiological function.

point mutation: a mutation that results from the substitution of one nitrogenous base by another.

prokaryote cell: a single-celled organism that lacks a nucleus.

proteins: three-dimensional molecules composed of amino acids that serve as structural components of animal bodies and as catalysts for biochemical reactions.

protein synthesis: the process by which proteins are produced from amino acids.

ribosome: a cytoplasmic organelle, made up of RNA and protein, where protein synthesis takes place.

RNA (ribonucleic acid): a single-stranded molecule, similar in structure to DNA. The three types of RNA are essential to protein synthesis.

sex chromosomes: in animals, those chromosomes involved with primary sex determination. The X and Y chromosomes.

sickle-cell anemia: a severe inherited disease that results from a double dose of a mutant allele, which in turn results from a single base substitution at the DNA level.

somatic cells: the cells of the body, excluding the cells involved with primary reproduction.

transcription: the formation of a messenger RNA molecule from a DNA template.

transfer RNA (tRNA): the form of RNA that binds to a specific amino acid and, during translation, transports them to the ribosome in sequence.

translation: the process of sequencing amino acids from a messenger RNA template into a functional protein or a portion of a protein.

triplet: a set of three nitrogenous bases on the DNA molecule.

trisomy: the present of three members of a chromosome pair instead of the usual two.

zygote: a cell resulting from the fusion of a sperm and an egg (ovum).

FILL-IN QUESTIONS

1. ___genetics___ is the study of how traits are transmitted from one generation to the next.

2. DNA is found within the ___nucleus___ of an eukaryotic cell.

3. The structures found in the cytoplasm that are responsible for energy production are the ___organelles___ .

4. The sole function of a gamete is to unite with a gamete from another individual to form a ___zygote___ .

5. An individual ___nucleotide___ consists of one dioxyribose sugar, one phosphate, and one of four nitrogenous bases.

6. Two long strands of nucleotides, formed into a double helix, describes the ___DNA___ molecule.

7. In the following illustration DNA is replicating. Put in the letter of the nitrogeous bases of the new strand of DNA in accordance with the principle of complementarity.

$$A - A - C - G - T - A$$

$$T - T - G - C - A - T$$

8. ___Enzymes___ are a group of substances that function in a myriad of ways, serving as structural components, as well as iniating and enhancing chemical reactions in the body.

9. In order for a protein to function properly its ___Amino___ ___acid___ must be arranged in the proper sequence.

10. In the DNA instructions, a _____ , or group of three bases, codes for a particular amino acid.

11. The genetic instructions for producing a protein are carried into the cytoplasm by a _____ _____ molecule.

12. The process in which a mRNA molecule is formed from DNA is called ___transcription___ .

13. The cytoplasmic organelles to which mRNAs attach are the

_____ .

14. The molecule which carries a specific amino acid and has a triplet which matches one of the mRNA codons is called _____ _____ .

15. A gene is a particular sequence of nucleotides along part of a chromosome that codes for the sequence of _____ _____ in a particular protein.

16. A change in the DNA of a gene results in a _____ .

17. The parts of a gene that code for specific amino acids are called _____ .

18. Some genes function by producing structural proteins; others are called _____genes that make enzymes, and other proteins, that control other segments of DNA.

19. The DNA of all life forms is composed of the same molecules and it carries out similar functions. We refer to this aspect of the genetic code as _____ .

20. Cell division results in _____ _____ .

21. The reason there are two strands of DNA when chromosomes become visible is because the DNA molecules have _____ .

22. Chromosomes that determine an individual's sex are referred to as _____ chromosomes.

23. Chromosomes that share genes for the same traits are said to be _____ .

24. Cell division in which the end result is two identical daughter cells with the full genetic complement of the species, from one parent cell, is called _____ .

25. In meiosis the end result is four gametes with _____ the original number of chromosomes.

26. _____ or _____-_____ is the process by which homologous pairs of chromosomes exchange genetic information.

27. The type of cell division that has the most importance for evolution is

_____ .

28. A boy is born with three chromosome 21s. This is a condition known as trisomy 21 or Down's Syndrome. The cause of this condition is the failure of the 21st chromosome to separate normally during meiosis in one of the parent's gametes. This failure to separate properly is called _____ .

MULTIPLE CHOICE QUESTIONS

1. The discipline that links or influences the various subdisciplines of physical (biological) anthropology is
   A. genetics.
   B. cell biology.
   C. paleontology.
   D. primatology.

2. A cell that has its DNA enclosed by a nucleus is called a
   A. karyote cell.
   B. prokaryote cell.
   C. eukaryote cell.
   D. prion.

3. The two nucleic acids that contain the genetic information that controls the cell's functions are
   A. ribosomes and Golgi apparati.
   B. mitochondria and desmosomes.
   C. the endoplasmic reticulum and ribosomes.
   D. DNA and RNA.

4. The organelles found in the cytoplasm that contains its own DNA are the
   A. ribosomes
   B. mitochondria
   C. lysosomes
   D. vacuoles

5. Which of the following is not a sex cell?
   A. gamete.
   B. ovum.
   C. sperm.
   D. skin cell.

6. A cell formed by the union of an egg and a sperm is called a
   A. gamete.
   B. zygote.
   C. neuron.
   D. ovum.

7. The smallest unit of DNA consists of one sugar, one phosphate, and one of four bases. This unit is called a
   A. sperm.
   B. nucleotide.
   C. nucleus.
   D. ribosome.

8. Researchers found that certain bases of the DNA macromolecule always pair. These bases are referred to as
   A. independently assorted.
   B. segregated.
   C. in equilibrium .
   D. complementary.

9. A parental chain of DNA provides the following template: AAT CGA CGT. Which of the following sequences of free nucleotides would pair with the parental template?
   A. TTA GCT GCA.
   B. AAT CGA CGT.
   C. GGC TAG TAC.
   D. UUA GCU GCA.

10. The end result of DNA replication is
    A. two new strands of DNA.
    B. the fusion of the mother's DNA with the father's DNA.
    C. the formation of a mRNA molecule.
    D. the production of an amino acid molecule.

11. A type of protein which helps to enhance chemical reactions in the body is
    A. bone.
    B. muscle.
    C. enzymes.
    D. hemoglobin.

12. Proteins consists of chains of
    A. triglycerides.
    B. monosaccarides.
    C. amino acids.
    D. fatty acids.

13. Which of the following is not true about RNA?
    A. it is single stranded.
    B. some forms of RNA are involved with protein synthesis.
    C. it has a different type of sugar than DNA has.
    D. it contains the base thymine.

14. The formation of a mRNA molecule from DNA is called
    A. transcription.
    B. translation.
    C. translocation.
    D. transforamation.

15. The reading of mRNA by a ribosomes to produce protein is called
    A. transcription.
    B. translation.
    C. translocation.
    D. transforamation.

16. A portion of a mRNA molecule that determines one amino acid in a polypeptide chain is called a
    A. nucleotide.
    B. gene.
    C. codon.
    D. nucleoside.

17. In protein synthesis all of the following occur except
    A. amino acids are initially bonded to specific tRNA molecules.
    B. animo acids are transported to the nucleus to bond with DNA molecules.
    C. the sequence of amino acids is determined by the codon sequence in mRNA.
    D. amino acids are bonded together to form a polypeptide chain.

18. What is the name of the molecule that amino acids bind to?
    A. messenger RNA (mRNA).
    B. ribosomal RNA (rRNA).
    C. transfer RNA (tRNA).
    D. mitochondral DNA (mtDNA).

19. The following segment of mRNA contains the bases UUA CGC UGA. Which triplets on three different tRNAs will line up in order during translation?
    A. UUA CGC UGA.
    B. AAT GCG ACT.
    C. AGU CGC AUU.
    D. AAU GCG ACU.

20. A series of DNA bases on the chromosome that code for a particular polypeptide chain is a(n)
    A. ribosome.
    B. amino acid.
    C. gene.
    D. polypeptide chain.

21. What is the characteristic number of chromosomes in human somatic cells?
    A. 23.
    B. 46.
    C. 48.
    D. 78

22. A genetically normal human female has
    A. 23 pairs of autosomes
    B. 23 pairs of autosomes and two X chromosomes
    C. 22 pairs of autosomes and two X chromosomes
    D. 22 pairs of autosomes, one X chromosome, and one Y chromosome.

23. Pregnant woman can have a procedure done called amniocentesis. In this procedure some of the fetal cells are obtained and photomicrographs are produced illustrating the fetus's chromosomes. Such a photomicrograph is called a
    A. banding pattern.
    B. CT scanning.
    C. karyotype.
    D. PET Imaging.

24. The end result of mitosis in humans is
    A. two identical "daughter" cells.
    B. four haploid cells.
    C. two cells with 23 chromosomes.
    D. two cells with mutations.

25. Which of the following is true for meiosis?
    A. it has only one division which duplicates the parent cell exactly.
    B. it produces gametes.
    C. when a mutation occurs it affects only the individual.
    D. it has no effect on evolution.

26. If chromosomes or chromosome strands fail to separate during meiosis seriour problems can arise. This failure to separate is called
    A. Turner's syndrome.
    B. nondisjunction.
    C. a monosomy.
    D. random assortment.

ANSWERS TO OUTLINE

I. THE CELL
- A. Unit
  1. multicellular
  2. single-celled
     - b. prokaryote (the word prokaryote actually means "before a nucleus")
  3. a. eukaryote (this word means "true nucleus")
- B. 2. cell membrane
  3. organelles
  4. nucleus
  5. a. 1. energy
           2. DNA
     - b. proteins
- C. 1. somatic
  2. reproduction
     - a. female
     - b. male
     - c. zygote

II. DNA STRUCTURE
- B. Two
  1. nucleotide
  2. complements
     - a. thymine (T)
     - b. cytosine (C)
     - c. exact

III. DNA REPLICATION
- A. genetic
  1. DNA
- B. 2. templates
  3. complementary
  4. two

IV. PROTEIN SYNTHESIS
- A. protein
- B. structural
- C. chemical
- D. amino
  1. 20
  2. sequence
- E. proteins
- F. ribosome
  1. single-stranded
  2. codons
- G. 1. amino

        2. mRNA
    H. 1. template
        2. transcription
    I. 1. ribosome
        2. amino acids
        3. tRNA
        4. protein
        5. translation
    J. gene
        1. polypeptide
        2. gene
    K. mutation
        1. protein
    L. 1. exons
        2. introns
    M. 1. regulatory
        2. genetic
            b. physical
    N. 1. universal
        2. common

V. CELL DIVISION: MITOSIS AND MEIOSIS
    A. cell division
    B. new, chromosomes
    C. 1. DNA
        2. single-stranded
        3. two
            a. centromere
            b. replication
    D. chromosomes
        1. 46
        2. pairs, homologous
            a. traits
            b. identical
                (1) alleles
    E. 1. autosomes
        2. sex
            a. X
            b. Y
    F. pair
    G. 1. mitosis
        2. growth
        3. c. centromere
            d. one
        4. daughter, identical
    H. 1. gametes

44

2. a. two
   b. four
   c. recombination
3. evolutionary
   a. mutation
   b. sexually reproducting
   c. genetic
      (1) mutation
I. 1. exact
   a. 23
   b. chromosome
2. miscarriages
3. nondisjunction
   b. 45
   c. 47
4. a. chromosome #21
   1. trisomy 21

ANSWERS & REFERENCES TO FILL-IN QUESTIONS

1. genetics, p. 44
2. nucleus, p. 44
3. mitochrondria, p. 45
4. zygote, p. 45
5. nucleotide, p. 46
6. DNA, p. 47
7. T-T-G-C-A-T, p. 47
8. proteins, p. 47
9. amino acids, p. 49
10. triplet, p. 49
11. messenger RNA, p. 50
12. transcription, p. 50
13. ribosomes, p. 51
14. transfer RNA, p. 51
15. amino acid, p. 52
16. mutation, p. 52
17. exons, p. 52
18. regulatory, p. 52
19. universal, p. 52
20. new cells, p. 53
21. replicated, p. 53
22. sex, p. 54
23. homologous, p. 53
24. mitosis, p. 55
25. half, p. 56

26. recombination (crossing-over), p. 57
27. meiosis: this is because meiosis has the potential to affect future generations, whereas, mitosis affects only the individual in which mitosis is occuring, p. 59
28. nondisjunction, p. 59

ANSWERS & REFERENCES TO MULTIPLE CHOICE QUESTIONS

1. A, p. 44
2. C, p. 44
3. D, p. 45
4. B, p. 45
5. D, p. 45
6. B, p. 45
7. B, p. 46
8. D, p. 46
9. A, pp. 46-47
10. A, p. 47
11. C, p. 47
12. C, p. 49
13. d, p. 50
14. A, p. 50
15. B, p. 51
16. C, p. 51
17. B, p. 51
18. C, p. 51
19. D, p. 51
20. C, p. 52
21. B, p. 53
22. C, p. 54
23. A, p. 55
24. B, p. 55
25. A, p. 57
26. B, p. 59

CHAPTER 4

HEREDITY AND EVOLUTION

LEARNING OBJECTIVES

After reading this chapter you should be able to

*   Discuss Mendel's Principle of Segregation (p. 65).

*   Recognize the patterns of inheritance for dominant and recessive traits (pp. 65-68).

*   Perform simple matings using a Punnett square (p. 67).

*   Discuss Mendel's Principle of Independent Assortment (p. 68).

*   Understand the complexity of inherited dominant and recessive traits (pp. 71)

*   Describe the difference between Mendelian traits and polygenic traits (pp. 71-73).

*   Understand the complexity involved between genetic and environmental factors (pp. 73-74).

*   Define biological evolution and note what entity evolves (pp. 74-75).

*   Describe the agents that are responsible for generating and distributing variation (pp. 74-76).

*   Discuss the revolutionary new approaches to the study of human genetics (pp. 76-78).

FILL-IN OUTLINE
Introduction

In the last chapter the structure and function of DNA was presented. In this chapter we look at the principles of heredity, originally studied by Gregor Mendel. More complex genetic inheritance, found in polygenic systems, is looked at. We close with a discussion of some of the new biotechnologies that are being applied to the world we live in.

I.   **THE GENETIC PRINCIPLES DISCOVERED BY MENDEL.**

A.   Introduction.

    1.   _____ (1822-1884) laid down the basic principles of heredity.

    2.   Mendel crossed different strains of purebred plants and studied their _____.

B.   Segregation.

    1.   Mendel crossed purebred plants that differed in one trait.

        a.   the plants used in this first cross were designated the _____, or P generation.

        b.   one of the traits disappeared in the _____ offspring.

        c.   the trait that was present in the F_1 generation was not _____

between the two traits as would be the case if _____ _____
theory was valid.

    d. when the F_1 generation self-fertilized the trait missing _____
in the F_2 generation.

    e. Mendel obtained a constant ratio of _____ dominants to _____ recessive in the
F_2 generation.

  2. Mendel's results could be explained if:

    a. the trait was the result of _____ units.

    b. these two factors _____ during sex cell formation.

    c. the idea that traits are controlled by two discrete units, which separate into different
sex cells, was Mendel's principle of _____ .

    d. today we know that _____ explains Mendel's principle of segregation.

C.   Dominance and Recessiveness

  1. Mendel called the trait that disappeared in the F_1 generation, but reappeared in the F_2
generation, _____.

  2. Mendel called the trait that was expressed in the F_1 generation _____.

  3. when two copies of the same allele are present the individual is _____
for that trait.

  4. when there are two different alleles at a locus the individual is _____.

  5. Mendel's results can be illustrated by a Punnett square (see Fig. 4-3).

    a. the Punnett square shows the _____ of offspring with
specific genotypes.

    b. the Punnett square is useful for predicting the proportions of _____ generation
genotypes.

D.   Independent Assortment

  1. Mendel next crossed two different characters which he considered _____.

  2. the F_1 generation expressed only the _____ traits.

  3. the ____ generation contained combinations of traits not present in either of the plants
of the P generation.

  4. Mendel deduced that these traits were inherited _____ of one
another.

  5. Mendel's second principle of inheritance is the principle of _____
_____ .

  6. by chance, Mendel did not use traits that were linked, i.e., genetic loci that are located
on the _____ chromosome.

    a. if Mendel had used linked traits his results would have been considerably different.

b. linked genes travel together during meiosis; consequently, they are not independent of one another and do not conform to the ratios predicted by independent _____ .

II. MENDELIAN INHERITANCE IN HUMANS

A. More Than _____ Traits are Known to be Inherited by Simple Mendelian Principles.

B. The Human _____ Blood System is an Example of a Simple Mendelian Inheritance.
   1. the A and B alleles are _____ to the O allele.
   2. neither the A or B allele are dominant to one another; they are _____ and both traits are expressed.

C. Genetic Disorders can be Inherited as Dominant or Recessive Traits.
   1. dominant disorders are inherited when _____ copy of a dominant allele is present. Such disorders include achondroplasia, brachydactyly, and familial hypercholesterolemia
   2. recessive disorders require the presence of _____ copies of the recessive allele.
      a. heterozygotes for such disorders are not affected, but because they carry one copy of the recessive allele they are _____ .
      b. some recessive conditions that affect humans are

      _____

      _____

      _____

D. Misconceptions Regarding Dominance and Recessiveness.
   1. A major misconception is that the presence of a recessive allele in heterozygotes has no effect on the _____ .
   2. today we know this is not true.
   3. we now know that recessive alleles exert an effect at the _____ level in heterozygotes.
   4. another misconception is that dominant alleles are more _____ .

III. POLYGENIC INHERITANCE

A. Mendelian Traits are Discrete Traits.
   1. _____ traits are fall into clear categories.
   2. because discrete traits are discontinuous, there are no _____ forms between discrete traits.
   3. Mendelian traits are governed by _____ genetic locus.

B. Polygenic Traits are Continuous Traits Governed by Alleles at More Than One Genetic Locus.

1. continuous traits show _____ .
   a. there is a series of _____ intermediate forms between the two extremes.
   b. the gradations formed by continuous traits produce a bell curve graphically
2. each locus in a polygenic trait contributes to the _____ ; we say these combined effects are additive, although the contribution of the alleles are not all equal.
3. a well known example of a polygenic trait is human _____ _____ , governed by perhaps 6 loci and at least 12 alleles.

C. Because Polygenic Traits <u>are</u> Continuous They can be Treated _____ .
   1. the _____ is a summary statistic which gives the average of a sample or population.
   2. a standard deviation measures _____ - _____ _____ .
   3. researchers are able to _____ continuous traits between different populations and to see if there are significant differences statistically.
   4. Mendelian characteristics are not as amenable to statistical analysis as polygenic characters are. However,
      a. Mendelian characteristics can be described in terms of _____ within populations and compared between populations.
      b. Mendelian characters can be analyzed for _____ of inheritance
      c. Mendelian characters are valuable because the approximate or exact _____ ___ _____ _____ for them is known.

IV.   GENETIC AND ENVIRONMENTAL FACTORS

A. The Terms Genotype and Phenotype Have Both a Narrow and Broad Definition.
   1. on the narrow level they both may be used in reference to a single trait, e.g., the genetic and physical expression of purple flowers vs. white flowers that Mendel studied on pea plants.
   2. at a broader level these two terms may refer to the individual's _____ genetic makeup and all of its observable characteristics.

B. The Genotype Sets Limits and Potentials for Development.
   1. the genotype also interacts with the organism's _____ .
   2. many aspects of the _____ is influenced by the genetic/environmental interaction.

   3. many _____ traits, such as height, are influenced by the environment.

4. Mendelian traits are _____ likely to be influenced by the environment.

5. even though polygenic traits are controlled by several loci and are more amenable to the environment, they still obey _____ principles at the individual loci.

V. HEREDITY AND EVOLUTION

A. There are Four Different Levels at Which Evolution Works: _____, cellular, _____, and populational.

   1. these different levels reflect different aspects of evolution

   2. they are all related and highly _____ in a way that eventually produces evolutionary change.

B   Mutation.

   1. the only source of _____ variation is mutation.

   2. _____ is an actual molecular alteration in genetic material.

   3. for a mutation to have any evolutionary significance it must occur in a _____ (or sex cell).

      a. such mutations will be carried on one of the individual's chromosomes.

      b. during meiosis the chromosome carrying the mutation will assort giving a _____ percent chance of passing the allele to an offspring.

C. A Modern Definition of Evolution is a Change in the _____ of Alleles in a Population From One Generation to the Next.

   1. an _____ frequency is the percentage of all the alleles at a specific locus accounted for by one specific allele.

   2. if a population shows change, it will do so as a result of change in _____ _____.

   3. for evolution to occur, a new allele must spread through the _____ and increase in frequency.

D. Other Factors That Lead to Increases in Allele Frequencies.

   1. _____ _____ is a random factor that is due mainly to sampling phenomena.

      a. gene drift is directly related to the _____ of the population.

      b. _____ populations are more prone to randomness in evolution, i.e. genetic drift.

      c. some alleles may be completely lost through genetic drift; in this case the remaining allele is referred to as "_____."

   2. the exchange of alleles between populations is called _____ _____.

E.   Directional Evolutionary Changes Can Only Be Sustained Through _____
     _____.

   1. natural selection works by some individuals with particular alleles leaving more offspring than other; this is called _____ _____.

   2. differential reproduction leads to changes in allele _____ and, hence, evolution.

VI. NEW FRONTIERS.

A.   Over the Last Fifty Years, the Field of Genetics has Revolutionized the Biological Sciences.

B.   The Goal of the Human Genome Project is to Sequence the Entire Human _____.

C.   New Technologies.

   1. polymerase chain reaction (PCR) makes it possible to analyze and identify segments of _____ as small as one molecule.

      a.   in this procedure the two strands of DNA are separated, an enzyme synthesizes complementary strands, and it is possible to produce over a _____ copies of the original DNA

      b.   PCR is very useful for analyzing evidence found at crime scenes or from fossils.

   2. _____ DNA techniques allow scientists to transfer genes from the cells of one species into the cells of another.

      a.   the most common use of recombinant technology is to insert human _____ into bacteria in order to produce useful gene products such as human insulin.

      b.   genes from other species can also be _____ into domesticated food crops to improve their characteristics, such as resistance to frost or the ability to resist insects.

         1.   genetic manipulation is controversial due to safety and environmental concerns.

         2.   the long-term effects on humans using genetically enhanced products is _____.

   2. cloning.

      a.   clones exist in nature (e.g., as in vegetative reproduction).

      b.   a _____ is an individual that is genetically identical to another individual.

KEY TERMS

allele: the alternative form of a gene.
allele frequency: the proportion of a particular allele to all the other alleles at a given locus in a population.

antigens: large molecules found on the surface of cells. Several different loci governing antigens on red and white blood cells are known. Foreign antigens provoke an immune response in individuals.

carrier: an individual who is a heterozygote for a recessive genetic disorder; the individual is unaffected.

clone: an organism that is genetically identical to another organism.

codominance: both alleles are expressed in the phenotype.

continuous traits: traits which have measurable gradations between the two end points, such as height in humans.

discrete traits: traits which fall into clear categories, such as a purple flower vs. a white flower in a garden pea.

dominant: the genetic trait that is expressed in the heterozygous state.

evolution (biological): a change in allele frequencies between generations.

F_1 generation: the hybrid offspring of purebreeding parents

gamete: a sex cell, in humans these are ova (eggs) and sperm.

gene: a sequence of DNA nucleotides that code for a particular polypeptide chain.

gene flow: exchange of genes between different populations of a species.

genetic drift: evolutionary changes in the gene pool of a small population due to chance (random factors).

genome: the complete genetic makeup of an individual or a species.

genotype: the genetic makeup of an organism.

heterozygous: the presence of two different alleles for a given genetic trait in an individual.

homozygous: the presence of the same alleles for a given genetic trait in an individual.

Human Genome Project: an international effort aimed at sequencing and mapping the entire human genome.

hybrid: parents who are in some ways genetically dissimilar. This term can also be applied to heterozygotes.

locus: position on a chromosome where a given gene occurs.

mean: a summary statistic which gives the average of a sample or of a population.

Mendelian traits: traits that are inherited at a single locus on a single chromosome

mutation: an alteration in the genetic material (a change in the base sequence of DNA).

natural selection: the evolutionary factor that causes changes in the allele frequencies in populations due to differential net reproductive success of individuals. The force of evolution that gives direction in response to environmental factors.

phenotype: the physical expression of an organism's genotype

phenotypic ratio: the proportion of one phenotype to other phenotypes.

population: a community of individuals, all of the same species, that occupy a particular area and breed among themselves.

polygenic: referring to traits that are influenced by genes at two or more loci.

polymerase chain reaction (PCR): a method of producing thousands of copies of a DNA segment using the enzyme DNA polymerase.

principle of independent assortment: Mendel's principle that states that alleles for different traits sort independently during gamete formation

principle of segregation: the principle expounded by Mendel that alleles occur in pairs which separate (segregate) during gamete formation. At fertilization the full number of alleles is restored.

recessive: the genetic trait that is not expressed in a heterozygous state

sickle-cell trait: a condition resulting from a point mutation of the gene coding for production of the beta-chain hemoglobin. A red blood cell with this trait is subject to collapse during periods of extreme stress or low blood oxygen levels.

standard deviation: a summary statistic which measures within-group variation.

Tay-Sachs disease: Mendelian disorder most common among Ashkenazi Jews; this disease manifests itself in a degeneration of the nervous system that results in death by the age of three.

variation (genetic): inherited differences between individuals. The basis of all evolutionary change.

FILL-IN QUESTIONS

1. The scientist who first described the basic principles of inheritance, based on his work with the common garden pea, was _____ .

2. A key characteristic of the different strains of pea plants that Mendel began his experiments with were that they always produced offspring that had the same traits as the parents. These are known as _____ plants.

3. When Mendel allowed the F_1 generation to self-pollinate he obtained a ratio of ___ dominant traits for ____ recessive trait.

4. Mendel's principle that any particular trait is governed by two different factors (alleles) which separate during the formation of gametes is called _____.

5. Using the Punnett square provided below, mate a heterozygous tall pea plant with a dwarf pea. The phenotypic ratios for this cross are _____:_____ .

6. What does Mendel's principle of independent assortment state? _____
   _____.

7. Mr. and Mrs. Blutrot both have type A blood. What are the possible phenotypes for blood groups that the offspring of Mr. and Mrs. Blutrot could produce? _____.

8. The <u>expression</u> of two different alleles for a trait, such as blood types AB and MN is called _____ .

54

9. Genetic disorders such as achondroplasia are expressed in the heterozygotes. This type of disorder is inherited as a _____ trait; other genetic disorders, often associated with the lack of an enzyme that blocks a metabolic pathway, requires both harmful alleles to be expressed - these are _____ traits.

10. Perform a mating in the Punnett square below between two normally pigmented individuals who each have a parent who is an albino. Of four children, what can we expect in terms of genotype? _____ What is the probability of albino offspring? _____.

11. Traits that are influenced by genes at two or more loci are called _____ traits.

12. Traits that fall into clearly defined categories are said to be _____ traits.

13. Polygenic traits are more likely to interact with the _____ than are discrete traits.

14. Even though polygenic traits are influenced by several loci, _____ principles still apply at the individual loci.

15. A change in allele frequencies from one generation to the next is the definition of _____ .

16. If the sequence of DNA that codes for a gene product has changed a _____ has occurred.

17. The force of evolution that is more likely to affect a small population rather than a large population is _____ .

18. The Afro-American gene pool in the northern United States is estimated to contain around 20% European alleles. This is an example of _____ .

19. Directional evolutionary changes can only be sustained by _____ _____ .

20. The international endeavor to map the DNA sequences of all of the human chromosomes is called the _____ _____ _____.

MULTIPLE CHOICE QUESTIONS

1. In a cross between two purebreeding strains of garden peas Mendel found that in the offspring
   A. both traits were represented in the F_2 generation.
   B. they were homozygous for the traits being studied.
   C. one of the traits disappeared.
   D. the traits were intermediate between the two parental traits.

2. Mendel used the term dominant for
   A. plants that were larger than others of the same variety.
   B. a trait that prevented another trait from appearing.
   C. a variety of pea plants that eliminated a weaker variety.
   D. a trait that "skipped" generations.

3. When Mendel crossed peas with Rr and Rr genotypes, the phenotypic ratio of the offspring was _____ (note: you may want to use a Punnett square to figure this out)
   A. 1:1.
   B. 3:1.
   C. 1:2:1.
   D. 2:2.

4. Genes exist in pairs in individuals; during the production of gametes, the pairs are separated so that a gamete has only one of each kind. This is known as the
   A. principle of segregation.
   B. principle of independent assortment.
   C. mitosis.
   D. unification theory.

5. What physiological process explains Mendel's principle of segregation?
   A. mitosis.
   B. meiosis.
   C. metamorphosis.
   D. metastasis.

6. Which of the following is characteristic of dominant alleles
   A. dominant alleles are expressed in heterozygous genotypes.
   B. dominant alleles are the alleles which are most common in a population.
   C. dominant alleles always cause more serious defects than recessive alleles.
   D. dominant alleles drive recessive alleles out of a population.

7.	A trait which is inherited as a recessive is expressed in the
	A. homozygous recessive individual.
	B. homozygous dominant individual.
	C. heterozygous individual.
	D. codominant individual.

8.	An alternative form of a gene is called a(n)
	A. nucleotide.
	B. locus.
	C. allele.
	D. epistasis.

9.	Homozygous means that an individual has
	A. two different alleles of the same gene.
	B. the same alleles of the same gene.
	C. the same alleles of different genes.
	D. two different alleles of different genes.

10.	The principle of independent assortment states that
	A. a pair of genes segregate during the production of gametes.
	B. genes recombine in a predetermined way.
	C. the distribution of one pair of genes does not influence the distribution of other pairs of genes on other chromosomes.
	D. mutations come from independent sources.

11.	A heterozygous genotype would be written as
	A. AA.
	B. Aa.
	C. aa.
	D. AA and aa.

12.	Mendelian traits are
	A. also known as traits of simple inheritance.
	B. controlled by alleles at more than one genetic locus.
	C. the product of several alleles on different chromosomes.
	D. only known for about 160 human traits.

13.	When there are two different alleles present in a heterozygote and both of these alleles are expressed, this condition is called
	A. recessive.
	B. dominance.
	C. codominance.
	D. sex-linked.

14. A certain form of albinism is inherited as a recessive. An albino and a normally pigmented person marry and have a child. This child meets and marries a person with the same background, i.e. an albino parent and a normally pigmented parent. What is the probability that the first offspring of the F_2 generation will be an albino?
    A. 0.
    B. 0.25.
    C. 0.50.
    D. 0.75.

15. In many polygenic traits the various loci each influence the phenotype producing
    A. a discrete trait.
    B. a discontinuous trait.
    C. an addititve effect.
    D. a new allele.

16. The **most complete** definition of biological evolution is
    A. change.
    B. a change in allele frequency from one generation to the next.
    C. mutation.
    D. survival of the fittest.

17. The only source for a new allele for a species gene pool is
    A. mitosis.
    B. natural selection.
    C. mutation.
    D. recombination.

18. When alleles are introduced into a population from another population it is a case of
    A. genetic drift.
    B. gene flow.
    C. founder effect.
    D. bottleneck effect.

19. An example of gene flow would be
    A. the Amerasian children of Vietnam.
    B. the isolated Amish of Pennsylvania.
    C. the American colonization of Antarctica.
    D. a small hunting and gathering society in Siberia with little outside contact.

20. The force of evolution which is significant when small human populations become isolated is
   A. gene flow.
   B. mutation.
   C. genetic drift.
   D. random mating.

Answers to Fill-In Outline

I. **THE GENETIC PRINCIPLES DISCOVERED BY MENDEL**
   A. 1. Mendel
      2. progeny
   B. 1. a. parental
         b. hybrid (F_1)
         c. intermediate; blending inheritance
         d. reappeared
         e. 3: 1
      2. a. two
         b. segregate (or separate)
         c. segregation
         d. meiosis
   C. 1. recessive
      2. dominant
      3. homozygous
      4. heterozygous
      5. a. proportions
      6. F_2
   D. 1. simultaneously
      2. dominant
      3. F_2
      4. independent
      5. independent assortment
      6. same
         b. assortment

II. **MENDELIAN INHERITANCE IN HUMANS**
   A. 1. 4,500
   B. ABO
      1. dominant
      2. codominant
   C. 1. one
      2. two
         a. carriers
         b. phenylketonuria, cystic fibrosis, Tay-Sachs disease, sickle-cell anemia, thalassemia and albinism. See Table 4-3 for a list and description of Mendelian disorders in humans.
   D. Misconceptions regarding Dominance and Recessiveness.

1. phenotype
3. biochemical
4. common

III. POLYGENIC INHERITANCE
A. 1. discrete or discontinuous
   2. intermediate
   3. one
B. 1. gradations
      a. measurable
   2. phenotype
   3. skin color
C. statistically
   1. mean
   2. within-group variation
   3. compare
   4. a. frequencies
      b. mode
      c. position of genetic loci

IV. GENETIC AND ENVIRONMENTAL FACTORS.
A. 2. entire
B. 1. environment
   2. phenotype
   3. polygenic
   4. less
   5. Mendelian

V. HEREDITY AND EVOLUTION
A. molecular; individual
   2. integrated
B. 1. new
   2. mutation
   3. gamete
      a. fifty
C. frequency
   1. allele
   2. allele frequencies
   3. population
D. 1. genetic drift
      a. size
      b. small
      c. fixed
   2. gene flow
E. Natural Selection
   1. differential reproduction
   2. frequency

VI. NEW FRONTIERS.
B. 1. DNA
      a. million

    2. recombinant
        a. genes
        b. inserted
            2. unknown
    3. b. clone

ANSWERS & REFERENCES TO FILL-INS

1. Gregor Mendel, p. 64.
2. purebred; genotypically a purebred is homozygous for the allele of the trait in question. For example, both alleles in a purebred tall pea plant would be the same, designated by Mendel as TT. A purebred dwarf pea plant would also be homozygous for this trait, tt, p. 64.
3. The F_1 pea plants are heterozygous and have a genotypes containing one dominant allele and one recessive allele; phenotypically they express the dominant allele. When they "self" they produce offspring of both phenotypes. The phenotypic ratio is 3:1, p. 65.
4. principle of segregation, p. 65.
5. a tall heterozygous pea plant has the genotype Tt, the dwarf pea plant is true breeding and is tt. This exercise is actually one of Mendel's test crosses and the phenotypic result is 1:1. See p. 67 & Fig. 4-3 for the explanation on how to use a Punnett square.
6. Mendel's units (genes) that code for different traits assort independently of each other during gamete formation, p. 68.
7. Blood type A and, if they both have AO genotypes, type O, p. 69.
8. Codominance, p. 69.
9. dominant, recessive. A dominant trait requires only one of the alleles to be expressed. Heterozygotes have one of the dominant alleles and, thus, express the trait. Because only one allele is needed to express a dominant trait most individuals affected with a dominant genetic disorder are heterozygous for that trait, p. 70, Table 4-3.
10. Each individual has an albino parent. This means that the mating between their parents would have been A_ X aa = Aa. (We do not know what the second allele was on the first parent, but because these two individuals are normal their genotype has to be Aa). Aa X Aa produces the genotype ratio of 1AA : 2Aa : 1aa. Phenotypically we can expect one albino child out of four, i.e. a 25% probability. See Fig. 4-3.
11. polygenic, p. 72.
12. discrete. Some examples in humans include blood types A, B, and O and the M and N blood types. There are no gradations in discrete traits. An individual either has the trait or does not have the trait, p. 71.
13. environment. Some examples in humans include height (influenced by nutrition) and intelligence (influenced by experience), p. 74.
14. Mendelian. If six loci help determine a trait, alleles at the individual locus still behave in a Mendelian fashion, i.e. there are alleles that are dominant and alleles that are recessive and, in some cases, alleles that are codominant at each locus, p. 74.
15. biological evolution, p. 75.
16. mutation. A mutation is defined as an alteration in the genetic material. p. 74.
17. genetic drift. Large populations are fairly immune to genetic drift; it is only in small populations where the increase or decrease of a few alleles can be reflected in dramatic changes in allele frequencies. Because most of human evolutionary history was spent as small hunter-gatherer bands genetic drift may have played a very important role during the course of human evolution, p. 75.

18. gene flow. Gene flow is the exchange of alleles between populations. The United States population as a whole is an example of gene flow, p. 75.
19. natural selection, p. 75.
20. Human Genome Project, p. 76.

ANSWERS & REFERENCES TO MULTIPLE CHOICE QUESTIONS

1. C, p. 65
2. B, p. 65
3. B, p. 67
4. A, p. 65
5. B, p. 65
6. A, p. 65
7. A, p. 67
8. C, p. 66
9. B, p. 67
10. C, p. 68
11. B, p. 67
12. A, p. 69
13. C, p. 69
14. B, because each of these individuals has an albino parent they must be heterozygotes. Therefore, the probability of is 0.25 for producing an albino in any mating, p. 70 & Table 4-3.
15. C, p. 72
16. B, p. 75
17. C, p. 74
18. B, p. 75
19. A, gene flow is the movement of alleles from one population into another. This is the case with the Amerasian children of Vietnam. Their fathers contributed alleles to the Vietnamese population. Note that the contributors do not have to become a part of the population to which they contributed their alleles. The American colonization of Antarctica did not involve a movement of alleles from the American population to the Antarctic population. While this colonization could be viewed as a movement of individuals, it did not involve any movement of alleles, p. 75.
20. C, p. 75

CHAPTER 5
AN OVERVIEW OF THE LIVING PRIMATES.

LEARNING OBJECTIVES
After reading this chapter you should be able to
- List and discuss primate evolutionary trends (pp. 83-86).
- Describe the influence of the arboreal environment on primate evolution (pp. 86-87).
- Compare and contrast the "arboreal hypothesis" with the "visual predation hypothesis" (p. 87).
- understand the possible affects of the evolution of flowering plants on primate evolution p. 87.
- Work out a dental formula (p. 90).
- Describe the major forms of locomotion found among primates and be able to name one type of primate for each form of locomotion (pp. 90-93).
- Explain how taxonomic classification reflects biological relationships (pp. 93-96).
- Explain how new genetic technologies have been used to deduce evolutionary relationships among the hominoids (pp. 93-96).
- Name, compare, and contrast the two major subdivisions of the primates (pp. 93-109).
- Name the major groupings of the anthropoids (pp. 98-109).
- Discuss the differences between New World monkeys and Old World monkeys (pp. 99-102).
- Name the two subdivisions of the Old World monkeys and the features that distinguish these two groups (pp. 100-102).
- Explain how monkeys and apes differ (pp. 102-103).
- Describe the major characteristics of the various apes that comprise the hominoids (pp. 102-108).
- Discuss the challenges facing primatologists today (pp. 109-110).

FILL-IN OUTLINE
Introduction.
    The preceding chapters have focused on the basic biological background for understanding human evolution. Now we will look at human evolution in more detail. In order to understand any organism it is important to have a frame of reference as to where that organism belongs - how it is similar and how it is different from other closely related organisms. This is done through a comparative approach. As primates the organisms that are useful to study are the other 190 species in the Order Primates. In this chapter we look at the physical characteristics that define the primates, an overview of the living members of the order, the molecular techniques that are used to deduce evolutionary relationships between primate species, and finish with a discussion of the conservation of our closest relatives.

I.   PRIMATE AS MAMMALS
A.   Primates belong to the vertebrate class, Mammalia.

    1. there are over 4,000 _____ of mammals.

    2. primates belong to the subgroup of placental mammals.

II. CHARACTERISTICS OF PRIMATES

A   As mammals, primates _____ a number of traits in common with other placental mammals. These are called primitive, or generalized, traits. These include

   1. fur, or, as it is referred to in humans, _____ _____.

   2. a relatively long gestation period followed by _____ birth.

   3. _____, the ability to maintain a constant body temperature through physiological mechanisms.

   4. _____ brain size.

   5. a great capacity for learning and behavioral _____.

B.   As an Order, primates have _____ many primitive mammalian traits and remain quite generalized.

   1. on the other hand, many other mammals have become increasingly _____.

     a. this leads to the modification of anatomical structures for the particular function that they become specialized for; e.g., the reduction of digits in horses.

     b. some mammals have specialized structures that are not found in any other mammalian group. An example is the four carnassial teeth found only in the Order Carnivora.

   2. because primates are generalized mammals they cannot be _____ by one or two common traits

     a. primates are defined by _____ trends.

       1. evolutionary _____ are traits that characterized the entire order to a greater or lesser degree

       2. it is important to note that primate evolutionary trends are a set of _____ tendencies not equally expressed in all primate species.

     b. the evolutionary trends that have been traditionally used by primatologists are a combination of primitive mammalian traits and common primate specialized traits. These traits characterize the _____ Primates.

C.   Limbs and Locomotion

   1. primates exhibit a tendency towards _____ _____, especially in the upper body, whether sitting, leaping, or standing.

2. primates possess a flexible, _____ limb structure which does not lock them into a specialized form of locomotion.

3. primate hands and feet possess a high degree of _____ (grasping ability). Other features of the hands and feet include

   a. retention of _____ digits on hand and feet

   b. an opposable _____ and, in most species, a divergent and partially opposable great toe.

   c. primates possess _____ on at least some digits

   d. primates have _____ pads enriched with sensory nerve fibers at the ends of digits which appears to enhance the sense of touch.

D. Diet and Teeth.

   1. primates lack dietary _____ and tend to eat a wide variety of foods.

   2. primates possess _____ dentition.

E. The senses and the brain.

   1. all primates rely _____ on vision. Primate evolutionary trends in vision include

      a. _____ vision in all diurnal primates. Nocturnal primates lack color vision.

      b. depth perception or _____ vision made possible by

         1. eyes positioned forward on the front of the face providing for _____ vision

         2. visual information from each eye is transmitted to the _____ centers in both hemispheres of the brain.

         3. visual information is organized into _____-dimensional images by specialized structures in the brain itself

   2. primates have a _____ reliance on the sense of smell (olfaction).

   3. the primate brain has expanded in size and become increasingly _____.

F. Maturation, learning, and behavior.

   1. primates possess the mammalian characteristic of the placenta, which provides for a more efficient means of _____ nourishment. Primates are marked by _____ periods of gestation, _____ numbers of offspring, _____ maturation, and _____ of the entire life span.

   2. primates exhibit a greater dependence on flexible, learned _____.

   3. primates tend to live in social groups. Males are _____ members of many primate social groups, a situation unusual among mammals.

   4. primates tend to be _____.

III. PRIMATE ADAPTATIONS

A. Evolutionary Factors

    1. _____ living was the most important factor in the evolution of the primates.

    2. arboreal life selected for _____ _____ in a three-dimensional environment.

    3. the primate grasping, prehensile hand is adapted to _____ in the trees.

    4. the tropical arboreal environment provided a variety of foods which led to the primate omnivorous _____ and _____ dentition.

    5. this view that the arboreal environment was the major factor influencing primate evolution is called the _____ _____.

    6. The visual predation hypothesis.

        a. the _____ _____ hypothesis is an alternative to the arboreal hypothesis.

        b. this hypothesis states that primates may have first evolved in the _____ _____ _____.

            (1) in this environment _____ - _____ eyes enabled early primates to judge distance when grabbing for insects.

        c. flowering plants, or _____, may have Influenced primate evolution,

    7. The visual predation and the arboreal hypotheses are not necessarily mutually exclusive explanations.

        a. many primate features may have begun in _____ settings.

        b. nevertheless, primates did move into the trees and, if they did have characteristics that evolved in another setting, they were "_____" for life in the trees.

B. Geographic Distribution and Habitats

    1. most living nonhuman primates live in the _____ or semitropical areas of the New and Old Worlds.

    2. most primates are _____, living in forest or woodland habitats

    3. some Old World monkeys have adapted to life on the _____.

    4. gorillas and chimpanzees spend considerable time on the _____.

    5. however, no nonhuman primate is _____ to a fully terrestrial environment. All spend some time in the trees.

C. Diet and Teeth

    1. primates are generally _____ and this is reflected in their generalized dentition.

    2. although the majority of primate species emphasize some food items over others, most

eat a combination of _____, _____, and _____.

  a. some primates (baboons and chimpanzees) occasionally kill and eat small

      _____.

  b. some primates, such as the colobine monkeys, are dietary specialists

      on_____.

3. most primates have _____ types of teeth.

  a. _____ and _____ function in biting and cutting.

  b. premolars and molars are used for _____.

4. a dental formula describes the _____ of each type of tooth that typifies a

   species.

  a. the order of each type of tooth is: _____ (s), _____ ,

      _____ (s), and _____ (s).

  b. the number of each type of tooth is presented for a _____ of the

      mouth. If these teeth are added up and multiplied by four the result is the number of

      teeth characteristic of that species.

      1. in the New World cebid monkey dental formula of 2.1.3.3, the teeth are added

          up, multiplied by four, and we can say that these monkeys have _____ teeth.

      2. the number of premolars present in these monkeys is _____ .

5. the dental formula for a primitive placental mammal is 3.1.4.3 which totals _____ teeth.

  a. primates and other mammals have reduced numbers of teeth than the primitive

      condition because of _____ trends in those lineages.

6. the primate generalized dentition is correlated with a lack of dental

   _____ . Unlike carnivore or herbivore specialists, primates

   possess low, rounded cusps that enable them to possess most foods.

D. Locomotion.

  1. almost all primates are, to some degree, quadrupedal - using all _____ limbs in

      their locomotion.

    a. many primates are able to employ more than one form of locomotion, a product of

        their generalized limb _____.

    b. the majority of quadrupedal primates are arboreal, but _____

        quadrupedalism is also fairly common

    c. limb ratios of quadrupeds differ.

1. the limbs of terrestrial quadrupeds are approximately of _____ length,

        with forelimbs being 90 per-cent as long as hind limbs.

      2. in arboreal quadrupeds, forelimbs are proportionately _____ and

          may only be 70-80 per-cent as long as hind limbs.

d. quadrupeds are also characterized by a relatively long and flexible lumbar
    _____ which positions the hind limbs well forward and enhances their
    ability to propel the animal forward.

2. vertical clinging and leaping is found in many _____.

3. brachiation (arm swinging) employs the forearms and is found among the _____.

    a. only the small _____ and _____ of Southeast Asia use
        this form of locomotion exclusively.

    b. brachiators are characterized by.

        1. arms _____ than legs.

        2. a short stable _____ spine.

        3. long _____ fingers.

        4. reduced _____ .

    c. brachiator characteristics have been inherited by the great apes from their ancestors
        who were either brachiators or _____.

    d. some monkeys that use a combination of leaping with some arm swinging are
        termed _____.

4. an aid to locomotion is a prehensile tail.

    a. among the primates prehensile tails are found only among the _____

        _____ _____.

    b. a _____ tail is like a fifth hand.

IV. A SURVEY OF THE LIVING PRIMATES

A. Primate Taxonomy

1. In taxonomic systems organisms are organized into increasingly _____
    categories.

    a. the highest level for the primates is the _____ .

    b. primates are subdivided into _____ large suborders.

        (1) the _____ includes lemurs, lorises and, traditionally, tarsiers.
        By grouping these primates together an evolutionary statement is made - these
        animals are _____ closely related to each other than they are to any of the
        anthropoids.

        (2) the _____ include the monkeys, apes, and humans.

    c. at each succeeding level finer distinctions are made until the _____
        level is reached.

    d. in this manner, classifications not only organize diversity into categories, but also
        illustrate evolutionary and genetic _____ between
        species and groups of species.

2. DNA
   a. The goal of taxonomy and systematics is to identify biological and evolutionary relationships   between groups of organisms.
      1. to achieve the goal of establishing evolutionary relationships classificatory schemes must be based on traits that species _____ because they are inherited from a common ancestor.
      2. emerging genetic technologies provide the means to compare DNA and DNA products directly.
         a. if two species share similar DNA it must be assumed that this DNA represents descent from a _____ ancestor.
         b. for the most part, the genetic data have reaffirmed the taxonomies based on _____ .
   b. Amino acid sequencing.
      1. the _____ of amino acids that comprise specific proteins can be examined for comparative purposes.
      2. amino acid sequencing of human and Africa ape _____ show remarkable similarities.
   c. DNA hybridization.
      1. DNA _____ is a technique in which a single strand of DNA from two separate species are combined to form a hybrid DNA molecule.
      2. DNA hybridization, like other genetic techniques, has reaffirmed most of the basic tenets of primate classification.
         a. DNA hybridization shows how genetically _____ humans and the African apes are.
3. Inherent shortcomings of the traditional method of classification: two cases.
   a. the place of tarsiers among the primates
   tarsiers are highly derived and display several unique characteristics.
     (1) traditionally they have been classified as _____ because they possess a number of prosimian traits.
     (2) however, they also share several traits with the _____.
     (3) with regards to chromosomes, they are _____ from both groups.
   b. the problem of where to place tarsiers has resulted in a taxonomic scheme which replaces the traditional _____ with alternative suborders.
      1. lemurs and lorises are placed in the suborder _____ (wet-nosed primates).

2. the tarsiers and anthropoids are placed in the suborder _____
(dry-nosed primates)

B. Prosimians.
1. prosimians are the _____ primitive of the primates.
2. primitive characteristics include
   a. greater reliance on _____ compared to the other primates
      1. this is reflected in the moist _____ at the end of the nose and
         the relatively long snout.
      2. prosimians mark their territories with _____.
   b. prosimians have more _____ placed eyes.
   c. the reproductive physiology, as well as the _____ gestation length and
      maturation periods, differ from the other primates.
   d. many prosimians possess a dental specialization called the " _____
      _____."
      1. this structure is formed by forward-projecting lower _____ and
         _____.
      2. the dental comb is used in both feeding and _____ .
3. lemurs.
   a. lemurs are found only on the island of _____ and several other
      closeby islands off the east coast of Africa.
      1. on Madagascar the lemurs _____ into numerous and
         varied ecological niches without competition from higher primates.
      2. lemurs became _____ elsewhere in the world.
   b. characteristics of lemurs.
      1. body size ranges from the small _____ _____ (5 inches in
         length, 2 ounces in weight) to the indri (over 2 feet, approximately 22 pounds)
      2. the _____ lemurs are diurnal and exploit a wide variety of vegetable
         foods ranging from fruit to leaves, buds, bark, and shoots.
      3. smaller lemurs are nocturnal and _____ (insect
         -feeding).
      4. there is great variation in lemur behavior from species to species.
         a. many forms are arboreal but some, such as the ring-tailed lemur, are more
            _____.
         b. some arboreal forms are quadrupedal, while others, such as the sifaka, are
            _____ _____ and _____.
         c. some species (e.g. ring-tailed lemurs and sifakas) live in _____ of

up to 25 animals, which includes both males and females of all ages.

      1. others, such as the indrii, live in _____ family units.

      2. most of the nocturnal species are _____.

  4. lorises.

    a. lorises are very similar in appearance to lemurs.

    b. lorises were able to survive in continental areas by adopting a nocturnal activity pattern. This enabled the lorises to avoid _____ with the more recently evolved monkeys.

    c. loris species are found in tropical forests and woodlands of India, Sri Lanka, Southeast Asia, and Africa.

    d. a member of the loris family is the _____, or bushbaby, which is found in forests and woodlands of sub-Saharan Africa.

    e. characteristics of lorises

      1. locomotion.

        a. _____ employ a slow cautious climbing form of quadrupedalism.

        b. _____ are active vertical clingers and leapers.

      2. diet.

        a. some lorises are almost completely _____.

        b. others supplement their diet with _____ of fruit, leaves, gums, and slugs.

        c. these animals frequently forage _____.

      3. ranges _____ and females frequently form associations for foraging or in sharing the same sleeping nest ("dormitories").

  5. both lemurs and lorises represent the same general primate _____ _____.

    c. these animals have longer _____ spans compared to other similar-sized mammals. This is an important primate characteristic associated with longer developmental and learning periods.

C. Tarsiers.

  1. tarsiers are small nocturnal primates found in the islands of _____ _____.

  2. tarsiers eat insects and small vertebrates which they catch by _____ from branches.

  3. the basic social pattern appears to be a family unit consisting of a _____ pair and their offspring.

4. the enormous _____ of tarsiers are unique.

D. Anthropoids.

 1. anthropoid characteristics that distinguish them from prosimians include

 a. generally _____ body size.

 b. larger _____ both in absolute size and in relation to body size.

 c. reduced reliance on the sense of _____ .

 d. increased reliance on _____ with forward-facing eyes placed at the front of the face.

 e. greater degree of _____ vision.

 f. _____ plate at the back of the eye socket.

 g. different pattern of blood supply than found in the prosimians.

 h. two sides of mandible are _____ .

 i. _____ specialized dentition.

 j. internal female reproductive anatomy is different than the prosimian condition.

 k. _____ gestation and maturation periods.

 l. _____ parental care.

 m. more mutual _____.

 2. monkeys represent about 70 percent of all primate species and are divided into two large groups: _____ _____monkeys and _____ _____ monkeys.

 a. New World monkeys.

  1. a characteristic that distinguishes the New World monkeys from the Old World monkeys is the shape of the _____.

   a. New World monkeys have widely flaring noses with nostrils that face _____. New World monkeys are placed in the infraorder Platyrrhini (flat-nosed).

   b. Old World monkeys have narrower noses with _____ facing nostrils. They are placed in the infraorder Catarrhini, which means "downward-facing nose."

  2. New World monkeys are almost exclusively _____ .

  3. like Old World monkeys all species, with the exception of the owl monkey, are

   _____.

  4. the New World monkeys are divided into two families: the Callitrichidae and the Cebidae.

   a. the _____ are the small marmosets and the tamarins.

    1. the marmosets and tamarins are considered to be the most

72

_____monkeys.

    a. they retain _____ instead of nails. The claws assist these quadrupedal monkeys in squirrel-like climbing of vertical trees trunks.

    b. they give birth to _____ (a prosimian trait among primates) instead of single infant.

  2. socially these monkeys live in family groups composed of either a mated pair, or a female and two adult males, plus the offspring. Males are heavily involved with _____ care.

b. there are 30 different cebid species.

  1. diet varies with most eating a combination of fruit and leaves supplemented by insects.

  2. the locomotor pattern of most cebids is _____.

    a. _____ monkeys are semibrachiators.

    b. some possess _____ tails.

  3. socially most cebids live in groups of both sexes and all ages, or as monogamous pairs with subadult offspring.

b. Old World monkeys.

  1. Old World monkeys are found from sub-Saharan Africa to the islands of Southeast Asia. Their habitats range from tropical forests to semiarid desert to even seasonally snow-covered areas in Japan and China.

  2. general characteristics of Old World monkeys.

    a. the locomotor pattern of most Old World monkeys is

_____.

    b. they are primarily arboreal. However, some have adapted to life on the ground.

    c. Old World monkeys sit erect and associated with this posture are areas of hardened skin, _____ _____, that serve as sitting pads.

  3. all of the Old World monkeys belong to one family, the Cercopithecidae, which is divided into two subfamilies, the cercopithecines and the colobines.

    a. cercopithecines.

      1. cercopithecines are more _____ than the more specialized colobines.

        a. they have a more omnivorous diet.

        b. a dietary adaptation is the presence of _____ _____

which enables these monkeys to store food while foraging.

    2. geographical distribution.

        a. most cercopithecines are found in _____.

        b. however, a number of species of _____ are also found in Asia.

  b. colobines.

    1. these animals are dietary specialists on _____.

    2. geographical distribution.

        a. the _____ monkeys are exclusively African.

        b. langurs are found in _____ and proboscis monkeys on Borneo.

4. locomotor behavior is varied.

  a. guenons, macaques, and langurs are _____ quadrupeds.

  b. baboons, patas, and macaques are _____ quadrupeds.

  c. _____ monkeys practice semibrachiation and leaping.

5. many cercopithecine species show a marked difference in size or shape between the sexes. This is called _____ _____ and is particularly pronounced in baboons.

6. females of several species exhibit pronounced cyclical changes of the external genitalia that advertises to the males that she is sexually receptive. This hormonally initiated period is called _____.

7. several types of social organization characterize Old World monkeys.

  a. colobines tend to live in small groups that contain only one or two adult _____.

  b. savanna baboons and most macaques live in _____ groups containing adults of both sexes and offspring of all ages.

E. Hominoids.

1. the superfamily _____ includes the "lesser" apes (family Hylobatidae, gibbons and siamangs), the great apes (family Pongidae), and the humans (family Hominidae).

2. hominoid characteristics that distinguish them from monkeys include

  a. _____ body size (gibbons and siamangs are exceptions).

  b. absence of a _____.

  c. _____ trunk (lumbar area relatively shorter and more stable).

  d. differences in position and musculature of the _____joint (adapted for suspensory locomotion).

  e. more _____ behavior.

      f.   more complex _____ and enhanced _____ abilities.

      g.   _____ period of infant development and dependency.

3. gibbons and siamangs.

      a.   gibbons and siamangs are found in the _____ areas of southeast Asia.

      b.   they are the _____ of the apes - gibbons weigh 13 pounds and siamangs 25 pounds.

      c.   gibbons and siamangs have anatomical features adapted for brachiation. These include

          1. extremely long _____.

          2. _____ fingers.

          3. _____ thumbs.

          4. powerful _____ muscles.

      d.   the highly specialized locomotor adaptations may be related to _____ behavior while hanging beneath branches

      e.   diet is composed largely of _____ with supplements of leaves, flowers, and insects.

      f.   the basic social unit is a _____ pair with their dependent offspring.

          1. _____ are very involved with the rearing of the offspring.

          2. the mated pair are territorial and delineate their territories with elaborate siren -like whoops and "_____."

4. orangutans (*Pongo pygmaeus*).

      a.   orangutans are found only in heavily forested areas of Borneo and Sumatra.

      b.   they are slow, cautious _____.

          1. they are almost completely _____.

          2. they do sometimes travel quadrupedally on the ground.

      c.   they are large animals (males = 200 pounds, females = 100 pounds) with pronounced_____ _____.

      d.   socially these animals are _____.

      e.   they are principally _____ (feed-eating).

5. gorillas (*Gorilla gorilla*).

      a.   gorillas are the _____ of the living primates and are confined to forested regions of central Africa.

      b.   gorillas exhibit marked sexual dimorphism, males can weigh up to 400 pounds, females 200 pounds.

      c.   because of their large size gorillas are primarily terrestrial employing a semiquadrupedal posture called _____ - _____.

    d. gorillas live in groups that consist of one (sometimes two) large

        _____ males, a few adult females, and their subadult offspring.

6. chimpanzees (*Pan troglodytes*).

    a. chimpanzees are found in equatorial _____.

    b. chimpanzees anatomically resemble gorillas in many ways particularly in

        _____proportions and _____ - _____ shape.

        1. this similarity is due to their mode of terrestrial locomotion, viz.

            _____ - _____.

        2. the _____ adaptations of chimps and gorillas differ with

            chimps spending more time in the trees.

    c. in size chimps are _____ than orangutans and gorillas; although they

        are also sexually dimorphic, it is not to the degree seen in the orangutans

        and gorillas.

    d. _____ includes quadrupedal knuckle-walking on the ground

        and brachiation (especially among younger chimps) in the trees.

    e. chimpanzees are omnivorous.

        1. they eat a large variety of both plant and animal foods

        2. chimps _____ and the hunting parties include both may and females.

            a. chimps kill and eat young monkeys, bushpigs, and antelope.

            b. prey is _____ among the group members.

    f. chimpanzees live in large, _____ communities of as many as 50 individuals.

        1. the core of the community are bonded _____ who never leave the group

            they were born into.

        2. chimp communities are fluid(individuals come and go) and consists of animals

            who occupy a particular territory, but the individual members are usually

            dispersed into small foraging parties.

        3. _____ frequently forage alone or in the company of their offspring

        4. females may leave the community either permanently or temporarily while in

            estrus. This latter behavior reduces the risk of mating with _____ male

            relatives (recall that males do not leave their birth group).

7. bonobos (*Pan paniscus*).

    a. _____ are another species of *Pan* and are only found in an area south

        of the Zaire River in Zaire.

    b. bonobos are the _____ studied of the great apes and their population is

        believed to number only a few thousand individuals.

c. bonobos differ from chimpanzees in several features.

    1. a more linear body build with _____ legs relative to arms.

    2. a relatively smaller head, a dark face from birth, and tufts of hair at the side of the face.

d. behavior.

    1. bonobos are more _____ than chimpanzees.

    2. they are less _____ among themselves.

    3. like chimps they live in _____ communities.

    4. bonobos exploit many of the same foods as chimps, including occasional _____ from killed small mammals.

5. among bonobos it is _____ - _____ bonds that constitute the societal core. This may be due to bonobo sexuality in which copulations are frequent and occur throughout the female's estrous cycle.

8. humans (*Homo sapiens*).

a. humans represent the only living species belonging to the family _____.

b. the primate heritage of humans is shown in a number of features including

    1. dependence on _____ for orientation to the world.

    2. lack of reliance on _____ cues.

    3. flexible limbs and _____ hands.

c. in diet, humans are _____ .

d. unique among animals, are the human cognitive abilities that are the result of dramatic increases in _____ size and other neurological changes.

e. humans are also completely dependent on _____ ; however, none of the technologies we have developed would have been possible without a biology that produced our highly developed cognitive abilities.

f. another unique characteristic of our species is the developed of _____ language.

    1. research with apes has revealed that these primates, while anatomically not capable of producing speech, can communicate with _____ .

g. aside from our cognitive abilities, the most distinctive characteristic that sets humans apart from other primates is our unique habitual _____ locomotion.

    1. bipedal locomotion has required significant structural modifications of the _____ and the limbs.

    2. as primates, our ancestors were already behaviorally preadapted for _____ .

V. ENDANGERED PRIMATES

A. Probably the greatest challenge facing primatologists today is the urgent need for conservation.

    1. over half of all living primates are endangered and many face immediate

    _____ .

    2. three main factors are leading to the endangerment of primate species.

        a. _____ _____ ; most primates live in tropical rain forests that are being logged or destroyed for their natural resources or for farm land.

        b. _____ for their meat.

        c. _____ _____ for either the local pet trade or to export to collectors.

    3. encompassing all of these factors is the burgeoning _____ population, which leads to competition between non-human primates and humans for scarce resources.

B. _____ per-cent of all primates live in the tropical forests of Africa, Asia, and Latin America.

C. Hunting of primates.

    1. in West Africa the most serious problem is hunting to provide " _____ _____ " to feed the growing human population.

    2. it is estimated that thousands of primates, including gorillas and chimpanzees, are killed and sold for meat every year; primates are also killed for commercial products.

D. Primates have also been live captured for zoos, biomedical research, and the exotic _____ trade.

    1. live capture has _____ dramatically in recent years.

    2. the implementation of the _____ ____ _____ ____ _____ _____ of Wild Flora and Fauna (CITES) in 1973 has made a difference. 87 countries have signed this treaty.

E. Conservation Efforts

    1. many developing countries such as Madagascar and Costa Rica have designated areas as national parks or biological _____.

    2. private organizations, such as the Rain Forest Information Center in Ecuador, have purchased land to set up biological reserves.

    3. it is only through such practices and through _____ programs that many primate species have any chance at escaping extinction.

adaptive niche: the entire way of life of an organism: where it lives, what it eats, how it obtains food, etc.

amino acid sequencing: a molecular technique in which amino acid sequences in proteins are mapped. They can then be compared between species in order to deduce evolutionary relationships.

anthropoid: any of the members of the primate suborder Anthropoidea. This suborder includes the monkeys, apes, and humans.

arboreal: living in the trees.

arboreal hypothesis: the view that primate characteristics, such as stereoscopic vision and grasping hands, are the result of evolutionary adaptation to arboreal habitats.

auditory bulla: a bony structure surrounding the middle-ear cavity that is partially formed from the temporal bone.

binocular vision: vision that results from forward facing eyes, hence overlapping visual fields. Binocular vision is a requirement for stereoscopic vision.

brachiation: a form of suspensory locomotion involving arm swinging. Found mainly among the apes.

bush meat: term used for primates and other game that are killed for food.

Callitrichidae: the family of New World monkeys that consists of the small marmosets and tamarins.

Cebidae: the family of New World monkeys that includes the capuchin, howler, squirrel, and spider monkeys. These monkeys are usually larger than the callitrichids.

Cercopithecidae: the one taxonomic family of the Old World monkeys.

cercopithecinae (cercopithecines): the subfamily of Old World monkeys that includes the baboons, macaques, and guenons.

colobinae (colobines): the subfamily of Old World monkeys that have evolved anatomical specializations in their teeth and in a large sacculated stomach for consuming a diet of leaves.

Convention on Trade in Endangered Species of Wild Flora and Fauna (CITES): a treaty aimed at the conservation of endangered organisms. This treaty has been signed by 87 nations.

cusps: the elevated portions (bumps) on the chewing surfaces of premolar and molar teeth.

dental formula: a morphological formula that gives the number of each kind of tooth for one-quarter of the mouth for a mammal. If the upper and lower dentition is different the dental formula will be presented for one-half of the mouth.

derived: refers to specialization found within a particular evolutionary lineage.

diurnal: an animal that is active during the day.

DNA hybridization: a molecular technique in which two single strands of DNA from two different species are combined to form a hybrid molecule of DNA. Evolutionary relationships can be deduced from the number of mismatched base pairs between the two strands of DNA.

estrus: period of sexual receptivity in female mammals that corresponds with ovulation. It differs from menstruation, the condition found in human females, in that the endometrial lining is reabsorbed rather than shed.

evolutionary trends: overall characteristics of an evolving lineage, such as the primates. Such trends are useful in helping categorize the lineage as compared to other lineages.

frugivory, -ous: a diet that consists mainly of fruit.

Hominoid: a member of the superfamily Hominoidea. This group includes apes and humans.

homoplasy: separate evolutionary development of similar characteristics in different groups of organisms.

intelligence: mental capacity; ability to learn, reason, or comprehend and interpret information, facts, relationships, meanings, etc.

ischial callosities: a pad of callused skin over the bone of the ischial tuberosity (a part of the pelvic bone) that serves as a sitting pad in Old World monkeys and gibbons.

Mammalia: the technical term for the formal grouping (class) of mammals.

morphology: the form (size, shape) of anatomical structures. This can include the entire organism.

nocturnal: an animal that is active during the night.

postorbital bar: a ring of bone that encloses the eye sockets in the primate skull.

postorbital plate: a plate of bone at the back of the eye orbit in primates.

primates: members of the mammalian order Primates. This includes prosimians, monkeys, apes and humans.

primatologist: a scientist that studies the biology of primates, including primate evolution.

primitive: in evolutionary terms, an organism that is most like the ancestor from which its lineage was derived. A more general member of its group. In primates the prosimians are the most primitive members.

prosimian: any of the members of the primate suborder Prosimii. Traditionally, this suborder includes lemurs, lorises, and galagos.

quadrupedal: using all four limbs to support the body during locomotion. This is the basic mammalian (and primate) form of locomotion.

rhinarium: the most, hairless pad at the end of the nose seen in most mammalian species.

sexual dimorphism: differences in physical features between males and females of the same species. Examples among primates include larger body size of males (baboons, gorillas among others) and larger canine teeth in males (baboons and chimpanzees are representative).

specialized traits: traits that have evolved to perform a particular function. Particular specialized traits are found in a specific lineage and serve to elucidate evolutionary relationships.

stereoscopic vision: a condition, due to binocular vision, in which visual images are superimposed upon one another. This is interpreted by the brain and results in the perception of depth or three-dimensional vision.

FILL-IN QUESTIONS

1. The Order Primates belongs to the more inclusive Class _____ .

2. The ability to maintain a constant internal body temperature through physiological processes is referred to as _____.

3   The overall characteristics of an evolving lineage, which may include both primitive features and specialized features, that are used to help define the lineage are called _____ _____.

4.   Primate hands and feet exhibit a high degree of _____.

5.   One of the hallmarks of the primates is the possession of a(n) _____ thumb.

6.   In most primate species, mammalian claws have been replaced by _____.

7.   The situation in which both eyes face forward, resulting in overlapping visual fields, is called_____ vision.

8.   The ability to perceive depth, i.e., see objects in three-dimensions, is called _____ vision.

9.   Primates have a heavy reliance on vision, while they have a decreased reliance on _____ _____.

10.   The single most important factor influencing the evolutionary divergence of the primates was the adaptation for _____ living.

11.   The idea that many primate characteristics are due to adaptations to life in the trees is called the _____ _____.

12.   An alternative hypothesis to many primate features being selected by the arboreal environment is the _____ _____ hypothesis. This hypothesis posits that early primates evolved in the bush layer of the forest where they traveled on thin vertical supports and fed on insects.

13.   A third suggestion Is related to angiosperms, or _____ _____.

14.   Most nonhuman primates are found in the _____ regions of the world.

15.   Primates have generalized dentition which is a result of the _____ diet.

16.   Locomotion which involves walking on all four legs is termed _____.

17.   A form of locomotion, found principally among prosimians, which involves pushing off of tree trunks, rotating in mid-air so that the feet land on the tree trunk that the animal is moving towards, is called _____ _____ and _____.

18.   A primate with arms longer than legs, a short stable lumbar spine, long curved fingers, and reduced thumbs would have _____ as its primary mode of locomotion.

19.   The traditional classification of primates divided the order into two suborders, the _____ and the _____.

20.   _____ _____ is a technique in which strands of DNA from two separate species are combined to form a "hybrid" molecule. This molecule can be examined for mismatched pairs to deduce genetic relatedness.

21.   Based on DNA, chimpanzees are most closely related to _____.

22.   The _____ are the most primitive group of primates.

23. A dental adaptation that assists lemurs in both grooming and feeding is the _____
    _____.

24. Lorises survived on continental areas, such as Africa and Asia, by adopting a
    _____ activity pattern.

25. Hardened skin over the ischial tuberosities of Old World monkeys, which are used as sitting
    pads, are called _____ _____.

26. The subfamily of the Cercopithedae that specialize on eating leaves is the _____.

27. Some terrestrial cercopithecines have a marked difference in body size between the males
    and the females. The males are sometimes twice the size of the females. This difference
    between the sexes is called _____ _____.

28. Female baboons (as well as some other cercopithecine species) have a pronounced swelling
    and color change in their external genitalia. These changes are associated with a type of
    reproductive cycling called _____.

29. Apes and humans belong to the superfamily _____.

30. The most distinctive feature of gibbons and siamangs relate to their functional adaptation
    for_____.

31. The largest living primate is the _____.

32. The genus *Pan* consists of two species. The common names for these two species are
    chimpanzees and _____.

33. The most distinctive characteristic of humans that has affected a number of anatomical
    traits and makes us unique among the primates is habitual _____.

MULTIPLE CHOICE QUESTIONS

1. Which of the following is **not** an evolutionary trend of primates?
   A. a tendency for males to be permanent members of primate social groups.
   B. a tendency for most species to be active at night, i.e. nocturnal.
   C. the lack of any dietary specialization.
   D. binocular vision.
   E. both A and B are not primate evolutionary trends.

2. Which of the following is **not** a primate trend?
   A. stereoscopic vision
   B. highly developed sense of smell
   C. orthograde or upright posture
   D. opposable thumbs and great toes
   E. retention of the clavicle

3. Binocular vision in primates results in
   A. color vision.
   B. dichromatic vision.
   C. panoramic vision.
   D. stereoscopic vision.
   E. lateral vision.

4. The formula 2-1-2-3 corresponds to what order of teeth?
   A. molar, pre-molars, canines, incisors.
   B. premolars, incisors, molars, canines.
   C. canines, premolars, incisors, molars.
   D. incisors, premolars, canines, molars.
   E. incisors, canines, premolars, molars.

5. The dental formula in all Old World monkeys, including apes, and humans is
   A. 3-1-4-4.
   B. 2-1-3-4
   C. 2-1-3-3
   D. 2-1-2-3
   E. 2-1-3-2

6. The tarsier has a dental formula of 2-1-3-3/1-1-3-3. How many incisors does a tarsier have?
   A. 2
   B. 3
   C. 4
   D. 6
   E. 8

7. Referring to the question above, how many teeth do tarsiers have?
   A. 17
   B. 18
   C. 34
   D. 36
   E. 38

8. Which of the following statements is correct?
   A. arboreal quadrupeds have slightly shorter forelimbs.
   B. terrestrial quadrupeds have nearly equal length forelimbs and hindlimbs.
   C. brachiators have longer hindlimbs than forelimbs.
   D. prehensile tails are only found in monkeys.
   E. both A and B are correct.

9. A form of locomotion found among some of the smaller lemurs and tarsiers is
   A. vertical clinging and leaping.
   B. quadrupedalism .
   C. scampering.
   D. bipedalism.
   E. brachiation.

10. Taxonomically tarsiers are classified with
    A. prosimians.
    B. anthropoids.
    C. strepsirhines.
    D. haplorhines
    E. both A and D, depending on the taxonomic scheme.

11. Prosimians are considered to be the most primitive of the primates. What does "primitive" mean in evolutionary biology?
    A. least derived.
    B. most like the ancestor.
    C. poorly adapted.
    D. inferior.
    E. both A and B.

12. In which type of primate would a "dental comb" be found
    A. lemur.
    B. New World Monkey.
    C. Old World Monkey.
    D. gibbon.
    E. orangutan.

13. Lemurs are found exclusively in
    A. Madagascar.
    B. India.
    C. Borneo.
    D. Sri Lanka.
    E. the Malay peninsula.

14. Lemurs seem to have survived on Madagascar because
    A. it was the center of their adaptive radiation.
    B. they were isolated from competition with higher primates.
    C. there were no birds for competition for arboreal resources.
    D. they lived on the ground.
    E. both B and C are correct.

15. Which of the following traits is characteristic of the ring-tailed lemur?
    A. terrestrial.
    B. completely enclosed bony orbits.
    C. solitary.
    D. prehensile tail.
    E. brachiation.

16. Which of the following is **not** true of tarsiers?
    A. nocturnal.
    B. insectivorous.
    C. can rotate their heads almost 180°.
    D. well developed color vision.

17. Which of the following is **not** generally a characteristic of anthropoids.
    A. a bony plate that encloses the orbit.
    B. decreased gestation period.
    C. a relatively larger brain.
    D. an absolutely larger brain.
    E. increased parental care.

18. The only nocturnal monkey is the
    A. baboon.
    B. chimpanzee.
    C. tamarin.
    D. howler.
    E. owl monkey.

19. Which of the following is **not** true regarding New World monkeys?
    A. some have prehensile tails.
    B. nostrils face downward.
    C. almost all are arboreal.
    D. one group retains claws.
    E. both B and C are true.

20. Which of the following structures are found in cercopithecines?
    A. dental comb.
    B. prehensile tail.
    C. claws.
    D. sacculated stomach.
    E. cheek pouch.

21. The term "sexual dimorphism" refers to
    A. differences in size and structure between males and females.
    B. differences in behavior between males and females.
    C. differences in reproductive physiology between males and females.
    D. females being biologically more important than males.
    E. parallel evolution between males and females of different species.

22. The reproductive cycle in non-human female primates is called
    A. estrus.
    B. menarche.
    C. menstruation .
    D. ischial callosities.
    E. hylobates.

23. Which of the following hominoids delineate their territories by śound?
    A. siamangs.
    B. orangutans.
    C. gibbons.
    D. gorillas.
    E. both A and C.

24. A frugivore is standing in front of a vending machine? Which item will the frugivore select?
    A. Koala Brother's Eucalyptus Cough Drops.
    B. Rainbow Fruit Bar.
    C. Rigney's Chewing Gum.
    D. Sunnyview Farms Sunflower Seeds.
    E. Rip Tyle's Chocolate-Covered Ants.

25. Which of the following applies to chimpanzees?
    A. insectivorous.
    B. live in monogamous family units.
    C. usually bipedal.
    D. occasionally hunt and eat young monkeys.
    E. smallest of the great apes.

26. In what way do bonobos differ from chimpanzees?
    A. more terrestrial than chimps.
    B. larger head relative to body size.
    C. longer legs relative to arms.
    D. larger body size.
    E. dietary specialists.

27. Which of the following statements is **not** true?
    A. genetic data is in conflict with taxonomies based on morphology.
    B. a problem with morphologically based taxonomy is similarities in species resulting from parallel evolution.
    C. humans have 46 chromosomes; chimpanzees have 48 chromosomes.
    D. DNA hybridization studies suggest that humans and chimpanzees are more closely related to each other than either is to the gorilla.
    E. humans and chimpanzees differ in only one amino acid in the hemoglobin beta chain.

28. Which of the following is not a reason that nonhuman primates are endangered?
    A. habitat destruction for logging, mining, and agriculture land.
    B. hunting for food and commercial products.
    C. live capture for either the exotic pet trade or biomedical research.
    D. establishment of biological reserves.
    E. pressures from the expanding human population.

ANSWERS TO OUTLINE

I. **PRIMATE AS MAMMALS**
    A. 1. species
II. **CHARACTERISTICS OF PRIMATES**
    A. share
        1. body hair
        2. live
        3. homeothermy
        4. increased
        5. flexibility
    B. retained
        1. specialized
        2. defined
            a. evolutionary
                (1) trends
                (2) general
            b. Order
    C. 1. erect posture
        2. generalized
        3. prehensility
            a. five
            b. thumb
            c. nails
            d. tactile
    D. 1. specialization
        2. generalized
    E. 1. heavily
            A. Color
            b. stereoscopic
                (1) binocular
                (2) visual
                (3) three
        2. decreased
        3. complex
    F. 1. fetal, longer, reduced, delayed, extension
        2. behavior
        3. permanent
        4. diurnal

III. PRIMATE ADAPTATIONS

- A.
  1. Arboreal
  2. depth perception
  3. climbing
  4. diet, generalized
  5. arboreal hypothesis
  6. a. visual predation
     b shrubby forest undergrowth
        (1) forward-facing
        (2) angiosperms
  7. a. nonarboreal
     b. preadapted
- B. Geographic Distribution and Habitats
  1. tropical
  2. arboreal
  3. ground
  4. ground
  5. adapted
- C.
  1. omnivorous
  2. fruit, leaves, insects
     a. mammals
     b. leaves
  3. four
     a. incisors, canines
     b. chewing
  4. number
     a. Incisor, Canine, Premolar, Molar
     b. quadrant
        1. 36
        2. three
  5. 44
     a. evolutionary
  6. specialization
- D.
  1. four
     a. structure
     b. terrestrial
     c. 1. equal
        2. shorter
     d. spine
  2. prosimians
  3. apes
     a. gibbons, siamangs
     b. 1. longer
        2. lumbar
        3. curved
        4. thumbs
     c. climbers

        d. semibrachiators
    4. a. New World monkeys
        b. prehensile

IV. A SURVEY OF THE LIVING PRIMATES
  A. Primate Taxonomy
    1. specific
       (a) order
       (b) two
          (1) Prosimii, more
          (2) Anthropoidea
       c. species
       d. relationships
    2. a (1) share
          (2) a. common
              b. morphology
       b. (1) sequence
          (2) proteins
       c. (1) hybridization
          (2) a. close
    3.   (1) prosimians
          (2) anthropoids
          (3) distinct
       e. suborders
          (1) Strepsirhini
          (2) Haplorhini
  B. Prosimians
    1. most
    2. a. olfaction
          1. rhinarium
          2. scent
       b. laterally
       c. shorter
       d. dental comb
          1. incisors, canines
          2. grooming
    3. Lemurs
       a. Madagascar
          1. diversified
          2. extinct
       b. 1. mouse lemur
          2. larger
          3. insectivorous
          4. a. terrestrial
              b. vertical clingers and leapers
              c. groups
                 1. monogamous
                 2. solitary

4. Lorises
    b. competition
    d. galago
    e. 1. a. lorises
              b. galagos
        2. a. insectivorous
              b. combinations
              c. alone
        3. overlap
5. adaptive level
    a. life

C. Tarsiers
  1. Southeast Asia
  2. leaping
  3. mated
  4. enormous

D. Anthropoids
  1. a. larger
      b. brain
      c. smell
      d. vision
      e. color
      f. bony
      h fused
      i. less
      k. longer
      l. increased
      m. grooming
  2. New World, Old World
      a. 1. nose
              a. outward
              b. downward
        2. arboreal
        3. diurnal
        4. a. callitrichids
                1. primitive
                    a. claws
                    b. twins
                2. infant
        b. 2. quadrupedalism
                a. spider
                b. prehensile
      b. 2. a. quadrupedalism
             c. ischial callosities
        3. a. 1. generalized
                b. cheek pouches
             2. a. Africa

                        b. macaques
                    b. leaves
                        2. a. colobus
                            b. Asia
                4. a. arboreal
                    b. terrestrial
                    c. colobus
                5. sexual dimorphism
                6. estrus
                7. a. males
                    b. large
    E. Hominoids
        1. Hominoidea
        2. a. larger
            b. tail
            c. shortened
            d. shoulder
            e. complex
            f. brain, cognitive
            g. Increased
        3. Gibbons and Siamangs
            a. tropical
            b. smallest
            c. 1. arms
                2. curved
                3. short
                4. shoulder
            d. feeding
            e. fruit
            f. monogamous
                1. males
                2. songs
        4. Orangutans
            b. climbers
                1. arboreal
            c. sexual dimorphism
            d. solitary
            e. frugivorous
        5. Gorillas
            a. largest
            c. knuckle-walking
            d. silverback
        6. Chimpanzees
            a. Africa
            b. limb, upper-body
                1. knuckle-walking
                2. ecological

          c. smaller

          d. locomotion

          e. 2. hunt

               b. shared

          f. fluid

               1. males

               3. females

               4. close

      7. Bonobos

          a. bonobos

          b. least

          c. 1. longer

          d. 1. arboreal

               2. aggressive

               3. fluid

               4. meat

               5. male-female

      8. Humans

          a. Hominidae

          b. 1. vision

               2. olfactory

               3. grasping

          c. omnivorous

          d. brain

          e. culture

          f. spoken

               1. primate

               2. symbols

          g. bipedal

               1. pelvis

               2. bipedalism

V. ENDANGERED PRIMATES

   A. 1. extinction

       2. a. habitat destruction

          b. hunting

          c. live capture

       3. human

   B. Ninety

   C. 1. bush meat

   D. pet

       1. declined

       2. Convention on Trade in Endangered Species

   E. 1. reserves

       3. educational

ANSWERS & REFERENCES TO FILL-IN QUESTIONS

1.   Mammalia, p. 82
2.   homeothermy, p. 83
3.   evolutionary trends, p. 83
4.   prehensility, p. 84
5.   opposable, p. 84
6.   nails, p. 84
7.   binocular, p. 84
8.   stereoscopic, p. 84
9.   the sense of smell or olfaction, p. 85
10. arboreal, p. 86
11. arboreal hypothesis, p. 87
12. visual predation, p. 87
13. flowering plants, p. 87
14. tropical, p. 87
15. omnivorous, p. 90
16. quadrupedalism, p. 90
17. vertical clinging and leaping, p. 92
18. brachiation, p. 92
19. Prosimii, Anthropoidea, p. 93
20. DNA hybridization, p. 95
21. humans, p. 95
22. prosimians, p. 96
23. dental comb, p. 96
24. nocturnal, p. 97
25. ischial callosities, p. 100
26. colobines, p. 101.
27. sexual dimorphism, p. 102
28. estrus, p. 102
29. Hominoidea, p. 102
30. brachiation, p. 103
31. gorilla, p. 104
32. bonobos, p. 107
33. bipedalism, p. 109

ANSWERS & REFERENCES TO MULTIPLE CHOICE QUESTIONS

1.   B, pp. 83-86
2.   B, pp. 84-86
3.   D, p. 84
4.   E, p. 90
5.   D, p. 90
6.   D, p. 90
7.   C, p. 90
8.   E, pp. 90-91
9.   A, p. 92
10. E. p. 95
11. E, p. 96

12. A, p. 96
13. A, p. 96
14. B, p. 96
15. A, p. 96
16. D, p. 98
17. B, p. 98
18. E, p. 99
19. B, p. 99
20. E, p. 101
21. A, p. 102
22. A, p. 102
23. E, p. 103
24. B, p. 104
25. D, p. 106
26. C, p. 107
27. A, p. 95
28. D, pp. 109-110

CHAPTER 6
PRIMATE BEHAVIOR

LEARNING OBJECTIVES

After reading this chapter you should be able to:

- Understand why anthropologists study nonhuman primate behavior, p. 121
- Understand the complexity of socioecology, pp. 122-123
- Have a general understanding of an evolutionary perspective in primatology, pp. 123-125
- Understand the problems in applying an evolutionary perspective to primate behavior, pp. 125-126
- Discuss aspects of social behavior found among all nonhuman primates, i.e., dominance hierarchies, communication, aggression, affiliative behaviors, grooming, reproductive strategies, mother-infant relationship, and cultural behaviors, pp. 126-139
- Recount various studies on primate cognition and language capabilities, pp. 139-143
- Comprehend that, although unique, humans are part of a biological continuum, pp. 143-144

FILL-IN OUTLINE

Introduction

In the last chapter the student was introduced to the primate order and some of the biological characteristics that distinguish different groups of primates. In this chapter we look at behavioral characteristics found among primates including dominance, grooming, reproductive strategies and mother-infant relationships. We discuss socioecology and the complexity of interpreting primate behaviors from an evolutionary perspective. We examine primate cultural behavior including tool use. An overview of studies done on primate language capabilities is presented. Finally, we end the chapter by looking at the human place in a biological continuum.

I. **THE IMPORTANCE OF PRIMATE STUDIES**
  A. Modern African apes and humans last shared a common ancestor between
        _____ and _____ million years ago.
  B. Since all living organisms must adapt to their environment, correlating aspects of social structure with _____ is informative.
  C. _____ monkeys have scarcely been studied.

II. **PRIMATE SOCIOECOLOGY**
  A. Socioecology refers to studying free-ranging primates by focusing on the relationship between social_____ and the natural
        _____.

  B. One of the underlying assumptions in socioecology is that various components of _____ systems evolved _____.

C. The environmental factors taken into consideration by primatologists include the quality and quantity of different _____.
D. Primatologists also look at the distribtuion of _____ resources, _____, _____ and _____ sites.
E. The relationships among ecological variables, social organization and behavior _____ _____ been worked out.
F. Multimale and multifemale groups are viewed as advantageous where _____ pressure is high.
G. _____males may _____ _____ to chase and attack predator.
   1. An example of this principle is the _____ _____.
   2. They have been known to kill domestic _____ and to attack _____ and _____.
H. Solitary foraging may be related to _____ and distribution of_____.
I. The loris is an example of a solitary feeder which _____ competition.
J. Solitary foraging may also be related to _____ avoidance.
K. Large-bodied females foraging alone or with offspring may have little to _____ from _____.
L. Feeding alone may maximize _____ to food.
M. Certain environmental factors such as _____ availability and _____ seem to exert strong influence on group size and structure.

III. THE EVOLUTION OF BEHAVIOR
A. An _____ _____ is the theoretical framework for interpreting primate behavior.
B. An evolutionary perspective looks at the evolution of behavior through the operation of _____ _____.
C. According to the evolutionary perspective, _____ is a phenotypic expression.
D. Individuals whose _____ influence behaviors may have higher _____ success.
E. The implication is that _____ code for specific _____.
F. Controversy arises when attempts are made to apply the evolutionary perspective to_____.
G. The fear is that if behaviors are explained in terms of _____ it could be used to support _____ views.
H. Among insects and lower vertebrates behavioral patterns are _____.
I. Among primates and humans most behavior results from _____.
J. In higher organisms some behaviors are influenced by gene _____, such as hormones.
K. Increased levels of _____ has been shown to increase aggressive behavior in many _____ species.
L. Behavior is the product of interactions between _____ and _____factors.

M. Problems arise when trying to apply the mechanics of behavioral evolution in complex _____ animals.

N. Sarah Blaffer Hrdy's explanation of _____ among Hanuman   langurs of India is cited as an example among primates.

O. Individuals act to maximize _____ _____ reproductive success.

P. When an infant dies the mother ceases to _____ and soon becomes _____ receptive.

   1. This is _____ to the male who has taken over.

Q. Infanticide is found in many primate species. It usually occurs in conjunction with the transfer of a _____ _____ into a group.

R. Many _____ surround the evolutionary perspective.

S. The five central problems with research from the evolutionary perspective include:

   (1)_____,

   (2)_____,

   (3)_____,

   (4)_____,

   (5)_____.

T. Evidence suggests that natural selection often works simply to "_____ _____."

U. The indri on Madagascar are not particularly _____.

V. The longest-term studies have been conducted on _____ and _____ and it still only includes two generations.

W. This approach provides an opportunity to study the effects _____ _____ has had in shaping primate behavior.

IV. PRIMATE SOCIAL BEHAVIOR

A. Dominance

   1. Dominance hierarchies impose a degree of _____ within the group.

   2. Dominant animals have priority access to _____ and _____ _____.

   3. Rank is not _____.

   4. Many factors influence one's status including _____, _____, level of _____, time spent in the _____, _____, perhaps_____, _____ and sometimes the _____'s social position.

   5. Position in the hierarchy is _____.

   6. _____ and _____ are indications of dominance and subordination.

   7. Young primates learn how to negotiate through social interactions by early contact with the _____ and exposure to _____.

B. Communication

   1. Raised body hair or enhanced body odor are examples of _____responses.

   2. Vocalizations, intense staring and branch shaking are examples of _____modes of communication.

3. _____ gestures might include a quick yawn to expose canines or bobbing back and forth in a crouched position.
4. Reassurance can take the form of _____, _____, _____ or holding _____.
5. The _____ _____ is seen in all primates to indicate fear and submission.
6. _____ are used to inform others that predators or food may be present.
7. _____ serve to communicate emotional states.
8. _____ is what makes social living possible.

C. Aggression
1. _____ is the area where a primate lives permanently.
2. _____ is the area that a primate might defend.
3. Jane Goodall and her colleagues witnessed _____ and _____ attacks of chimpanzees by other chimpanzees.
4. Territoriality and acquisition of _____ are the motives suggested for chimpanzee male aggression.

D. Affiliative Behaviors
1. _____ group stability.
2. Pertain to _____ associations between individuals.
3. Most affiliative behaviors involve _____ _____.
4. _____ is one of the most important affiliative behavior among primates.
5. Grooming is not only _____ by keeping each other clean but it is immensely _____.
6. Grooming _____ social bonds.
7. Hugging, kissing and grooming are all forms used in _____
8. _____ or _____ are used to enhance the status of members of a group.
9. _____ behaviors benefit another and pose some risk or sacrifice to the performer.

V. **REPRODUCTION AND REPRODUCTIVE STRATEGIES**
A. Patterns of Reproduction
1. Females are sexually receptive when they are in _____.
2. Visual cues to a female's sexual readiness include _____ and changes in color of the skin around the _____ _____.
3. The temporary relationship between male and female savanna baboons for mating purposes is called _____.
4. Male and female _____ may mate even when the female is not in estrus.
   a. This behavior is not typical of _____ male and females.
B. Reproductive Strategies
1. The _____ is to produce and rear to_____ as many offspring as possible.

2. _____-_____ refers to the production of a few young with an investment of parental care.

3. _____-_____ refers to the production of many offspring with little parental care.

4. Primates are _____ at birth.

5. Primates learn within a _____ environment.

6. _____ and _____ have different strategies to meet life's challenges.

7. The _____ demands on female primates due to pregnancy, lactation and caring for offspring is _____.

8. Many female primates are viciously _____ to protect resources.

9. To increase his genetic contribution to the next generation, male primates will secure as many _____ as possible.

10. Male competition for mates and mate choice in females are both examples of _____.

11. Female birds frequently select males with _____ _____ plumage.

12. Males of many primate species are _____ than females.

VI. MOTHERS AND INFANTS

A. Except in those species in which _____ or _____ occurs, males do not participate in rearing offspring.

B. For a non-human primate mother to properly care for her offspring she should have had a _____ _____ with her own mother.

C. In an experiment where monkeys were raised with no mother, they were _____ of forming lasting _____ ties.

D. Monkeys need to _____ rules of social behavior.

E. The close mother-infant relationship does not always end with _____.

VII. NONHUMAN PRIMATE CULTURAL BEHAVIOR

A. Most biological anthropologists feel that it is appropriate to use the term _____ in referring to nonhuman primates as well as humans.

B. Cultural behavior is _____ and passed on from one generation to the next.

C. Young primate infants learn appropriate _____.

D. Imo was a Japanese macaque who began _____ her sweet potatoes before eating them.

E. Dietary habits and _____ preferences are learned.

F. Examples of chimpanzee tools include _____ fishing sticks (or rods), _____ sponges, twigs as _____ and _____ as weapons.

G. Chimpanzees exhibit regional _____ in their tool use.

H. Kanzi learned to strike two stones together and make _____-_____ flakes.

I. Kanzi resolved his difficulties in making flakes by throwing the stone onto a _____ _____.

J. Evolution is not _____ directed.

K. Nonhuman primate behaviors that have been recently documented by humans are not _____ _____ in our nonhuman primate relatives.

VIII. PRIMATE COGNITIVE ABILITIES

A. Vervet monkeys have three different vocalizations to indicate _____.

B. Humans have the ability to think _____.

C. Human language, as a mode of communication is _____.

D. Humans and apes have differences in the anatomy of the _____ _____ and the _____-related structures in the brain.

E. Washoe learned _____.

F. Sara learned to recognize _____ _____ as symbols for objects.

G. Koko, a female _____ uses more than _____ signs of _____.

H. A male orangutan named Chantek learned to sign in reference to objects that were not _____.

I. Chimps have also shown that they can _____ unfamiliar objects.

J. Kanzi _____ acquired language and used symbols by age 2-1/2 years.

K. For human evolution _____ became very important.

IX. THE PRIMATE CONTINUUM

A. When traits or behaviors are seen to continuously _____ into one another so that there are no discrete _____ it is said to be part of a continuum.

B. The differences in some human and chimpanzee behaviors is one of _____.

KEY TERMS

affiliative: friendly relations between individuals.

agonistic: aggressive or defensive social interactions

alloparenting: individuals other than the parents take care of infants.

altruism: helping another individual at some risk or cost but with no direct benefit to oneself.

anthropocentic: interpreting nonhuman traits and behaviors from the perspective of human values and experiences. Viewing humans as the most important entity in the world.

autonomic: involuntary physiological responses

biological continuum: traits and behaviors that continuously grade into one another with no discrete categories in organisms that are related through common ancestry.

bisexual: refers to both sexes

consortships: temporary relationship between one adult male and an estrous female

core areas: a portion of a home range where reliable resources are found such as food, water and sleeping trees.

displays: physical movements that convey an emotional state

diurnal: active during the day

dominance hierarchies: systems of social organization wherein individuals are ranked relative to one another based on priority access to food and sex.

ecological: the relationship between organisms and all aspects of their environment

encephalization: a predictable relationship between brain size and body size.

estrus: period of sexual receptivity in female mammals (except humans) correlated with ovulation.

evolutionary ecology: behavioral attributes that have evolved due to demands imposed by a particular environment.

evolutionary perspective: a theoretical framework which looks at behavior within an evolutionary context. If a behavior has a genetic basis it will be subject to natural selection. (Formerly referred to as "sociobiology.")

free-ranging: noncaptive animals living in their natural habitat

grooming: picking through fur to remove dirt, parasites or any other material that may be present.

home-range: the geographic area, usually permanent, exploited by an animal or social group for food, water and sleeping areas.

inclusive fitness: the total contribution of an individual's genes to the next generation, including those genes shared by close relatives.

infanticide: the killing of infants

inter: between (i.e., intergroup)

intra: within (i.e., intragroup)

K-selected: a reproductive strategy wherein the individuals produce fewer offspring but increase parental investment of care, time and   energy

monogamous pair: a mated pair and its young.

natal group: the group in which an individual is born.

nocturnal: active at night

philopatric: remaining in one's natal group or home range as an adult.

Physiology: the physical and chemical phenomena involved with the functions and activities of an organism or any of its various parts

polyandry: one female with multiple males.

presenting: a subordinate animal presents his/her rear to a dominant animal

reproductive strategies: behavioral patterns that contribute to an individual's reproductive success, i.e., producing and successfully rearing to adulthood as many offspring as possible.

sexual selection: a type of natural selection operating on one sex (usually males). It may be the result of males competing for mates or female preference in choosing sexual partners.

social grooming: grooming done for pleasure. Common among primates and reinforces social relationships.

social intelligence: the ability to assess a social situation before acting and storing information related to social interactions.

social structure: the composition, size and sex ratio of a group of animals.

socioecology: attempts to find patterns of relationship between environment, biological needs and social behaviors when studying animals

sympatric: two or more species who live in the same area.

territory: the part of the home range that animals will defend

FILL-IN QUESTIONS

1. _____ monkeys have barely been studied.

2. Primatologists are attempting to analyze the relationship between social behavior and the natural environment. This approach is called _____.

3. Primate social structure is integrated. To understand the function of any single aspect of primate social structure one must look at its relationship with numerous other aspects of the environment including _____, _____,
_____, _____, _____,
_____, _____, _____
and _____..

4. Solitary foraging may be related to _____ and distribution of _____.

5. The assumption of the evolutionary perspective is that if a behavior has a genetic basis it will be subject to natural selection. The problem of applying this approach to primate behavior is that much of primate behavior is _____

_____.

6. One of the fears that arise when applying the concept of specific genes coding for specific human behaviors is that it would be used to support _____ and _____ views.

7. The ability of an organism to adjust physiologically to differing conditions is called

_____.

8. Explain how infanticide among Hanuman langurs is used as an example of behavioral evolution. _____

_____.

9. Lack of long-term data makes testing hypotheses difficult in _____.

10. Two possible explanations are offered for why primates live in social groups. These explanations include _____ and _____.

11. One of the disadvantages offered for primates living in social groups is competition for

_____

_____.

12. Dominance hierarchies are learned, change throughout life and are determined by priority access to food and sex. These factors help to _____ physical violence within primate social groups.

13. Since high-ranking females have greater access to food than subordinate females they are provided with more energy for _____ production and _____.

14. A young primate's position in the hierarchy is part of its learning experience. In particular, observing its _____ and how other members _____ to her. It also learns through _____ with age peers.

15. Communication is a critical aspect of primate social structure. It can be unintentional or deliberate. Unintentional communication that conveys an emotional state is called autonomic and raised body_____ or enhanced body _____ would be an example of it.

16. An example of deliberate nonhuman primate communication could include_____, _____ or _____.

17. Certain nonhuman primate behaviors are meant to convey friendly, submissive or reassuring messages. Baboons may convey submission by presenting their _____.

18. The chimpanzee and bonobo fear grin indicates _____ and _____.

19. Affiliative behaviors can be used in reconciliation, reassurance or just to be friendly. Examples of affiliative behaviors might include _____ or _____.

20. Grooming has hygenic and social functions. One of its social functions would be to reinforce _____.

21. Reconciliation takes many forms including _____, _____ and _____.

22. To defend territories between groups and to protect resources, _____ may be used.

23. Estrus is the period of female sexual receptivity associated with ovulation in female non-human primates. A male non-human primate would know that a female was in estrus by certain physical cues, namely, _____ and _____ of skin around the _____ area.

24. Consortships are temporary relationships that last while the female is _____.

25. Sexual selection is a type of natural selection that usually acts on males. Two selective agents discussed in the text include male competition for _____ and choice in _____.

26. The presence or absence of sexually dimorphic traits is a reasonably good indicator of mating structure. What is the probable mating structure where pronounced sexual dimorphism is found?

_____ or _____.

27. The mother-infant relationship among primates is critical. However, for a female to be a good mother studies have shown that she must have had a normal experience with her

_____.

28 Most infant primates are cared for by the mother. However, in a polyandrous mating system such as the _____ and _____ the males participate greatly ion caring for infants.

29. Nonhuman primates do not deliberately teach their young "cultural" behaviors. Rather, their offspring learn these behaviors through _____.

30. Chimpanzees carefully select a piece of vine, bark or twig, strip the leaves and modify it to make a termite stick. It could be said that they are _____ a tool.

31. To open nuts chimpanzees in West Africa use _____ with _____.

32. Chimpanzees are the only nonhuman primate that consistently and habitually _____ and _____ tools.

33. Among chimpanzees we see regional variation in tool use and food preferences. These differences are similar to human cultural variations particularly because they are not related to

_____.

34. Kanzi showed brilliant problem-solving ability in attempting to learn how to make cutting implements out of stone. He realized that if he _____ the stone on a hard _____ it would shatter and produce plenty of cutting tools. He would then use these tools to cut open a bag containing food.

35. Although it is probable that early hominids used tools in much the same way that nonhuman primates do today, this does not mean that nonhuman primates are "_____" to becoming human.

36. In most animal species altruistic behaviors are limited to protecting _____

_____.

37. Among chimpanzees the adoption of orphaned youngsters is common. They are usually adopted by older _____.

38. Vervet monkey vocalizations refer to _____ components of the external environment.

39. Human language is composed of symbols that in themselves have no relationship to what they stand for. Human language is therefore said to be _____.

40. Nonhuman primates lack the anatomical structures for speech but they do not necessarily lack the _____ to interpret visual signs and use them to communicate.

41. In 1966 two psychologists taught ASL to a chimpanzee named _____.

42. In later years Washoe deliberately _____ another chimpanzee, Loulis, some signs.

43. Two gorillas, Koko and Michael, communicate with each other via _____.

44. Bonobo Kanzi and his sister were exposed to lexigrams while their _____ was being trained.

45. In language studies with nonhuman primates it appears that they show some capabilities in symbolic thought. From this, primatologists have hypothesized that perhaps the last common _____ between apes and humans possessed abilities to _____ similar to those we now see in apes.

46. In recent years it has become apparent that humans are part of a _____.

MULTIPLE CHOICE QUESTIONS

1. Among primates, _____ can be viewed as adaptive responses to environmental demands
   A. Behaviors
   B. Blood types
   C. bone density
   D. All of the above

2. One of the underlying assumptions of socioecology is that
   A. intelligent organisms can manipulate their environment
   B. The various components of ecological systems evolved together
   C. Social structures are independent of ecological structures
   D. The distribution of sleeping sites determines a species activity pattern

3. Group size and composition of nonhuman primate species
   A. Is well understood
   B. Appears to be related to obtaining food
   C. Appears to be related to avoiding predators
   D. All of the above
   E. B & C only

4. Where predation pressure is high we find group composition to be
    A. Multi-male/multi-female
    B. One male
    C. Monogamous pair
    D. Solitary

5. Savannah baboons
    A. Sleep on the ground
    B. Sleep in trees
    C. Spend much of the day on the ground
    D. Spend much of the day in trees
    E. B & C only

6. An evolutionary perspective holds that
    A. Behavior is learned
    B. Behavior has a genetic basis
    C. A primatologist should consider the environmental influences affecting primate behavior
    D. All of the above

7. The behavior of insects is
    A. Largely under genetic control
    B. Innate
    C. Learned
    D. All of the above
    E. A & B only

8. To support the theoretical framework of an evolutionary perspective among primates
    A. Infanticide is used
    B. Genotype-phenotype interactions are used
    C. Behavior and reproductive success are used
    D. All of the above

9. Dominance hierarchies
    A. Increase aggression and fighting within a group
    B. Have no apparent function in social groups
    C. Provide a degree of order
    D. Are limited to adult males

10. Dominance hierarchies
    A. Guarantee that dominant males are more reproductively successful
    B. Result in dominant individuals having priority access to food
    C. Don't guarantee a reproductive advantage to dominant males
    D. Are permanent
    E. B & C only

11. Unintentional modes of communication among nonhuman primates might include
    A. Enhanced odor
    B. Raised body hair
    C. Gestures
    D. Facial expressions
    E. A & B only

12. Which of the following is not a threat gesture among nonhuman primates?
    A. A quick yawn to expose canines
    B. An intense stare
    C. Bobbing back and forth
    D. Mounting

13. Displays
    A. Communicate an emotional state
    B. Reassure others in the group
    C. Console others
    D. All of the above

14. Affiliative behaviors
    A. Are amicable behaviors
    B. Defuse potentially dangerous situations
    C. Promote group cohesiveness
    D. All of the above
    E. A & C only

15. Grooming
    A. Occurs in a variety of contexts
    B. Is usually associated with mother and offspring
    C. Is usually associated with mating
    D. Usually occurs with family members

16. Bonds between individual nonhuman primates
    A. Usually end at adolescence
    B. Can last a lifetime
    C. Usually develop in adulthood
    D. Are inconsistent

17. Regarding the geographic areas in which nonhuman primates eat, sleep and mate:
    A. Home ranges won't overlap
    B. Core areas will be defended
    C. Core areas may overlap
    D. Territories may overlap

18. The reproductive strategy among primates
    A. Is similar for males and females
    B. Is termed K-selected
    C. Is termed r-selected
    D. Requires an enormous investment from at least one parent
    E. B & D only

19. Sexual selection
    A. Is a type of natural selection
    B. Operates on only one sex
    C. Usually operates on males
    D. May refer to female choice in mates
    E. All of the above

20. Mothering among primates appears to be
    A. innate
    B. Learned
    C. Dependent on a normal experience with one's own mother
    D. B & C only

21. Human behavior is
    A. No more complex than that of other primates
    B. Predominantly learned
    C. Predominantly genetic
    D. Similar to that of early hominids

22. Modern African apes and humans last shared a common ancestor
    A. 20 m.y.a.
    B. 15 m.y.a.
    C. 8 to 5 m.y.a.
    D. 11 m.y.a.

23. The "famous" example(s) of nonhuman cultural behavior cited in the book include:
    A. Japanese macaque females opening nuts using rocks
    B. A Japanese macaque named Imo began washing her sweet potatoes
    C. Kanzi learned to clean sand out of grain
    D. A & B only
    E. B & C only

24. All but which of the following tool use has been seen among chimpanzees?
    A. Termite fishing
    B. Leaf sponges
    C. Washing sweet potatoes
    D. Toothpicks

25. Kanzi has shown abilities in all but which of the following areas?
    A. Problem-solving capabilities
    B. Food preparation
    C. Tool manufacturing
    D. Goal-directed activities

26. Vervet monkey communication
    A. Dispelled the previously held belief that primate vocalizations could not
       include external events or objects
    B. Is limited to scent marking and an occasional bark
    C. Includes specific sounds for different categories of predators (air, tree or ground)
    D. A & c

27. Apes cannot speak because
    A. They lack the intelligence
    B. They lack the anatomical structures necessary
    C. They don't have anything they want to say
    D. All of the above

28. Sara is a chimpanzee who
    A. Learned ASL from her mother
    B. Learned to recognize plastic chips as symbols for various objects
    C. Spontaneously began signing after observing others
    D. Taught an infant ASL

29. Koko
    A. Is a female lowland gorilla
    B. Has learned over 500 signs of ASL
    C. Communicates with a male gorilla named Michael using ASL
    D. All of the above
    E. B & C

30. Kanzi
    A. Is an orangutan
    B. Has learned to make stone tools
    C. Spontaneously learned language through observation
    D. All of the above
    E. B & c

31. Ape language experiments
    A. Show that apes are not capable of symbolic thought
    B. May suggest clues to the origins of human language
    C. Show that all signing apes have the same understanding of the
       relationship between symbols and the objects they represent
    D. Have no value in assessing the evolutionary relationship between humans and apes

ANSWERS TO FILL-IN OUTLINE

I. THE IMPORTANCE OF PRIMATE STUDIES
A. 5, 8
B. habitats
C. arboreal

II. PRIMATE SOCIOECOLOGY
A. Behavioral, environment
B. Ecological, together
C. Foods
D. food, water, predators, sleeping
E. Have not yet
F. Predation
G. adult, join forces
   1. Savannah baboons
   2. Dogs, leopards, lions
H. diet, resources
I. Reduces
J. Predator
K. Fear, predators
L. Access
M. Resource, predation

III. EVOLUTION OF BEHAVIOR
A. evolutionary perspective
B. Natural selection
C. Behavior
D. Genotypes, reproductive
E. Genes, behaviors
F. Humans
G. Genes, racist
H. Innate
I. Learning
J. Products
K. Testosterone, nonhuman
L. Genetic, environmental
M. Social
N. Infanticide
O. Their own
P. Lactate, sexually
   1. Advantageous
Q. New male
R. Criticisms

S. Lack of long-term data on demographics and social behavior of large groups of individually known animals, lack of long-term data on distribution of resources in time and space, lack of information on genetic relatedness through the male line, difficulty in assigning reproductive and other costs and benefits to particular behaviors, ignorance of the genetics of primate social behavior and many sociobiological models are untestable.
T.   To get by
U.   Well adapted
V.   Baboons
W.   Natural selection

IV.   PRIMATE SOCIAL BEHAVIOR
A.   Dominance
  1.   Order
  2.   Food, mating partners
  3.   Permanent
  4.   Sex, age, level of aggression, time spent in group,
              intelligence, motivation, mother's social position
  5.   Learned
  6.   Gestures, behaviors
  7.   Mother, peers
B.   Communication
  1.   Autonomic
  2.   Deliberate
  3.   Threat
  4.   Touching, patting, hugging, holding hands
  5.   Fear grin
  6.   Dominance
  7.   Vocalizations
  8.   Communication
C.   Aggression
  1.   Home range
  2.   Core Area
  3.   unprovoked, brutal
  4.   mates (or females)
D.   Affiliative Behaviors
  1.   promote
  2.   amicable
  3.   physical contact
  4.   Grooming
  5.   hygenic, pleasurable
  6.   reinforces
  7.   reconciliation
  8.   Alliances, coalitions
  9.   Alruistic

V. REPRODUCTION AND REPRODUCTIVE STRATEGIES
   A.   Patterns of Reproduction
   1.   Estrus
   2.   Swelling, genital area
   3.   Consortships
   4.   Bonobos
      a.   chimpanzee
   B.   Reproductive Strategies
   1.   Goal, adulthood
   2.   K-selected
   3.   R-selected
   4.   Helpless
   5.   Social
   6.   Male and female
   7.   Metabolic, enormous
   8.   Competitive
   9.   Mates
   10. Sexual selection
   11. Vividly colored
   12. Larger
   13. Testes
   14. Monogamous

VI. MOTHERS AND INFANTS
   A.   Monogamy, polyandry
   2.   Normal experience
   3.   Incapable, affectional
   4.   Learn
   5.   Weaning

VII. NONHUMAN PRIMATE CULTURAL BEHAVIOR
   A.   culture
   B.   learned
   C.   behaviors
   D.   washing
   E.   food
   F.   termite, leaf, toothpicks & stones
   G.   variation
   H.   sharp-edged flakes
   I.   onto a hard floor
   J.   goal directed
   K.   newly developed

VIII. PRIMATE COGNITIVE ABILITIES
   A.   predators
   B.   symbolically

C.   open
     D.   vocal tract, language
     E.   American Sign Language (ASL)
     F.   plastic chips
     G.   gorilla, 500, ASL
     H.   present
     I.   categorize
     J.   spontaneously
     K.   communiction

IX.   THE PRIMATE CONTINUUM
     A.   grade, categories
     B.   degree

ANSWERS & REFERENCES TO FILL-IN QUESTIONS

1.   arboreal, p. 121
2.   socioecology, p. 122
3.   Quantity and quality of foods, distribution of food, body size, water, predators, sleeping sites, activity patterns, relationships with other nonpredator species, and impact of human activities, p. 122
4.   diet, resources, p. 123
5.   learned, p. 124
6.   racist, discriminatory, p. 124
7.   plasticity, . 124
8.   infanticide, p. 125
9.   evolutionary perspective, p. 125
10.   resources, p. 122
11.   food, p. 123
12.   reduce, p. 126
13.   offspring, care, p. 126
14.   mother, respond, play, p. 127
15.   autonomic, hair, odor, p. 127
16.   gestures, facial expressions, vocalizations, p. 127
17.   hindquarters, p. 127
18.   fear, submission, p. 127
19.   grooming, consolation, p. 130
20.   social relationships, p. 130
21.   hugging, kissing, grooming, p. 131
22.   aggression, p. 129
23.   swelling, redness, genital, p. 132
24.   in estrus, p. 132
25.   mates, females, p. 134
26.   multi-male, polygynous, p. 134
27.   own mother, p. 136

ANSWERS AND REFERENCES TO MULTIPLE CHOICE QUESTIONS

CHAPTER 7
MAMMALIAN/PRIMATE EVOLUTIONARY HISTORY.

LEARNING OBJECTIVES
After reading this chapter you should be able to
* Recognize the place of humans in nature (p. 148).
* Understand the ways in which evolutionary biologists deduce relationships between organisms (pp. 148-151).
* Use the classification chart of animal taxonomy (p. 149).
* Recount the major events of vertebrate evolution (pp. 152-153).
* List the major adaptive complexes of mammals (pp. 153-154).
* Distinguish the three major mammalian groups and be able to discuss their reproductive differences (p. 155).
* Discuss the difficulties of distinguishing the primates of Paleocene from other placental mammals of that time. (pp. 155-156).
* State during which Epoch , and in what geographical locations, the earliest undoubted primates appear; what type of modern primate do the earliest primates most resembles (pp. 156-157).
* Explain what rafting is and why this concept is important in primate evolution (p. 157).
* List the types of primates found at the Fayum in the Oligocene (p. 157).
* Discuss the groupings of Miocene hominoids and what these groupings mean evolutionarily (pp. 158-160).
* Compare and contrast the Miocene hominoids of Africa, Europe, and Asia (pp. 159-160).
* Compare and contrast modes of evolutionary change (pp. 160-161).
* Discuss the problems of classifying fossil forms at both the species and genus levels (pp. 163-164).

FILL-IN OUTLINE
Introduction.

In the preceding chapters we surveyed the genetic mechanisms that are the foundation of the evolutionary process. Chapters 5 -6 looked at our closest relatives, the nonhuman primates, and how their study helps us to understand ourselves. In this chapter the process of macroevolution is studied. A synopsis of the key innovations in vertebrate, and particularly mammalian, evolution is examined over the great depth of time of these major groups. We will look at the fossil history of the primates over the last 60 million years and, by so doing, look at our own evolutionary history as well. With what you have learned about primate anatomy, ecology, and social behavior, you will be able to "flesh out" the bones and teeth that make up the evolutionary record of primate origins. This chapter ends with the processes of macroevolution and an examination of the genus and species concepts.

I.   THE HUMAN PLACE IN THE ORGANIC WORLD

A.   Considering both living and extinct organisms the amount of biological _____

is staggering.

1. in order to understand this diversity biologists have constructed a
   _____ system.
2. the classificatory system that biologists have devised organizes life into convenient
   groupings.
   a. this helps to _____ the complexity.
   b. these groupings indicate _____ relationships.

B. The place of humans in nature.
   1. humans belong to a broad group of organisms that move about and ingest food
      which are called _____ .
   2. humans belong to the group of animals that are multicelled, the _____ .
   3. within the metazoa humans belong to the phylum _____, animals that
      possess
      a. a _____ , a stiff supporting rod along the back.
      b. _____ slits (at some stage of development).
   4. within the chordates humans belong to the _____.
      a. these animals are characterized by a _____ _____.
      b. vertebrates have a well developed _____.
      c. additionally, vertebrates have _____ sensory structures for sight, smell,
         and balance.
   5. _____ are divided into six classes: bony fishes, cartilaginous fishes,
      amphibians, reptiles, birds and mammals.

II TAXONOMY

A. The field that specializes in delineating the rules of classification is _____.
   1. one of the criteria for classifying organisms is _____ similarities.
   2. the crucial criteria for classification, however, is evolutionary _____ .

B. Taxonomic concepts
   1. structures that are shared through descent from a common ancestor are called
      _____.

   2. structures in organisms that are used for the same function, but have developed
      independently and are not the result of common descent, are called

      _____.
      a. recall from Chapter 5 that homoplasy is the process by which similarities can
         develop in different groups of organisms.
      b. _____ can develop through homoplasy in unrelated organisms; at
         the same time, _____ can also develop through homoplasy, but
         in related organisms.

      b. _____ is more recent and predominants among anthropologists.

3. _____ Is the current method used In attempting to Interpret evolutionary relationships.

4. cladistics focuses on _____.

5. cladistics precisely _____ the types of homologies that yields useful information; some homologous characters are more informative than others.

      a. traits that reflect the ancestral condition of the organisms being studied are said to be _____ (or primitive).

      b. traits that are shared by all members of a group, but not present before the group's appearance, are said to be shared _____ characteristics; these are the traits considered to be most important to cladistics.

III. TIME SCALE

A. In addition to the vast array of life, evolutionary biologists must also contend with vast periods of time.

B. Geologists have formulated the geological _____ _____.

    1. this organizes time into hierarchies.

    2. very large _____ spans are subdivided into eras, periods, and epochs.

IV. VERTEBRATE EVOLUTIONARY HISTORY: A BRIEF SUMMARY

A. There are three geological eras: the Paleozoic, Mesozoic, and Cenozoic.

B. The first vertebrates.

    1. the earliest vertebrates are present in the _____ record early in the Paleozoic, after 500 m.y.a.

    2. later in the Paleozoic, several varieties of _____, _____ , and _____ appeared.

    3. at the end of the Paleozoic (c. 250 m.y.a.) several types of _____-like reptiles are present, probably including the ancestor of modern mammals.

C. The Mesozoic.

    1. the reptiles underwent an adaptive radiation, a rapid expansion into a variety of _____ _____.

    2. the first mammals are known from fossil traces early in the _____.

3. the _____ mammals do not appear until late in the Mesozoic, around 70 m.y.a.

D. The Cenozoic
    1. the Cenozoic is divided into two periods.
      a. the _____ last for about 63 million years.
      b. the Quaternary begins 1.8 m.y.a. and continues to the _____.
    2. to be more precise, paleontologists usually refer to the seven _____ of the Cenozoic.

V. MAMMALIAN EVOLUTION

A. After the dinosaur extinctions _____ underwent an adaptive radiation in which they filled a wide variety of ecological niches.
    1. this mammalian diversification was so successful that the Cenozoic is sometimes referred to as the Age of _____.
    2. mammals and birds _____ reptiles as the dominant terrestrial vertebrates.

B. Factors contributing to the mammalian success.
    1. the _____, which controls higher brain functions, came to comprise the majority of brain volume
    2. this _____ in brain size led to a greater ability to learn and a general flexibility of behavior in mammals.
    3. an efficient mode of prenatal internal _____ is found among the mammals
      a. this is associated with the need for the longer development of the larger _____.
      b. mammals are viviparous, i.e. they give birth to _____ young.

VI. MAJOR MAMMALIAN GROUPS.

A. There are _____ major subgroups of living mammals: monotremes, marsupials, and placental mammals.

B. Monotremes are _____ -laying and are extremely primitive; there are only two types existing today.

C. Marsupials
    1. the young are born extremely _____.
    2. the young complete birth in an external _____.

D. Placentals
    1. the placenta is a structure that prevents the mother's immune system from _____ the fetus.

2. the longer _____ period allows the central nervous system to develop more completely in the fetus

3. mammals also have the "bond of _____" between the mother and the offspring

   a. this period of association between the mother and the offspring provides for a wider range of _____ stimuli

   b. it is not sufficient that the young mammal has a brain capable of learning; mammalian _____ systems provides it with ample learning opportunities.

VII. EARLY PRIMATE EVOLUTION.

A.   Primate origins begin in the _____ _____ radiation at the start of the Cenozoic.

   1. primates diverged very _____ from the primitive placental mammals.

   2. discerning early primates from these very early generalized mammals is quite difficult.

B.   Plesiadapiforms.

   1. until recently plesiadapiforms were considered to be the earliest _____.

      a. only fragmentary evidence of _____ and _____ were known.

      b. subsequent fossil material, including elements of the hand and wrist (where primate characteristics would be obvious), suggest these mammals are more closely related to colugos.

   2. this group has been removed from the Order Primates.

   3. nevertheless, plesiadapiforms are probably closely linked to the early roots of the primates, but the primates had already _____ by the appearance of this group.

   4. The bottom line: we are left with extremely scarce traces of the beginnings of the primate radiation.

C.   The earliest undoubted primates appear in the Eocene.

   1. these forms are found in North America, Europe, and Asia, which were all geographically connected.

   2. summary of Eocene primates:

      a. it is certain these mammals were _____ .

      b. these animals were widely distributed.

      c. by the end of the Eocene most of these primates are _____ .

      d. some of these forms are probably the ancestors of the _____ .

         1. others appear to have given rise to the tarsiers.

         2. some recent discoveries from North Africa, the Persian Gulf, and China may be anthropoid ancestors from the late Eocene.

D. The Oligocene (34-22.5 m.y.a.)

    1. Most of our knowledge of primate Oligocene evolution comes from a site in Egypt, the
        _____ .

    2. it is believed that New World and Old World monkeys share a _____ ancestor.

        a. some of the earliest _____ primates appear to be close to the ancestry of both
           groups of monkeys.

        b. monkeys may have reached South America by "_____ " (see Chapter 5)
           from Africa.

        c. regardless of how monkeys reached South America, New World and Old World
           forms have had a separate lineage since about _____ m.y.a.

    3. Fayum forms.

        a. some paleontologists have suggested that the genus _____ lies near,
           or even before, the evolutionary divergence of New and Old World anthropoids.

        b. *Aegyptopithecus*

           1. this is the _____ of the Fayum primates, weight estimated at
               between 13 to 18 pounds.

           2. *Aegyptopithecus* had a small brain, large snout, and does not show any of the
               _____ traits of either Old World monkeys or the hominoids.

              a. this primate may be close to the ancestry of _____ Old World
                 monkeys and apes

              b. _____ is found in geological beds dated
                 between 35-33 m.y.a., suggesting that the evolutionary divergence of
                 hominoids from other Old World anthropoids occurred after this time.

VIII. MIOCENE (23-5 M.Y.A.) FOSSIL HOMINOIDS

A. The _____ was the "heyday" of the hominoids, marked by a spectacular
    hominoid

    radiation and could be called "the golden age of hominoids"

B. The Miocene hominoid assemblage is large and complex. Consequently, they are often
    treated geographically.

    1. African forms (23-14 m.y.a.).

        a. the best known of these fossils is _____ and this genus exhibits
           considerable variation

        b. the range in Africa for hominoids extends over 1800 miles.

    2. European forms (13-11 m.y.a.)

        a. these forms are quite _____ .

        b. the best known of these forms are assigned to the _____ *Dryopithecus* .

3. Asian Forms (16-7 m.y.a.)
   a. this is the _____ and most varied group from the Miocene fossil hominoid assemblage.
   b. these forms are _____ derived.
   c. the best known genus is _____ .

C. Four general points can be made about the Miocene hominoid fossils.
   1. they are _____ geographically.
   2. these hominoids were _____ .
   3. they span a considerable portion of the Miocene.
   4. these hominoids are _____ understood. However, we can make the following conclusions:
      a. these primates are _____ .
      b. they are mostly _____ -bodied hominoids.
      c. most of the Miocene forms are so _____ that they are improbable ancestors to any living form.
      d. *Sivapithecus* shows some highly derived facial features that suggest a close link to the modern _____ .
      e. there are no known _____ from any Miocene-dated locale.

IX. **MODES OF EVOLUTIONARY CHANGE**
   1. The major evolutionary factor underlying _____ change is speciation.
   2. The way new species are produced involves some form of _____
      a. geographical isolation
         1. involves some isolating factor such as a geographical _____ or great distance.
         2. members of a single species that become geographical isolated cannot exchange _____.
            a. over time isolation leads to genetic _____ accumulating in populations that have been separated.
            b. genetic drift will cause _____ frequencies to change in both populations.
            c. because drift is _____ the effects should not be the same in both populations.
            d. if the populations are inhabiting difference environments _____ _____ will cause them to have even more genetic differences
         3. the end result of geographical isolation will be two populations that can no

longer_____.

    b. behavioral _____ can work in maintaining the genetic differences of two new species even if they come back into contract again

        1. behavioral isolation includes differences in behaviors between closely related species.

        2. behavioral isolation has been well demonstrated in the courtship behavior of birds.

3. The consensus has been that _____ evolution is explained by microevolutionary changes accumulated into macroevolutionary changes. This is now being challenged.

4. Gradualism vs. punctuated equilibrium.

    a. the traditional view of evolution, as put forth by Darwin, is called _____ _____.

        1. according to gradualism, evolution works by gradual _____ accumulating.

        2. there should be a series of intermediate, or _____, forms in any line.

        3. the reason that such forms are rarely found is attributed to the incompleteness of the _____ record.

    b. the concept of punctuated equilibrium challenges the idea of gradualism.

        1. _____ _____ posits that species may persist for long periods with little or no change.

            a. this period of "stasis" comes to an end with a "spurt" of _____.

            b. this uneven, nongradual process of long stasis and quick _____ is called punctuated equilibrium

        2. punctuated equilibrium does not challenge that evolution has occurred; it challenges the "_____" and "_____" of gradualist evolution.

            a. rather than long periods of gradual change, this alternate view postulates long periods of _____ change, punctuated only occasionally by sudden bursts of speciation.

            b. rather than gradual accumulation of small changes (microevolution) in a single lineage, an additional evolutionary mechanism, accelerated _____ , directs macroevolution in a way quite distinct from gradualism.

c. speciation events and the longevity of these transitional species are so
_____ that they are not preserved in the fossil record.

c. the fossil record and punctuated equilibrium.

1. the fossil record for marine invertebrates _____ punctuated equilibrium.

2. the primate evolutionary record, on the other hand, _____ _____ appear to support the model of punctuated equilibrium.

X. THE MEANING OF GENUS AND SPECIES.

A. Our study of fossil primates has introduced us to a number a taxonomic names for extinct primates.

1. what do these names mean in evolutionary terms?

2. our goal is to make meaningful _____ statements when we assign taxonomic names.

3. all populations contain _____.

a. _____ variation will exist

b. _____ -dependent variation exists.

1. in hominoids there is a difference in the number of adult teeth vs. the milk teeth.

2. it would be a mistake to not recognize that members of the same species may have different numbers of teeth at different ages; otherwise _____ species would be described when there should only be one.

c. _____ _____ can be a confounding factor when describing a fossil species; males and females may have different structural traits.

B. Definition of species.

1. the most precise taxonomic level that we would like to assign fossil primates to is the

_____.

a. recall from Chapter 2 that a living biological species is a group of interbreeding, or potentially interbreeding, organisms that are reproductively isolated and produce viable and fertile offspring.

2. a question that must be answered in dealing with the species concept is what is the biological significance of the _____ that is present? There are two possible answers.

a. variation is accounted for by individual, age, and sex differences, i.e., _____ variation.

b. or, variation represents differences between reproductively isolated groups, i.e., _____ variation.

124

c. making the choice.
1. in order to make a choice between the two possibilities we must use _____ species as models and observe their reproductive behavior.
2. if the amount of morphological variation observed in fossil samples is consistent with the variation of modern species of closely related forms, then we should not "_____" our sample into more than one species.
3. one serious problem with fossil species is that not only is their variation over space, but there is also variation in _____ .
    a. even more variation is possible in _____ because individual specimens may be separated by thousands, perhaps millions, of years.
    b. standard Linnaean taxonomy is designed to account for the variation present at a particular time (in living species) and, basically, describes a _____ situation (no change, or evolution, occurring).

C. Definition of genus.
1. the next higher level of taxonomy from the species is the _____ . The classification of fossils at the genus level presents its own problem.
    a. one definition of a genus is a group of _____ composed of members more closely related to each other than they are to species from another genus. This often becomes very subjective.
    b. in order to have more than one genus there must be at least _____ species.
2. another definition of a genus is a number of species that share the same broad _____ _____ .
    a. this represents a general _____ lifestyle more basic than the particular ecological niches characteristic of species. This ecological definition is more useful for applying to fossil genera.
    b. _____ are the most often preserved parts and they are excellent ecological indicators.
3. cladistic analysis also provides assistance in making judgements about evolutionary relationships; members of the same genus should all share _____ characters not seen in members of other genera.

KEY TERMS

adaptive radiation: the rapid expansion and diversification of an evolving group of organisms adapting to a variety of new niches.

analogies: similarities between organisms based strictly on common function with no assumed descent from a common ancestor. E. g., the wings of an insect and the wings of a bat.

ancestral (primitive) trait: referring to a character that reflects the ancestral condition within a lineage.

Apidium: the fossil primate genus from the Fayum that has three premolars. It may be ancestral, or related to whatever was, to the New World monkeys.

classification: the ordering of organisms into categories, such as phyla, orders, and families to show evolutionary relationships.

Cenozoic: the geological era during which primate evolution occurred. It encompasses the last 65 million years.

cerebrum: the outer portions of the brain.

Chordata (Chordates): the phylum of the animal kingdom that includes the vertebrates.

cladistics: an approach to taxonomy that groups taxa based on shared derived characteristics.

cladogram: a chart showing evolutionary relationships as determined by cladistic analysis. It is based solely on interpretation of shared derived characters. No time component is indicated, and ancestor-descendant relationships are not inferred.

continental drift: the movement of continents on sliding plates of the earth's surface. This has resulted in dramatic movement of the earth's land masses over time.

derived trait: referring to a character that reflects specialization within a lineage and is more informative about the evolutionary relationship between organisms.

Dryopithecus: the Miocene hominoid genus that inhabited Europe. This hominoid was characterized by thin molar enamel.

ecological niche: the positions of species within their physical and biological environment.

endothermy: production of heat within the animal by means of metabolic processes within cell (mainly muscle cells). Birds and mammals are the endothermic animals.

epochs: categories of the geological time scale; subdivision of periods.

evolutionary (phylogenetic) systematics: a traditional approach to classification (and evolutionary interpretation) in which presumed ancestors and descendants are traced in time by analysis of homologous characters.

Fayum: a rich paleontological site in Egypt that yields late Eocene primates and is the only site for Oligocene primates.

genus: a group of closely related species.

geological time scale: the organization of earth history into eras, periods, and epochs.

Gondwanaland: the southern continents that broke off of Pangea. Gondwanaland (AKA Gondwana) included South America, Africa, Antarctica, Australia, and India).

heterodonty: the condition in which there are different kinds of teeth specialized for different functions.

hominids: popular form of Hominidae, the family to which modern humans belong; includes all bipedal hominoids back to the divergence from African great apes.

homologies: similarities between organisms based on descent from a common ancestor. E. g., the bones in the wing of a bird and the bones in the arm of a human.

homoplasy: separate evolutionary development of similar characteristics in different groups of organisms.

homeothermy: the ability to maintain a constant body temperature. Through physiological feedback mechanisms heat generated through endothermy is either dissipated or retained within the normal range of body temperature for the species.

interspecific: refers to between two or more species.

intraspecific: refers to within one species.

large-bodied hominoids: those hominoids including "great" apes and hominids, as well as all ancestral forms back to the time of divergence from small-bodied hominoids.

Laurasia: the northernmost continents that had been part of Pangea. Laurasia included North America, Europe, and Asia.

Metazoa: the multicellular animals, a major division of the animal kingdom. The metazoa are all of the animals except the sponges.

neocortex: the outer layer of brain tissue of the cerebrum, which has expanded during the evolution of the vertebrates, particularly in primates, and most especially in humans. The neocortex is associated with high mental functions.

paleospecies: groups of fossil organisms that are assigned to the same species. Paleospecies exhibit more variation than in living species. This is because of the time span involved; in humans *Homo erectus* covers more than one million years.

Pangea: the supercontinent that included all of the present-day continents. Pangea began to break up in the early Mesozoic.

phyletic gradualism: the evolutionary concept, first postulated by Charles Darwin, that evolutionary change takes place slowly with slight modifications in each generation.

phylogenetic tree: a chart showing evolutionary relationships as determined by phylogenetic systematics. It contains a time component and infers ancestor-descendant relationships.

Proconsul: the genus of Miocene hominoid from Africa. *Proconsul* was the most primitive of the Miocene hominoids.

punctuated equilibrium: the evolutionary concept that there are long periods, in the history of a species, in which no change takes place (stasis) followed by a quick spurt of evolutionary change (speciation).

shared derived trait: referring to a character shared in common by two forms and considered the most useful for making evolutionary interpretations.

Sivapithecus : the Miocene hominoid found in Asia that has several derived characteristics that link it to the orangutan.

speciation: the process by which new species are produced from earlier species. The most important mechanism of macroevolutionary change.

vertebrates: animals with bony backbones; includes fishes, amphibians, reptiles, birds, and mammals.

viviparity: the reproductive process in which the young are born live.

FILL-IN QUESTIONS

1. Animals that are characterized by a stiff, flexible rod running along their back and the presence of pharyngeal gill slit, at least at some time in their lives, belong to the phylum

    _____.

2. Fishes, amphibians, reptiles, birds, and mammals, animals with backbones, are all
   _____.

3. In order for similarities between organisms to be useful they must reflect common
   _____ _____.

4. Amphibians, reptiles, birds, and mammals all have a very similar upper arm bone called the
   humerus. The humerus in these animals are said to be _____.

5. The taxonomic approach that emphasizes shared derived characteristics is called
   _____.

6. Characters that are modified from the ancestral condition in a particular lineage are referred
   to as _____ or modified traits.

7. A useful tool for geologists and paleoanthropologists is the organization of earth history into
   eras, periods, and epochs and called the _____ _____ _____.

8. The earliest vertebrates are present in the fossil record early in the _____,
   about 500 million years ago.

9. The diversification of many new species from a common stock that expand into new
   ecological niches is called an _____ _____.

10. Almost all mammals give birth to live young a characteristic called _____.

11. The ancestor of the modern _____ is sometimes confused as an one of the earliest
    primates. Despite their close relationship these two groups had already diverged by
    Paleocene times.

12. The first fossil forms that are clearly identifiable as primates appear during the
    _____.

13. The most important Oligocene fossil primate locality in the Old World is the _____.

14. The Oligocene primate that best bridges the gap between the Eocene prosimians and the
    Miocene hominoids is _____.

15. The great hominoid radiation, the epoch of apes, occurred during the _____.

16. The best known Miocene ape from Asia belongs to the genus _____.

17. The major evolutionary factor underlying macroevolutionary change is _____.

18. The way that new species are first produced involves some form of _____.

19. Darwin described a type of evolution in which there should be a series of forms, many
    intermediate, between each ancestor and its descendant. This type of evolution is called
    _____ _____.

20. The mode of evolution which emphasizes a long period of stasis which is interrupted by a
    quick spurt of speciation is called _____ _____.

21. The way (or the how) that evolution actually works, whether by gradualism or punctuated events, is the _____ of evolution.

22. How quickly, or how slowly, evolution actually works, is the _____ of evolution.

23. Variation within a species is known as _____ variation.

24. Variation between different species is called _____ variation.

MULTIPLE CHOICE QUESTIONS

1. Humans are
   A. Animals.
   B. Parazoa.
   C. Metazoa.
   D. chordates.
   E. all of the previous except B.

2. The scientific discipline that delineates the rules of classification is
   A. paleontology.
   B. stratigraphy.
   C. homology.
   D. taxonomy.
   E. geology.

3. The primary basis for classifying organisms is similarities in
   A. physical structure.
   B. physiology.
   C. diet.
   D. ecology.
   E. analogies.

4. Bats have wings that allow them to fly. So do birds and insects. Similarities such as wings in different animals that have a common function
   A. does not mean a common ancestry.
   B. are called homologies.
   C. are called analogies.
   D. are derived traits.
   E. both A and C are correct.

5. Humans and other apes have certain characteristics in common such as a broad sternum, a Y-5 cusp pattern on the molars, and the lack of a tail. These traits are all
   A. analogies.
   B. primitive traits.
   C. shared derived traits.
   D. general traits.
   E. ancestral traits.

6. Continental drift is explained by
   A. parallel evolution.
   B. The Big Bang.
   C. the Cenozoic.
   D. the continents "float" on huge plates
   E. Pangea.

7. In the early Mesozoic, Pangea broke into two large continents, Gondwana and Laurasia. Laurasia consisted of the present day continents of
   A. South America and Africa.
   B. South America, Africa, and Australia.
   C. South America, Africa, Australia, India, and Antarctica.
   D. North America and Europe.
   E. North America, Europe, and Asia.

8. The dominant terrestrial life forms of the Mesozoic were the
   A. crossopterygians
   B. amphibians
   C. reptiles
   D. birds
   E. mammals

9. Which of the following is **not** one of the mammalian innovations that has led to their success?
   A. ectothermy.
   B. larger brain.
   C. viviparity.
   D. internal fertilization.
   E. longer period of growth.

10. A "pouched" mammal Is a(n)

    A. monotreme
    B. therapsid
    C. marsupial
    D. A & C

11. The fossil material that is available for most vertebrates, including primates, are
    A. pelves.
    B. humerus and other arm bones.
    C. dermal ossicles.
    D. teeth.
    E. femurs, which are the largest bones in any vertebrate.

12. The group of mammals that reproduce by laying eggs and generally have more primitive traits than the other mammals are the
    A. monotremes.
    B. metatherians.
    C. marsupials.
    D. placentals.
    E. eutherians.

13. An important aspect of viviparity is a barrier that protects the fetal tissues from the mother's immune system. This barrier is the
    A. placental.
    B. lymphatic system.
    C. hard-shelled egg.
    D. human lymphatic antigen.
    E. "bond of milk."

14. After birth a young mammal has a period of neural development coupled with learning. Some refer to this period of close association between the young mammal and its mother as the
    A. rehearsal period.
    B. placental connection.
    C. "park."
    D. biosocial perspective.
    E. "bond of milk."

15. The early primate evolution of the Paleocene
    A. is well represented by the genus *Plesiadapis* .
    B. is quite fragmentary
    C. is represented mainly by limb bones with few skull parts preserved.
    D. both B and C are correct.
    E. indicates that primates had not yet diverged from the colugos and bats.

16. The time of radiation of the probable ancestors of prosimians was during the
    A. Paleocene.
    B. Eocene.
    C. Oligocene.
    D. Miocene.
    E. Pleistocene.

17. Which of the following statements about New World monkey evolution is **not** correct?
    A. it is very unlikely that the Old and New World primates have shared any evolutionary history since the early Oligocene.
    B. the fossil history of the New World monkeys is rich in South America.
    C. in the early Oligocene, South America was much closer to Africa than it is today.
    D. *Apidium* may be related to whatever was the ancestor of the New World monkeys.
    E. New World and Old World monkeys have been separate after about 35 m.y.a.

18. According to most primate evolutionary biologists, *Aegyptopithecus*
    A. is the ancestor of the hominoids.
    B. is near, or even before, the split of Old and New World anthropoids.
    C. is the direct ancestor of the New World anthropoids.
    D. precedes the major split in catarrhine evolution.
    E. both B and D are correct.

19. The living hominoids today are
    A. the most diverse group of primates that has ever existed.
    B. the most diverse group of hominoids that has ever existed.
    C. a small remnant of a very successful Miocene radiation.
    D. the most successful hominoids that have ever lived.
    E. confined to the tropical rain forests of Southeast Asia.

20. Which of the following is a Miocene African hominoid?
    A. *Dryopithecus* .
    B. *Sivapithecus* .
    C. *Proconsul* .
    D. *Pliopithecus* .
    E. *Lufengpithecus.*

21. Which of the following is **not** as closely related as the other four?
    A. orangutan.
    B. gorilla.
    C. chimpanzee.
    D. human.
    E. gibbon.

22. The Miocene ape that bears a striking resemblance to the modern orangutan in the face, but not in the postcranium, is
    A. *Dryopithecus* .
    B. *Sivapithecus* .
    C. *Proconsul* .
    D. *Pliopithecus* .
    E. *Kenyapithecus.*

23 There are two bird species on a midwestern prairie that look very much alike physically and are probably descended from a common ancestor. During courtship, however, the males of one species stands on one leg while looking at the female. The males of the second species uses both feet to drum on the prairie floor. The females will only mate with those males who behave appropriately during courtship. This is an example of
    A. parallel evolution.
    B. convergent evolution.
    C. behavioral isolation.
    D. geographical isolation.
    E. both A and B are correct.

24. The fossil record of many marine invertebrates shows long periods where there is very little change in species. Then a new species appears without any transitional species. These observations best support the idea of
   A. convergent evolution.
   B. punctuated equilibrium.
   C. phyletic gradualism.
   D. small microevolutionary changes lead to transspecific evolution.
   E. the broken stick model.

25. The primate fossil record does not seem to support
   A. slow gradual change from ancestor to descendant.
   B. punctuated equilibrium.
   C. phyletic gradualism.
   D. small microevolutionary changes lead to transspecific evolution.
   E. either B or D.

26. A major different between paleospecies and biological species is that a paleospecies
   A. is more variable.
   B. adds a temporal component.
   C. does not interbreed among itself.
   D. is static.
   E. both A and B are correct.

27. Closely related species are grouped together in a
   A. species.
   B. subspecies
   C. genus.
   D. subgenus.
   E. family.

28. Species that share the same broad adaptive zone is another definition for a
   A. species.
   B. genus.
   C. family.
   D. infraorder.
   E. order.

Answers to Outline

I.   THE HUMAN PLACE IN THE ORGANIC WORLD
   A. diversity
      1. classification
      2. a. reduce
         b. evolutionary
   B. 1. animals
      2. metazoa

3. chordata
   a. notochord
   b. gill
4. vertebrates
   a. vertebral column
   b. brain
   c. paired
5. vertebrates

II. TAXONOMY
A. taxonomy
   1. physical
   2. descent
B. 1. homologies
   2. analogies
      b. analogies, homologies
   3. cladistics
   4. homologies
   5. defines
      a. ancestral
      b. derived

III. TIME SCALE
A. time scale
B. time

IV. VERTEBRATE EVOLUTIONARY HISTORY
B. 1. fossil
   2. fishes, amphibians, reptiles
   3. mammal
C. 1. ecological niche
   2. Mesozoic
   3. placental
D. 1. a. Tertiary
      b. present
   2. epochs

V. MAMMALIAN EVOLUTION
A. mammals
   1. mammal
   2. replaced
B. 1. neocortex
   2. expansion
   3. development
      a. brain
      b. live

VI. MAJOR MAMMALIAN GROUPS
A. three
B. egg
C. 1. immature
   2. pouch

D. 1. rejecting
   2. gestation
   3. milk
      a. learning
      b. social

VII. EARLY PRIMATE EVOLUTION
A. placental mammal
   1. early
B. 1. primates
      a. jaws, teeth
   3. diverged
C. 2. a. primates
      c. extinct
      d. prosimians
D. 1. Fayum
   2. common
      a. Fayum
      b. rafting
      c. 35
   3. *Apidium*
      b. 1. largest
         2. derived
            a. both
            b. *Aegyptopithecus*

VIII. MIOCENE FOSSIL HOMINOIDS
A. Miocene
B. 1. a. *Proconsul*
   2. a. derived
      b. genus
   3. a. largest
      b. highly
      c. *Sivapithecus*
C. 1. widespread
   2. numerous
   4. poorly
      a. hominoids
      b. large
      c. derived
      d. orangutan
      e. hominids

IX. MODES OF EVOLUTIONARY CHANGE
A. 1. macroevolutionary
   2. isolation
      a. 1. barrier
         2. genes
            a. differences
            b. allele

                    c. random
                    d. natural selection
             3. interbreed
         b. isolation
      3. transspecific
   B. Gradualism vs. Punctualism
      1. phyletic gradualism
         a. changes
         b. transitional
         c. fossil
      2. a. punctuated equilibrium
             (1) speciation
             (2) spurts
         b. tempo, mode
             (1) no
             (2) speciation
             (3) short
      3. a. supports
         b. does not

X. THE MEANING OF GENUS AND SPECIES
   A. 2. biological
      3. variation
         a. individual
         b. age
             2. two
         c. sexual dimorphism
   B. 1. species
      2. variation
         a. intraspecific
         b. interspecific
         c. 1. contemporary
             2. split
             3. time
                a. paleospecies
                b. static
   C. 1. genus
         a. species
         b. two
      2. adaptive zone
         a. ecological
         b. teeth
      3. derived

ANSWERS & REFERENCES TO FILL-IN QUESTIONS
1. chordates, p. 148
2. vertebrates, p. 148
3. evolutionary descent, p. 150

ANSWERS & REFERENCES TO MULTIPLE CHOICE QUESTIONS

1. E, p. 148
2. D, p. 148
3. A, p. 150
4. E, p. 150
5. C, p. 151
6. D, p. 156
7. E, p. 156
8. C, p. 153
9. A, pp. 153-154
10. C, p. 155
11. D, p. 155
12. A, p. 155
13. A, p. 155
14. E, p. 155
15. B, p. 155
16. B, p. 156
17. B, p. 157
18. A, p. 158
19. C, p. 158
20. C, p. 159
21. E, p. 160
22. B, p. 160

23. C, p. 161
24. B, p. 162
25. B, p. 162
26. E, p. 164
27. C, p. 164
28. B, p. 164

Chapter 8
HOMINID ORIGINS

Learning Objectives

After reading this chapter you should be able to:

- List the important distinguishing characteristics of a hominid, pp. 168-169
- Discuss what mosaic evolution is and the mosaic nature of human evolution, pp. 168-169
- Explain a biocultural approach to the study of human evolution, pp. 169-171
- Explain how and why paleoanthropology is a multidisciplinary science, 171-172
- Outline the steps and the types of individuals involved in finding an early hominid site through the interpretation of the site, pp. 171-172
- Compare relative dating techniques to chronometric techniques, 172-174
- Describe the various dating techniques in terms of how they are used and for what time periods (if applicable) they can be used for, 172-174
- Locate the East African Rift Valley and appreciate its unique features, pp. 174-175
- Match major hominid sites in Africa with specific fossil finds, pp. 175-186
- Understand the geological complexities and resultant dating problems in South Africa, pp.185-186
- Explain the effects of bipedalism on hominid body structure, pp. 186-191
- Recount the four broad groupings for the Plio-Pleistocene African hominids as an alternative to a proposed phylogeny, pp. 192-201
- Compare and contrast the "robust" and "gracile" australopithecines, pp. 195-198 understand the biological implications in making a genus-level or species-level distinction in interpreting fossil relationships, pp. 201-204
- Interpret various proposed phylogenies, p. 205-206

Fill-In Outline
Introduction

We have seen in previous chapters that humans are a primate and we share our evolution and even much of our behavior with other primates. At some point, however, our ancestors took their primate heritage and went off in another direction to become the unique primate we are today. Some primitive hominoid may have begun this process before 10 m.y.a., but after 5 m.y.a. there is certainly definite hominid fossil evidence in Africa. Culture as the adaptive strategy of humans again makes us aware of the biocultural nature of our evolution. The difficulties in reconstructing the culture of our ancient ancestors is addressed. This chapter looks at the multidisciplinary nature of paleoanthropology, dating techniques, the significance of the bipedal adaptation, major hominid sites, and ends with a broad grouping of the numerous ancient fossils.

I. DEFINITION OF HOMINID

   A. Modern humans and our hominid ancestors are distinguished from our closest relatives in a number of characteristics. Various researchers have pointed to certain hominid characteristics as being significant (at some stage) in defining what a hominid is.

      1. large _____ size.

      2. _____ behavior.

      3. _____ locomotion.

   B. Mosaic evolution.

      1. all of the above mentioned characteristics did not evolve

         _____.

      2. the evolutionary pattern in which different features evolve at different_____ is called mosaic evolution.

      3. the major defining characteristic for all hominid evolution is _____

         _____.

         a. bipedal locomotion predates other specialized traits that makes hominids unique.

         b. thus, skeletal evidence for bipedal locomotion is the only truly reliable _____ of hominid status.

   C. Biocultural evolution: the human capacity for culture.

      1. the most distinctive behavioral feature of modern humans is our extraordinary elaboration and dependence on _____ .

      2. culture encompasses much more than just toolmaking capacity.

         a. culture integrates an entire _____ _____ involving cognitive, political, social, and economic components.

         b. the material culture, tools and other items, is but a small portion of this_____ complex.

      3. the record of earlier hominids is almost exclusively remains of _____culture, especially residues of stone tool manufacture.

         a. thus, it is difficult to learn anything about the _____ stages of hominid cultural development before the regular manufacture of stone tools, circa 2.5 m.y.a.

         b. without "_____" evidence we cannot know exactly what the earliest hominids were doing.

            1. before they began making stone tools, hominids were probably using other types of _____ (such as sticks) made of "soft" perishable materials.

            2. we also cannot know anything about the cultural behavior of these earliest humans.

         4. the fundamental basis for human cultural elaboration relates directly to_____ abilities.

         a. when did the unique combination of cognitive, social, and material cultural adaptations become prominent in human evolution?

            1. care must be taken to recognize the manifold nature of culture and to not expect it always to contain the same elements across species or through _____.

2. we know that the earliest hominids did _____ regularly manufacture stone tools.
   a. the earliest members of the hominids,_____, date back to approximately 7-5 m.y.a.
   b. the protohominids may have carried objects such as naturally sharp stones or stone flakes, parts of carcasses, and pieces of wood. At the least, we would expect them to have displayed these behaviors to the same degree as is found in living _____.

b. over periods of _____ million years numerous components interacted, but they did not all develop simultaneously.
   1. as cognitive abilities _____, more efficient means of communications and learning resulted.
   2. as a result of _____ reorganization, more elaborate tools and social relationships also emerged.
   3. more elaborate tools and social relationships selected for greater _____, which in turn selected for further neural elaboration in a positive feedback loop.
   4. these mutual dynamics are at the very heart of hominid _____ evolution.

II. PALEOANTHROPOLOGY AS A MULTIDISCIPLINARY SCIENCE
A. The task of recovering and interpreting the remains of early _____ is the province of paleoanthropology.
   1. _____ is the study of ancient humans.
   2. paleoanthropology is a diverse _____ field that seeks to reconstruct the dating, anatomy, behavior, and ecology of our ancestors.
B. Site survey.
   1. _____ do the initial survey work to locate potential early hominid sites.
   2. Paleontologists can generally give quick estimates of the geological age of a site based on _____ remains. In this way fossil beds of a particular geological _____, in which we might find humans, can be isolated.
C. Site excavation.
   1. the search for hominid traces is conducted by _____.
   2. hominid sites do not need to contain actual fossilized skeletal material for us to know that they _____ the site.
      a. _____ provide behavioral clues of early hominid activities.

III. DATING METHODS
A. One of the essentials of paleoanthropology is putting sites and fossils into a _____ framework (i.e., how old are they?).
B. The two types of dating methods used by paleoanthropologists are _____ dating and _____ (absolute) dating.
C. Relative dating.
   1. relative dating tells you which object is older or younger than another object, but not in actual _____.

2. one type of relative dating is _____, the study of the sequential layering of deposits.
   a. stratigraphy is based on the law of _____ , i.e., that the oldest stratum (layer) is the lowest stratum and higher strata are more recent.
   b. problems associated with stratigraphy.
      1. earth _____ such as volcanic activity, river activity, mountain building, or even modern construction companies, can shift strata making it difficult to reconstruct the chronology.
      2. the _____ period of a particular stratum is not possible to determine with much accuracy.
      3. fluorine analysis.
         a. this relative dating technique can only be used on _____.
         b. when a bone is buried it is exposed to fluorine in the groundwater which seeps into the bone and deposits _____ during the fossilization process.
            1. the _____ a bone is in the ground, the more fluorine it will contain.
         c. fluorine analysis can only be done with bones found at the same _____, i.e., this method is "site specific."
      4. biostratigraphy
         a. is based on the fairly _____ changes seen in dentition of animals.
   3. paleomagnatism
      a. the earth's _____ pole has shifted several times in the past.
D. Chronometric (absolute) dating.
   1. chronometric dating provides an estimate of age in years and is based on _____ decay.
      a. certain radioactive isotopes of elements are unstable and they disintegrate to form an isotope of another _____.
      b. this disintegration occurs at a constant rate.
         1. by _____ the amount of disintegration in a particular sample, the number of years it took for the amount of decay may be calculated.
   2. potassium/argon (K/Ar) dating involves the decay of _____ into argon gas.
      a. K/Ar has a half-life of 1.25 _____ years.
      b. this technique can only be done on _____ matrix; it will not work on organic material such as bone.
         1. however, fossil bones are often associated with matrix and can be indirectly dated by its association.
         2. the best type of rock to perform K/Ar dating on is _____ rock.
            a. when the lava is laid down in its molten state the _____ gas present is driven off. After solidification any argon that has been trapped in the rock is the result of potassium decay.

b.   to obtain the date of the rock, it is reheated and the escaping argon is
_____.

3.   _____ _____ is a radiometric method commonly used by
archeologists.
a.   Carbon 14 has a half-life of 5730 years.
b.   this method can be used to date materials as recent as a few _____
years.
c.   the probability of _____ of Carbon 14 increases
after 40,000 years

IV THE EAST AFRICAN RIFT VALLEY
A.   The Great _____ Valley of Africa is a stretch of 1,200 miles
1.   this area has experienced active geological processes over the last several
_____ years in which the area is being rifted (separated).
2.   because of this geological activity earlier sediments are thrown to the
_____ where they become exposed and can be located by a
paleoanthropologist.
B.   Rifting has stimulated _____ activity.
1.   volcanic sediments provide a valuable means for _____
dating many sites in East Africa.
2.   the datable hominid sites along the Rift Valley have yield crucial information
concerning the precise _____ of early human evolution.

V. EAST AFRICAN HOMINIDS
A.   Earliest Traces.
1.   the oldest specimen that is believed to be a hominid comes from Lothagam,
Northern Kenya.
a.   this specimen is very _____.
b.   several other fragmentary specimens from around the same area of East Africa
have also been found. All are represented by only a _____
specimen.
2.   these early specimens all come from the time period _____ m.y.a.
B.   Aramis.
1.   this site has been radiometrically dated at 4.4 m.y.a., making the group of fossils
from this site the oldest _____ (rather than single specimens) of
hominids yet discovered.
2.   remains recovered include jaws, teeth, partial crania and upper limb bones, hand
and foot bones. In addition, 40% of a complete _____ has recently
been recovered.
3.   because many of the discoveries have only been partially described, only
provisional interpretations are possible at this time.
a.   there is anatomical evidence of _____, the criterion for
hominid status.
1.   the _____ _____ is positioned further forward
than in quadrupeds.
2.   features of the humerus suggest that the forelimb was not _____ -
_____.

4. Tim White and his co-workers has suggested that the _____ hominids be assigned to a new genus and species, *Ardipithecus ramidus* . The basis for this recognition of a new genus is
    a. these specimens are much more _____ than *Australopithecus* (the other hominid genus closest to this time period)
    b. _____ enamel caps on the molars in contrast to the thicker enamel caps of *Australopithecus*
C. Kanapoi and Allia Bay (East Turkana).
    1. These hominid sites had been dated between _____and _____ m.y.a.
    2. The _____ enamel on the molars conform to the condition found in *Australopithecus*
    3. it has been suggested that these specimens be assigned to the genus *Australopithecus*, but to a separate species, i.e., *A. anamensis*.
D. Laetoli.
    1. a rare find was fossilized hominid _____ imprinted into volcanic tuff.
        a. one group of footprints suggests _____, possibly, _____ individuals. Analysis of the footprints indicate one individual was 4' 9" and the other was 4' 1".
        b. despite agreement that these individuals were bipedal, some researchers feel they were _____ bipedal in the same way as modern humans. They suggest that the Laetoli hominids moved in a "strolling" fashion with a short stride.
E. Hadar (Afar Triangle).
    1. the most recent dating calibrations suggest a range of dates from 3.9-____ m.y.a.
    2. two of the most extraordinary discoveries of human paleontology were found at Hadar.
        a. _____ percent of an *Australopithecus afarensis* female, nicknamed "Lucy," was recovered here. This is one of the two most complete humans from before 100,000 years ago.
        b. the first "catastrophic" assemblage
            1. a group of bones representing at least 13 individuals, including 4 _____, was found at Hadar.
            2. it has been suggested that these individuals represented a single _____ that died at the same time in a catastrophe.
                a. the precise _____ of the site has not been completely explained and the assertion that these individuals were contemporaries must be viewed tentatively.
                b. considerable cultural material has been recovered. Some stone tools may be 2.5 million years old, making them the _____ cultural evidence yet found.
F. Bouri (Middle Awash)
    1. These new hominid discoveries have been classified as *Australopithecus* _____.
    2. These fossils are quite _____ from other Plio-Pleistocene hominids.
    3. The _____ proportions are unusual.

4. Animal bones found with these fossils show clear signs of _____.
G. Koobi Fora (East Lake Turkana)
   1. the specimens recovered at Koobi Fora represent at least _____ individuals.
   2. Next to Olduvai sites on the east side of Lake Turkana have yielded the most information concerning the _____ of early hominids.
H. West Turkana
   1. The "black _____" dated 2.4 mya was found here.
I. Olduvai Gorge
    A. The greatest abundance of paleoanthropological information concerning the behavior of early hominids comes from Olduvai Gorge in Tanzania.
       1. continuous excavations were done by Louis and Mary Leakey since the 1930's.
       2. Olduvai is a steep-sided valley with a deep ravine that resembles a miniature_____ _____.
         a. the semi-arid pattern of modern Olduvai is believed to be similar to most of the past environments preserved there over the last ___ million years
    B. The greatest contribution of Olduvai to paleoanthropological research is the establishment of an extremely well documented and correlated sequence of geological, paleontological, archeological, and hominid remains over the last ___ million years.
       1. at the very foundation of all paleoanthropological research is a well-established_____ _____. Another hominid site can be accurately dated relative to other sites in the Olduvai Gorge by cross-correlating known marker beds.
       2. paleontological evidence includes more than 150 species of _____
         a. this evidence provides clues to the _____ conditions that the earliest humans lived in.
       3. the archeological sequence is well documented for the last 2 million years.
         a. the earliest hominid site is from around _____ million years ago.

VI. CENTRAL AFRICA
  A. A hominid mandible was discovered in Chad dating from _____ - _____ m.y.a.
  B. Preliminary analysis suggests that this fossil's closest affinities is to

_____ .

VII. SOUTH AFRICAN SITES
  A. Earliest Discoveries
   1. Darwin had predicted that the earliest humans would be found in Africa.
   2. The first australopithecine described was discovered in South Africa.
     a. this was a child from a quarry at _____ .
     b. Raymond Dart, the researcher who analyzed this fossil, observed several features that suggested that this child was a _____.
       1. the foramen magnum was farther _____ than in modern apes (although not as far forward as in modern humans).
       2. the slant of the forehead was not as _____ as in apes.

3. the milk _____ were exceedingly small and the first molars were large, broad teeth.
4. in all respects this fossil resembled a hominid rather than a pongid with the glaring exception of the very small _____ .
   c. Dart named this species _____ and he believed it represented a "missing link" between the apes and the humans.
      1. this was not well received.
B. South African Hominids Aplenty
   1. More _____ discoveries were made during the 1930's and 1940's.
      a. additional sites include Sterkfontein, Kromdraai, Swartkrans, and Makapansgat.
      b. as the number of discoveries accumulated, it became increasingly difficult to insist that the australopithecines were simply aberrant _____ .
         1. among the fossils recovered were postcranial bones that indicated bipedalism in these hominids.
         2. The acceptance of the australopithecines as hominids required revision of human evolutionary theory.
            a. it had to be recognized that the greatest hominid brain expansion came _____ earlier changes in teeth and locomotor anatomy.
            b. the _____ nature of human evolution had to be recognized.

VIII. THE BIPEDAL ADAPTATION
A. Efficient bipedalism among primates is found only among _____.
B. The process of bipedal walking.
   1. to walk bipedally a human must _____ on the "stance" leg while the "swing" leg is off the ground.
   2. during normal walking, both feet are simultaneously on the ground only about _____% of the time.
C. Structural/anatomical modifications for bipedalism.
   1. to maintain a _____ center of balance many drastic anatomical modifications in the basic primate quadrupedal pattern are required.
   2. the most dramatic changes occur in the hominid _____ and its associated musculature.
   3. the gluteus maximus is a(n) _____ extensor of the thigh and provides additional force, particularly during running and climbing.
   4. unlike the straight great ape vertebral column, the human spine has a forward _____ bringing the center of balance forward.
   5. a longitudinal _____ develops.
D. All the _____ structural changes required for bipedalism are seen in early hominids from East and South Africa.
E. Other human structural characteristics are also present in these early hominids.
   1. the vertebral column shows the same _____ as in modern humans.
   2. the lower _____ were lengthened to almost the same degree as in modern humans.

3. early hominid foot structure is known from sites in both South and East Africa.
   a. these specimens indicate that the _____ and longitudinal _____ were well adapted for a bipedal gait.
   b. some paleontologists suggest, however, that the great toe was _____ unlike the pattern seen in later hominids.
      1. this would have aided the foot in _____ , enabling early hominids to more effectively exploit arboreal habitats.
         -some researchers believe that these early humans spent considerable amount of time in the _____.

IX. PLIO-PLEISTOCENE HOMINIDS OUTSIDE AFRICA
   A. For years it was assumed that early hominids were confined to the African continent. New fossils and dating techniques now establish hominids in Asia by _____ m.y.a. and possibly in Europe prior to _____ m.y.a.

X. MAJOR GROUPS OF PLIO-PLEISTOCENE HOMINIDS
   A. In recent years numerous new discoveries have been made. We now have specimens of close to _____ individuals from South Africa and more than _____ from East Africa.
   B. To avoid the problems associated with establishing phylogenetic relationships, this material has been divided into four _____ groupings.
      1. SET I. Basal Hominids (4.4 m.y.a.)
         a. The earliest and most primitive remains are those from _____. They have been classified as _____, a different genus from all other Plio-Pleistocene forms.
      2. SET II. Early Primitive *Australopithecus* (4.2-3.0 m.y.a.)
         a. The hominids from Laetoli and Hadar are assigned to *Australopithecus* _____.
         b. *A. afarensis* is more _____ than any of the later species of *Australopithecus*.
            1. the teeth of *A. afarensis* are quite _____ .
               a. the _____ are often large, pointed teeth that overlap.
               b. the tooth rows are _____.
            2. the cranial parts that are preserved also exhibit several primitive _____ features.
               a. cranial capacities are difficult to estimate but they seem to range from _____ cm^3 to 500 cm^3.
                  1. it appears that the smaller cranial capacities are for the _____ and the larger cranial capacities are for _____.
                  2. one thing that is certain is that *A. afarensis* had a _____ brain.
         3. stature has been estimated.
            a. *A. afarensis* was a short _____.
            b. there appears to have been considerable sexual _____. If this is true,
               1. _____ was around 3 1/2 feet tall.
               2. males could be up to _____ feet tall.

3. *A. afarensis* may have been as sexually dimorphic as _____ living primate.

4. *A. afarensis* is so primitive in the majority of dental and cranial features that if it were not for evidence of _____ this primate would not be classified as a hominid.

3. SET III. Later, more derived *Australopithecus* (2.5-1.0 m.y.a.)

   a. These forms have been grouped into two subsets, the "robust" and the "gracile" australopithecines.

      1. Robust Australopithecines

         a. The "robust" forms are clearly more robust in the _____ and _____.

         b. The term "_____" is a term for larger body size.

         c. WT 17000, or "the black skull," has a mixture of primitive and derived characteristics.
-a cranial capacity of 410 cm^3 WT 17000 has the_____ definitely ascertained brain volume of any hominid yet found.
-compound _____ in the back of the skull.
-_____ upper face.
-upper dental row _____ in back.
-it has been placed in a separate species, *Australopithecus* _____.

         d. by 2 m.y.a., even more _____ members of the robust lineage were on the scene in East Africa. Robust australopithecines have
-_____ cranial capacities (510-530 cm^3).
-very large, broad _____
-_____ back teeth and lower jaws
-the East African robust hominids are assigned to *Australopithecus* _____.

         e. all members of the robust lineage appear to be specialized for a diet of _____ food items such as seeds and nuts.

      2. "Gracile" australopithecines.

         a. the gracile australopithecines are only known from _____ _____.

         b. historically, it had been thought that there was significant differences in _____ between the gracile and robust forms.

           1. it is now understood that there is not much difference in body size between the gracile and robust forms

           2. most of the differences between the two types of australopithecines is found in the_____ and in the _____ .

         c. the differences in the relative proportions of teeth and jaws noted above best define a _____, as compared to a robust australopithecine.

         d. most differences in skull shape can be attributed to contrasting _____ function in the two forms.

4. SET IV. Early *Homo* (2.4-1.8 m.y.a.)
   a. Early remains of *Homo* have been found in East Africa and _____.
   b. the earliest appearance of our genus, _____, may be as ancient as the robust australopithecines.
      1. the earliest evidence of *Homo* is a temporal bone from _____ m.y.a.
      2. these earliest humans are already beginning to _____ .
   c. when L. S. B. Leakey named these specimens _____ _____ (which means "handy man") it was meaningful from two perspectives:
      1. it inferred that *Homo habilis* was the early Olduvai_____.
      2. by calling this group *Homo* Leakey was arguing for at least _____ separate branches of hominid evolution in the Plio-Pleistocene. By calling one group *Homo* Leakey was guessing at which group led to us.
   d. *H. habilis* differs from *Australopithecus* in cranial _____ and dental _____ .
      1. the estimated _____ cranial capacity for *H. habilis* is 631 cm^3.
      2. the _____ in cranial capacity is at a minimum 20% greater over the australopithecines.

XI. INTERPRETATIONS: WHAT DOES IT ALL MEAN?
   A. Number fossil specimens is an attempt to keep designations _____.
   B. Formal _____ comes later.
   C. The first step in interpreting hominid evolutionary events is to _____ and _____ a site.
   D. Hominids that are on an evolutionary side branch from human ancestors must have become _____.

XII. CONTINUING UNCERTAINTIES--TAXONOMIC ISSUES
   A. Plio-Pleistocene hominids come from _____ and _____ Africa.
   B. The Plio-Pleistocene hominids span from _____to _____ m.y.a.
   C. Researchers generally agree to a _____-level assignment for most Plio-Pleistocene hominids.
   D. At the _____-level very little concensus can be found.
   E. Evolution is not a _____ process.
   F. _____ is at the heart of scientific research.
   G. *Ardipithecus* is
      1. _____ million years old.
      2. from _____.
      3. Known to have had thin _____ on the back teeth.
      4. different looking from any known _____ species.
   H. At Hadar and Laetoli
      1. Some paleoanthropologists think that a least ____ species exist.
      2. It is clear that australopithecines are highly _____.
      3. It is good practice not to overly _____ fossil samples.
   I. *Australopithecus anamensis*
      1. fossils have been quite _____.
      2. anatomical differences compared to *Australopithecus afarensis* are not _____.

J. Regarding the number of genera of *Australopithecus*
1. In the _____ and _____ most researchers lumped all forms into the genus *Austraopithecus*.
2. In the last decade there has been an increasing tendency to split the _____ group into a separate clade.
3. The robust forms have been generically termed _____.
4. The robust forms include _____, _____ and _____.
5. This text continues to lump these closely related taxa because it simplifies _____.

K. Regarding the number of species of early *Homo*.
1. The current debate will not likely be _____ soon.
2. The key issue is whether the variation we see is _____ or _____ specific.

XIII. INTERPRETING THE INTERPRETATIONS
A. All proposed phylogenies in the text postdate _____.
B. Proposed phylogenies prior to this date did not include _____.
C. The new finds, _____ and _____ need to be incorporated into these proposed phylogenies.

KEY TERMS

absolute dating techniques: see chronometric dating techniques.

Ardipithecus ramidus : a provisional species of the most primitive hominid yet discovered. It dates from 4.4 million years ago.

artifacts: material remnants or traces of hominid behavior. Very old artifacts are usually of made of stone or, occasionally, bone.

australopithecine: the common name for members of the genus *Australopithecus* . Originally this term was used as a subfamily designation. North American researchers no longer recognize this subfamily, but the term is well established in usage.

Australopithecus : a genus of Plio-Pleistocene hominids with at least five species. The genus is characterized by bipedalism, a relatively small brain, and large back teeth.

biostratigraphy: dating method based on evolutionary changes within an evolved lineage.

"the black skull": a fossil cranium, designated WT 17 000, that was recovered from West Lake Turkana. This member of the robust group has been provisionally assigned to *Australopithecus aethiopicus* and lived about 2.5 million years ago.

chronometric dating techniques: dating techniques that gives an estimate in actual number of years, based on radioactive decay. AKA absolute dating.

endocast: a solid impression of the inside of the skull, showing the size, shape, and some details of the surface of the brain.

family, the: a collection of the remains of at least 13 *Australopithecus afarensis* individuals who may have been contemporaries.

faunal analysis: see biostratigraphy.

fluorine analysis: a relative dating technique in which the amount of fluorine deposited in bones is compared. Bones with the most fluorine are the oldest.

foramen magnum: the large opening at the base of the cranium through which the spinal cord passes and where the vertebral column joins the skull.

gracile australopithecine: the South African species, *Australopithecus africanus*, that is more lightly built than the stouter species inhabiting the same area.

habitual bipedalism: refers to the usual mode of locomotion of the organism. Used in reference to humans in the text, there are other habitual bipedal animals (e.g., large terrestrial flightless birds and kangaroos), although many hop rather than walk.

half-life: in chronometric dating, the amount of time that it takes for one-half of the original (parent) isotope to decay into its daughter isotope.

<u>**Homo habilis**</u> : a species of early *Homo*, well known in East Africa, but also perhaps from other regions.

"Lucy": a female Australopithecus afarensis for which 40 percent of the skeleton was recovered.

mosaic evolution: the evolutionary pattern in which different characteristics evolve at different rates.

obligate bipedalism: refers to the fact that the organism cannot use another form of locomotion efficiently.

os coxa: the structure that consists of three bones (fused together in the adult) that, together with another ox coxa and the sacrum, constitutes the pelvis. It is also referred to as the coxal by some anatomists and as the innominate bone by an earlier generation of anatomists.

paleoecology: the study of fossil communities and environments.

paleomagnetism: dating methods based on the earth's shifting magnetic poles.

paleontology: the recovery and study of ancient organisms.

palynology: the study of fossil spores, pollen, and other microscopic plant parts.

precision: refers to the closeness of repeated measurements of the same quantity to each other.

protohominid: the earliest members of the hominid lineage. No fossils of this hypothetical group have yet been found.

relative dating: a type of dating in which objects are ranked by age. Thus, some objects can be said to be older than other objects, but no actual age in years can be assigned.

robust australopithecine: any of the three species of *Australopithecus* that are characterized by a stouter body frame, larger back teeth relative to front teeth, a more vertical face, and sometimes a sagittal crest.

sagittal crest: a ridge of bone running along the midline (i.e., sagittal plane) of the cranium. The temporalis muscle, used in chewing, attaches to the sagittal crest in those mammals that possess this structure.

sectorial premolar: a premolar with a bladelike cutting edge that sections food by shearing against the cutting edge of the upper canine. The shearing action also sharpens both teeth.

stratigraphy: study of the sequential layering of deposits.

taphonomy: the study of how bones and other materials came to be buried and preserved as fossils.

Fill-In Questions

1. The distinctive characteristics of a hominid include _____ locomotion, _____ brain size and _____.
2. Different rates of evolution for function systems (dentition, locomotion and brain size) is termed _____.

3. The most important defining characteristic of a hominid is _____.
4. The distinct behavioral characteristic of humans is our elaboration of and dependence on _____.
5. _____ abilities are directly related to human cultural elaboration.
6. _____ are the earliest members of the hominid lineage.
7. The diversity of paleoanthropolgy makes it a _____ pursuit.
8. Paleontologists are used at an archeological site to analyze _____ remains.
9. Behavioral clues at an archeological site are referred to as _____.
10. Chronometric dating is also called _____ dating.
11. _____ is a dating technique using sequential layering of deposits.
12. The shifting of the earth's geomagetic pole has resulted in a type of relative dating technique called _____.
13. _____ dating is based on radioactive decay.
14. The chronometric dating technique with a half-life of 5,730 years is _____.
15. Since each type of dating technique has a degree of error _____-_____ is done in an attempt to confirm dates.
16. The rich hominid site that is 1,200 miles long, through Ethiopia, Kenya and Tanzania is the _____ of Africa.
17. The gap in our knowledge of early hominid evolution is between ___ and ____ m.y.a.
18. The oldest PROBABLE hominid comes from _____.
19. The earliest collection of probable hominids comes from _____.
20. More than _____ individuals are represented from the Aramis collection.
21. *Ardipithecus ramidus* has _____ enamel on the molars, a trait not found among the other early hominids.
22. The hominids found at Kanapoi and Allia Bay hae been classified as _____ _____.
23. A 75 foot long trail of footprints was found at _____.
24. These footprints allowed us to determine that these early hominids were fully _____.
25. The extraordinary discovery of 40% of a complete skeleton at Hadar, Ethiopia is known as "_____."
26. Also found at Hadar was a group of bones representing at 13 individuals who all died at about the same time. It is the first "_____" assemblage ever found.
27. _____ was found at the Bouri site in Ethiopia close to animal bones displaying clear signs of _____.
28. The "black skull" was found on the _____ side of Lake _____.
29. _____ is located in the Serengeti Plain of northern Tanzania and resembles a miniture Grand Canyon.
30. The paleoanthropological research at Olduvai has been extremely well documented and correlated a _____ of geological, _____, archeological and _____ remains.
31. Hominid remains from Olduvai range in time from _____ m.y.a. to fairly recent *Homo sapiens*.
32. The hominid mandible found in Chad, in central Africa, is associated with _____ remains and is dated to _____-_____ m.y.a.
33. The scientist who made the first discovery of an australopithecine is _____.

34. The Taung child was classified as _____.
35. The most productive hominid site in southern Africa is _____.
36. Only hominids engage in _____ as their primary mode of locomotion.
37. The major structural changes required for bipedalism are found in the _____.
38. The large extensor muscle used during running or jumping is the _____.
39. Hominid evidence prior to 2 m.y.a. comes from _____.
40. Attempting to interpret the fossil record is extremely _____.
41. The hypotheses for human evolution for the period between 4.5 and 1 m.y.a. is
    _____ and _____.
42. A diagram showing a proposed family tree is called a _____.
43. *Ardipithecus ramidus* has been classified as a _____ hominid.
44. The tooth rows of *Australopithecus afarensis* are _____ which is primitive.
45. *Australopithecus afarensis* appears to have been quite _____
    since males were much larger than females.
46. The oldest of the robust australopithecines is WT 17000, also known as the "_____."
47. *Australopithecus boisei* is a _____ australopithecine from _____.
48. Raymond Dart is associated with the _____ child, the first South African hominid
    to be named _____.
49. The face and dentition are different between the robust and _____ australopithecines.
50. *Australopithecus africanus* has a face that is somewhat _____-_____.
51. The remains of early *Homo* have been found in _____ and _____ Africa.
52. The cranial capacity of *Homo habilis* is much _____ than the australopithecines.
53. The average cranial capacity of *Homo habilis* is _____.
54. Early members of the genus *Homo* lived _____ with australopithecines.
    They lived "side by side" for over _____ years.
55. In order to keep designations neutral, specimens are _____.
56. Once a fossil site is located a logical sequence should be followed to avoid later confusion.
    The steps would include selecting, _____ and excavating the site, recovering,
    _____ and describing fossils, comparing fossils _____ and with
    known _____ found in closely related groups. If the previous steps have all
    been followed, the last would be assigning a _____ name.
57. The Plio-Pleistocene fossils from East and South Africa date from _____-_____ m.y.a.
58. One thing research agree unanimously on is that these forms are _____.
59. Very little agreement can be found for _____-level distinctions.
60. The number of species at Hadar and Laetoli is unknown for certain since australopithecines
    were highly _____.
61. Many people think that the robust australopithecines should be put into a separate genus,
    _____.
62. The issue of how many species of early *Homo* existed is based on whether the variation
    we see is _____ or _____ specific.
63. The proposed phylogenies presented in the text are _____ since so many
    fossils are still being described and analyzed.

MULTIPLE CHOICE QUESTIONS

1. The acceptance of the australopithecines as hominids by the scientific community required a complete revision of the thinking of the time, namely that
    A. large brains have always been part of the hominid line
    B. the manufacture and use of stone tools and dental modifications occurred simultaneously
    C. the brain expanded after modifications in the dental and locomotor systems
    D. to be human requires a minimal cranial capacity of 750 cm3

2. Evolution in which structures evolve at different rates is termed
    A. convergent evolution.
    B. parallel evolution.
    C. mosaic evolution.
    D. punctuated equilibrium

3. Human evolution can be characterized as
    A. parallel.
    B. convergent.
    C. homologous.
    D. mosaic.

4. Which of the following is an aspect of material culture that would be a vestige of the earliest hominids?
    A. a fragment of a stone tool.
    B. cognitive abilities.
    C. economic systems.
    D. social systems.

5. Initial surveying and locating potential hominid sites is the primary task of
    A. physical anthropologists.
    B. geologists.
    C. paleoecologists.
    D. archeologists.

6. The primary task of an archeologist at a paleoanthropological site is to
    A. search for hominid "traces."
    B. reconstruct the ancient environment of the site.
    C. establish the relationships of any fossil humans recovered.
    D. perform dating techniques to establish the time period.

7. A disadvantage to fluorine analysis is that it
   A. can only be done on volcanic beds.
   B. can only be done on bones found in the same area.
   C. is not effective for materials older than 50,000 years.
   D. has a range of error of 12,000 years.

8. Chronometric techniques are based on
   A. radioactive decay.
   B. superposition.
   C. stratigraphy.
   D. the works of Oldowan Kanobe.

9. A half-life
   A. differs for the isotopes of different elements.
   B. is the amount of time it takes for the original amount of an isotope to decay into another
      isotope.
   C. is set at 5,730 years for K/Ar.
   D. both A and B are correct.

10. The dating technique used extensively in paleoanthropology for the time period 1-5 m.y.a. is
    A. uranium 238.
    B. carbon 14.
    C. fluorine analysis.
    D. potassium-argon.

11. Several different dating techniques are used to cross-check the age of a
    paleoanthropological site because
    A. there are gaps in the periods covered.
    B. sources of error differ in the various techniques.
    C. because the techniques are all done on the same material duplication adds reliability.
    D. spectrophotometers must be transported to field sites where field conditions can cause
       error.

12. One of the reasons that East Africa is such an excellent area for following the evolution
    of humans is
    A. the soil is acidic, making preservation of fossils more likely
    B. it was once a sea and the fossilization of the shells of marine organisms provide
        for excellent stratigraphy
    C. there is a great deal of commecial development occurring and these developers find
        fossil remains and alert paleoanthropologists
    D. there is a great deal of geological activity, which not only churns up earlier
        sediments but also provides datable material

13. Which of the following is NOT a characteristic of *Ardipithecus ramidus*?
    A. large canines
    B. a sectorial premolar
    C. the foramen magnum is positioned forward, consistent with bipedalism
    D. the pelvis is narrow with a long iliac blade

14. Which hominid species has been recovered from Aramis?
    A. *Ardipithecus ramidus*
    B. *Australopithecus anamensis*
    C. *Australopithecus garhi*
    D. *Australopithecus africanus*

15. What is the good hard evidence from Laetoli that hominids were bipedal by 3.5 m.y.a.?
    A. a fossilized foot
    B. fossilized footprints imprinted in volcanic tuff
    C. the forward position of the foramen magnum on a cranium that has been recovered
    D. a fossil pelvis

16. Which hominid species has been recovered from Kanapoi & Allia Bay?
    A. *Ardipithecus ramidus*
    B. *Australopithecus anamensis*
    C. *Australopithecus garhi*
    D. *Australopithecus africanus*

17. Which hominid species has been recovered from Bouri?
    A. *Ardipithecus ramidus*
    B. *Australopithecus anamensis*
    C. *Australopithecus garhi*
    D. *Australopithecus africanus*

18. *Ardipithecus*
    A. resembles most *Australopithecus* species
    B. shows distinct evidence of sexual dimorphism
    C. shows thin enamel on the back teeth
    D. may not have been bipedal

19. Which of the following was found at Hadar?
    A. "Lucy"
    B. a "catastrophic" assemblage
    C. the "black skull"
    D. "Zinj"
    E. both A & B

20. The rich fossil site identified with Louis and Mary Leakey, located in the Serengeti Plain of northern Tanzania which resembles a miniature Grand Canyon is
    A. Koobi Fora
    B. Olduvai Gorge
    C. Sterkfontein
    D. Omo

21. The Taung skull was found due to
    A. deforestation
    B. locals probing for a water source
    C. quarry activity
    D. children playing and stumbling upon this unique fossil

22. Raymond Dart is associated with
    A. The Taung child
    B. the "black skull"
    C. *Australopithecus boisei*
    D. *Australopithecus africanus*
    E. A & D

23. Which of the following is NOT one of the hominid sites from south Africa?
    A. Omo
    B. Kromdraai
    C. Makapansgat
    D. Swatkrans

24. What factor led to humans becoming bipedal?
    A. protohumans started standing upright in order to free hands for carrying objects and making tools
    B. being bipedal reduced the amount of solar radiation hitting the skin and preventing protohominids from overheating
    C. protohominids stood bipedally to get a view over the tall grasses of the savanna in order to detect predtors
    D. we do not know what the initiating factor for bipedalism was

25. The gluteus maximus is the largest muscle in the human. Why?
    A. it provides a "cushion" for when we sit
    B. it is a powerful muscle for throwing
    C. it is a powerful extensor muscle of the upper leg and important in bipedal walking
    D. its main purpose is energy storage in the form of fat

26. Which of the following statements is true?
    A. the human vertebral column is fairly straight
    B. the earliest hominid, *Homo erectus*, is completely bipedal
    C. all the major structural changes required for bipedalism are seen in the early
        hominids from east and south Africa
    D. the earliest hominids have all the major features of bipedalism except the os cosa
        is still long and bladelike

27. A foot that is highly capable of grasping and climbing is less capable as a stable
    platform during bipedal locomotion. This is because anatomical remodeling is limited
    by functional
    A. contingencies
    B. constraints
    C. paradoxes
    D. drift

28. Which of the following is NOT a major feature of hominid bipedalism?
    A. development of curves in the human vertebral column
    B. the "straightening" of the human fingers from the curved condition found in apes
    C. the forward repositioning of the foramen magnum underneath the cranium
    D. the modification of the pelvis into a basin-like shape

29. A phylogeny is
    A. a grouping into which early hominids are placed
    B. a diagram representing ancestor-descendant relationships
    C. a branch on a family tree
    D. all of the above

30. Basal hominids are represented by
    A. *Ardipithecus ramidus*
    B. *Australopithecus afarensis*
    C. *Australopithecus africanus*
    D. the robus australopithecines

31. The Plio-Pleistocene hominid fossils from Africa
    A. Range from 6 m.y.a. to 1.5 m.y.a.
    B. Are widely dispersed geographically
    C. range from 4.4-1.0 m.y.a.
    D. None of the above

32. What makes *Australopithecus afarensis* a hominid?
    A. large thickly enameled molars
    B. bipedalism
    C. the front teeth are hominid
    D. the presence of a sagittal crest

33. The earliest species of robust australopithecine is
    A. *Australopithecus boisei*
    B. *Australopithecus robustus*
    C. *Australopithecus aethiopicus*
    D. *Australopitecus africanus*

34. The smallest ascertained cranial capacity in a hominid is found in
    A. *Australopithecus boisei*
    B. *Australopithecus robustus*
    C. *Australopithecus aethiopicus*
    D. *Australopitecus africanus*

35. Which of the following hominids is found in south Africa
    A. *Australopithecus boisei*
    B. *Australopithecus robustus*
    C. *Australopithecus aethiopicus*
    D. *Australopitecus africanus*

36. By assigning certain specimens to the genus *Homo*, L.S.B. Leakey was
    A. stating that these hominids were more closely related to the south African australopithecines than to the East African australopithecines
    B. arguing for at least two separate branches of hominid evolution in the Plio-Pleistocene
    C. indicating that this was the only species making tools in east Africa
    D. both B & C

37. You have measured the cranial capacity of an east African hominid from around 1.7 m.y.a. The measurement you obtained is 700 cm3. Which species below does your specimen most likely belong?
    A. *Australopithecus boisei*
    B. *Australopithecus robustus*
    C. *Australopithecus aethiopicus*
    D. *Homo habilis*

38. Early *Homo* is distinguished from the australopithecines largely by
    A. larger cranial capacity
    B. shorter stature
    C. larger back teeth
    D. the presence of a chin

39. Regarding the Plio-Pleistocene hominid fossils from Africa
    A. researchers don't agree as to their locomotion
    B. researchers generally agree to a genus-level distinction
    C. not all researchers aree that they are members of the family Hominidae
    D. more coplete specimens are needed

40. The species-level distinctions of the African Plio-Pleistocene hominids
    A. are fairly clear
    B. are the subject of ongoing disputes
    C. are being resolved through dating
    D. require immediate splitting

41. *Australopithecus anamensis*
    A. Is not much different than *Australopithecus afarensis* anatomically
    B. has been represented by an almost complete skeleton
    C. requires further study and analysis before it can be confirmed as a separate species
    D. A & C

42. The australopithecines are
    A. sometimes divided into two different genera
    B. are clearly one genus
    C. sometimes divided into four different genera
    D. very similar in their adaptive levels

43. The key issue with early *Homo* is
    A. dating
    B. evaluating intraspecific variation
    C. evaluating interspecific variation
    D. evaluating the observed variation as being either intraspecific OR interspecific

ANSWERS TO FILL-IN OUTLINE
I.   DEFINITION OF HOMINID
    A. 1.   brain
       2.   toolmaking
       3.   bipedal
    B. 1.   simultaneously
       2.   rates
       3.   bipedal locomotion
       b.   indicator
    C. 1.   culture
       2.   a.   adaptive strategy
          b.   cultural
       3.   material
          a.   earliest
          b.   hard
             1.   tools
       4.   cognitive
          a.   1.   time
             2.   not
                a.   protohominids
                b.   chimpanzees

160

        b. several
            1. developed
            2. neurological
            3. intelligence
            4. biocultural

II. PALEOANTHROPOLOGY AS A MULTIDISCIPLINARY SCIENCE
   A. hominids
       1. paleoanthroplogy
       2. multidisciplinary
   B. 1. geologists
       2. faunal
   C. 1. archaeologists
       2. occupied
           a. artifacts

III. DATING METHODS
   A. chronoloical
   B. relative, chronometric
   C. relative dating
       1. years
       2. stratigraphy
           a. superposition
           b. problems associated with stratigraphy
               1. disturbances
               2. time
               3. fluorine analysis
                   a. bone
                   b. fluorine
                       1. longer
                   c. location
               4. biostratigraphy
                   a. regular
       3. paleomagnatism
           a. geomagnetic
   D. Chronometric (absolute) dating
       1. radioactive
           a. element
           b. 1. measuring
       2. potassium
           a. billion
           b. rock
               2. volcanic
                   a. argon
                   b. measured
       3. Carbon-14
           b. hundred

c. error

IV. THE EAST AFRICAN RIFT VALLEY
A. Rift
1. million
2. surface
B. volcanic
1. chronometrically
2. chronology

V. EAST AFRICAN HOMINIDS
A. Eariest Traces
1. a. fragmentary
   b. single
2. 5.7
B. Aramis
1. collection
2. skeleton
3. a. bipedalism
   1. foramen magnum
   2. weight-bearing
4. Aramis
   a. primitive
   b. thin
C. Kanapoi and Allia Bay (East Turkana)
1. 4.2-3.9
2. thick
D. Laetoli
1. footprints
   a. two, three
   b. not
E. Hadar (Afar Triangle)
1. 2.3
2. a. 40%
   b. the first "catastrophic" assemblage
   1. infants
   2. social unit
      a. deposition
      b. oldest
F. Bouri (Middle Awash)
1. *garhi*
2. different
3. limb
4. butchering
G. Koobi Fora (East Lake Turkana)
1. 100
2. behavior

H. West Turkana
  1. skull
I. Olduvai Gorge
  A. 2. Grand Canyon
      a. 2
  B. 2
    1. geological picture
    2. extinct animals
      a. ecological
    3. a. 1.85

VI. CENTRAL AFRICA
  A. 3.5-3.0
  B. *Australopithecus afarensis*
VII. SOUTH AFRICAN SITES
  A. Earliest Discoveries
    2. a. Taung
      b. hominid
        1. forward
        2. receding
        3. canines
        4. brain
      c. *Australopithecus africanus*
  B. South African Hominids Aplenty
    1. australopithecine
      b. apes
        2. a. after
          b. mosaic
VIII. THE BIPEDAL ADAPTATION
  A. hominids
  B. The process of bipedal walking
    1. balance
    2. 25
  C. Structural/anatomical modifications for bipedalism
    1. stable
    2. pelvis
    3. important
    4. curve
    5. arch
  D. major
  E. Other human structural characteristics are also present in these early hominids
    1. curvature
    2. limb

3. a. heel, arch
    b. divergent
        1. grasping
            -trees

IX. PLIO-PLEISTOCENE HOMINIDS OUTSIDE AFRICA
   A. 1.8, 1.5

X. MAJOR GROUPS OF PLIO-PLEISTOCENE HOMINIDS
   A. 200, 300
   B. broad
       1. SET I. Basal Hominids (4.4 m.y.a.)
           a. Aramis, *Ardipithecus ramidus*
       2. SET II. Early Primitive *Australopithecus* (4.2-3.0 m.y.a.)
           a. *afarensis*
           b. primitive
               1. primitive
                   a. canines
                   b. parallel
               2. hominoid
                   a. 375
                       1. females, males
                       2. smaller
               3. a. hominid
                   b. dimorphism
                       1. Lucy
                       2. 5
                       3. any
               4. bipedalism
       3. SET III. Later, more derived *Australopithecus* (2.5-1.0 m.y.a.)
           1. Robust Australopithecines
               a. skull, dentition
               b. robust
               c. -smallest
                   -crest
                   -projecting
                   -converges
                   -aethiopicus
               d. derived
                   -small
                   -faces
                   -mosaic
                   -boisei
               e. hard
           2. "Gracile" australoithecines
               a. south Africa
               b. body size

                2. face, dentition
        c. gracile
        d. jaw
    4. SET IV. Early *Homo* (2.4-1.8 m.y.a.)
        a. south Africa
        b. *Homo*
                1. 2.4
                2. diversity
        c. *Homo habilis*
                1. toolmakers
                2. two
        d. capacity, proportions
                1. average
                2. increase

XI. INTERPRETATIONS: WHAT DOES IT ALL MEAN?
A. neutral
B. naming
C. select, survey
D. extinct

XII. CONTINUING UNCERTAINTIES--TAXONOMIC ISSUES
A. south, east
B. 4.4, 1
C. genus
D. species
E. simple
F. debate
G. *Ardipitecus* is
    1. 4.4
    2. Aramis
    3. enamel
    4. australopithecine
H. At Hadar and Laetoli
    1. two
    2. variable
    3. split
I. *Australopithecus anamensis*
    1. fragmentary
    2. striking
J. Regarding the number of genera of *Australopithecus*
    1. 1960's, 1970's
    2. robust
    3. *Paranthropus*
    4. *aethiopicus, boisei, robustus*
    5. terminology

K. Regarding the number of species of early *Homo*
    1. resolved
    2. inter, intra

XIII. INTERPRETING THE INTERPRETATIONS
A. 1979
B. *Australopithecus afarensis*
C. *Ardipithecus, anamensis*

ANSWERS & REFERENCES TO FILL-IN QUESTIONS

1. bipedal, large, toolmaking, p. 168
2. mosaic evolution, p. 168
3. bipedal locomotion, p. 168
4. culture, p. 169
5. cognitive, p. 170
6. protohominids, p. 170
7. multidisciplinary, p. 171
8. faunal, p. 171
9. artifacts, p. 171
10. absolute, p. 172
11. stratigraphy, p. 172
12. paleomagnetism, p. 173
13. chonometric, p. 173
14. carbon 14, p. 174
15. cross-correlating, p. 174
16. Great Rift Valley, 174
17. 8, 5, p. 175
18. Lothagam, p. 176
19. Aramis, p. 176
20. 40, p. 177
21. thin, p. 177
22. *Australopithecus anamensis*, p. 178
23. Laetoli, p. 178
24. bipedal, p. 179
25. Lucy, p. 179
26. catastrophic, p. 180
27. *Australopithecus garhi*, butchering, p. 180
28. west, p. 181
29. Olduvai Gorge, p. 181
30. sequence, paleontological, hominid, p. 182
31. 1.85, p. 182
32. 3.5-3.0, p. 183
33. Raymond Dart, p. 183
34. *africanus*, p. 184
35. Swartkrans, p. 186

36. bipedalism, p. 186
37. pelvis, p. 188
38. gluteus maximus, p. 188
39. Africa, p. 189
40. complications, p. 189
41. opposing, conflicting, p. 191
42. phylogeny, p. 192
43. basal, p. 192
44. parallel, p. 194
45. sexually dimorphic, p. 194
46. black skull, p. 196
47. robust, East Africa, p. 196
48. Taung, *Australopithecus*, p. 198
49. gracile, p. 198
50. dish-shaped, p. 198
51. east, south, p. 198
52. larger, p. 200
53. 631 cubic centimeters, p. 200
54. contemporaneously, 1 million, pp. 200-201
55. numbering, p. 202
56. surveying, numbering, chronologically, variations, taxonomic, p. 202
57. 4.4, 1, p. 202
58. hominids, p. 202
59. species, p. 202
60. variable, p. 203
61. *Paranthropus*, p. 204
62. inter, intra, p. 204
63. speculative, p. 63

ANSWERS & REFERENCES TO MULTIPLE CHOICE QUESTIONS

1. D, p. 168
2. C, p. 168
3. D, p. 168
4. A, p. 170
5. B, p. 171
6. A, p. 171
7. B, p. 173
8. A, p. 173
9. D, p. 173
10. D, p. 174
11. B, p. 174
12. D, pp. 174-175
13. D, p. 177
14. A, p. 177

15. B, p. 178
16. B, p. 178
17. C, p. 180
18. C, p. 177
19. E, p. 180
20. B, p. 181
21. C, p. 183
22. E, p. 184
23. A, p. 186
24. D, pp. 186-189
25. C, p. 188
26. C, p. 188
27. B, p. 189
28. B, pp. 190-191
29. B, p. 192
30. A, p. 192
31. C, p. 190
32. B, pp. 194-195
33. c, p. 196
34. C, p. 196
35. D, p. 198
36. B, p. 200
37. D, p. 200
38. A, p. 200
39. B, p. 202
40. B, p. 202
41. D, p. 203
42. A, p. 204
43. D, p. 204

CHAPTER 9
HOMO ERECTUS

LEARNING OBJECTIVES
After reading this chapter you should be able to

- Discuss the temporal and geographic distribution of *Homo erectus,* pp. 211-212 & p. 219
- Briefly describe the time frame and glacial movements of the Pleistocene, p. 213
- Describe the physical characteristics of *Homo erectus,* pp. 213-218
- Discuss scientists and the *erectus* finds they are associated with, pp. 218-220
- Describe the fossil remains and related archeological evidence of Java, China and Africa, pp. 218-227
- Compare African and Asian *erectus* fossils, pp. 218-227
- Describe the cultural stages of *Homo erectus,* p. 222
- Understand some of the disputes in interpreting *erectus* fossils and archeological evidence particularly with regard to European fossils, p. 227
- Analyze the technological advances reflected in the *erectus* tool kit, pp. 228-230

FILL IN OUTLINE
Introduction
In the previous chapters we looked at early hominid evolution by examining the genera *Australopithecus* and early *Homo*. In this chapter we move on chronologically to examine *Homo erectus*, believed by most to be the ancestor of modern *Homo sapiens*. We look at the geographic and temporal distribution of *Homo erectus*, physical characteristics typical of *erectus*, the history of *erectus* discoveries, variation exhibited by African and Asian *erectus* fossils and the technological advances made by *erectus* over approximately 1.5 million years.

I. INTRODUCTION
    A. Hominid evolution has been characterized by _____.

    B. We need to look at the _____ capacities of *H. erectus* in concert with _____ changes to understand its success as a hominid species.

II. HOMO ERECTUS – TERMINOLOGY AND GEOGRAPHICAL DISTRIBUTION
    A. The name first given for the Javanese fossils was _____.

    B. After _____ the previous taxonomic splitting was combined under the classification *Homo erectus*.

    C. Finds in E. Africa have been radiometrically dated to _____.
    D. Two sites in _____ have dates that compare to those in E. Africa.
    E. Evidence indicates that hominids left Africa before _____.
    F. A likely route that can be reconstructed for the *erectus* migration out of Africa would be _____.

    G. The fossil remains from the Gran Dolina site in Spain are approximately _____ years old.
III. THE PLEISTOCENE (1.8 m.y.a. - 10,000 y.a.)

    A. Also known as the "_____" or "_____"

B. _____ was covered with ice.

C. New evidence indicates approximately ____ major cold periods and ____ minor advances.

D. *Homo erectus* _____ and _____ during the Pleistocene.

IV. THE MORPHOLOGY OF <u>HOMO</u> <u>ERECTUS</u>

A. Brain Size

1. In *Homo erectus* ranges from _____ to _____.

2. Has a mean of _____ in *erectus*.

3. Is related to overall _____.

4. *Homo erectus* was considerably _____ than later members of the genus *Homo*.

B. Body Size

1. *Homo erectus* displays a dramatic _____ in body size.

2. Adults are estimated to have weighed on average _____.

3. Average adult height is estimated at _____.

4. *Homo erectus* was quite _____ as indicated by the East African specimens.

C. Cranial Shape

1. Has a distinctive _____.

2. Thick cranial bones are found in the _____ specimens.

3. Supraorbital tori refer to _____.

4. The forehead is _____.

5. Maximum breadth is _____.

D. Dentition

1. _____ incisors are a typical characteristic.

2. Shovel-shaped incisors have been found in _____ specimens and also in an individual from _____ in Africa.

V. HISTORICAL OVERVIEW OF <u>HOMO</u> <u>ERECTUS</u> DISCOVERIES

A. Java

1. _____ was the first laboratory scientist to go to work in the field.

2. The first fossils unearthed were a _____ and a _____.

3. These fossils were classified as _____.

4. _____ evolved before the enlargement of the brain.

B. *Homo erectus* from Java

1. All the fossils from Java have been found come from _____ sites.

2. _____ is a problem because of complex Javanese geology.

3. New dating techniques have revealed dates ranging from _____ to _____.

4. The Ngandong individuals date from _____ to _____.

5. If the Ngandong dates are correct it would make *Homo erectus* _____ with *Homo sapiens*.

6. In Java, no_____ have been found that can be associated with *Homo erectus*.

C. Peking
   1. "_____" were known to be used as medicine and as aphrodisiacs.
   2. Near the village of _____ a remarkable fossil skull was found.
   3. The bones from were packed for shipment and _____.
D. Zhoukoudian *Homo erectus*
   1. More than _____ male and female adults and children have been found.
   2. Features include the _____ in front and the _____ behind.
   3. The skull is keeled by a _____.
      4. The face _____ and the incisors are _____.

   5. The skull shows the greatest breadth near the _____.
   6. Cultural Remains
      a. More than _____ artifacts have been unearthed.
      b. The site was inhabited intermittently for almost _____ years.
      c. Occupation has been divided into _____ cultural stages.
      d. Early tools are _____ and _____.
      e. Materials used to make tools include _____, _____ and

         _____.
      f. Drinking bowls were made out of _____.
      g. Food included _____, _____, _____,

         _____, _____ and _____.
      h. It is _____ that they used language.
      i. The life span of *Homo erectus* was not very _____.

      j. _____% of the bones found were of individuals less than 14 years old.
      k. ____% of the bones found were of individuals in the 50-60 year range
E. Other Chinese Sites
   1. Chenjiawo and Gongwangling are often referred to as "_____."
   2. Lontandong Cave is often referred to as "_____."
   3. Chenjiawo finds is provisionally dated at _____.
   4. Gongwangling finds are provisionally dated at _____.
   5. In the Lontandong Cave a _____ was found exhibiting several _____ characteristics.

   6. In Yunxian County two relatively complete skulls were found dating
      to _____ y.a.

   7. The Yunxian County crania show a mid-facial morphology similar to
      that of _____.

F. East Africa
   1. Olduvai
      a. _____ unearthed OH9.
      b. OH9 dates to _____.
      c. OH9's cranial capacity is estimated at _____.
      d. OH9 is the _____ of the African *erectus* finds.
   2. East Turkana
      a. ER 3733 is an almost complete _____.

b. ER 3733 dates to _____.
c. Not many _____ have been found.
3. West Turkana
   a. WT 15,000 was found at a site known as _____.
   b. WT 15,000 is the most complete *H. erectus* _____ ever found.

   c. WT 15,000 dates to _____.
   d. WT 15,000 was a boy about _____ years old.
   e. If WT 15,000 had grown to his full height he would have been more than _____ tall.

   f. WT 15,000's adult cranial capacity would have been _____.
4. Ethiopia
   a. An abundance of _____ tools have been found.
   b. A robust mandible has been found dating to _____.
5. Summary of East African *Homo erectus*
   a. African *erectus* finds show several _____ from the Java and Chinese fossils

   b. The crania of the East African specimens have thinner cranial bones than those found in _____.

   c. Some scientists would argue that the African and Asian *erectus* finds should be classified as _____.

   d. It appears that the African and Asian populations are separated by more than _____.

6. South Africa
   a. Disagreement exists over how to classify the _____ found at Swartkrans.
7. North Africa
   a. Remains are almost entirely made up of _____.
   b. Tenerife remains are quite _____.
   c. Tenerife remains date to _____.
   d. Moroccan material is less _____ than that from Tenerife.
8. Europe
   a. Evidence suggests that the first hominids dispersed to Europe prior to _____ y.a.

   b. The European fossil material from the early Pleistocene is _____ and only _____ discovered.

   c. Taxonomic assessment of these remains has been _____.

VI. TECHNOLOGICAL AND POPULATION TRENDS IN THE MIDDLE PLEISTOCENE
A. Technological Trends
   1. _____ exists over the physical and cultural changes of *erectus*.
   2. The text takes a _____ regarding changes.
   3. A core stone that was worked on both sides is called a _____.

These tools are commonly called _____ and _____.

4. The _____ stone tool was an all purpose tool for more than a million years. It has been found in _____, _____ and later in _____. It has never been found in _____ or

_____.

5. Early toolmakers used a hammer made of _____.
6. Later toolmakers began using _____ and _____ which gave them more _____

7. Widespread evidence for _____ exists. Thousands of Acheulian hand axes have been found in association with _____.
8. *Homo erectus* is seen as a potential _____ and _____.

B. Population Trends
1. *Homo erectus* had a penchant for _____.
2. Hunters-scavengers and gatherers are _____.
3. Stone tools found on the island of Flores, 375 miles east of Java suggest that *erectus* may have had the capability of constructing _____ vessels.
4. *Homo erectus* embraced _____ as a strategy of adaptation.

KEY TERMS

Acheulian: a tool technology from the lower and middle Pleistocene characterized by bifacial

tools usually made of stone.

artifacts: objects or materials made or modified for use by hominids

biface: a stone tool consisting of a core stone worked on both sides. Commonly called

hand axes and cleavers. Associated with *H. erectus* in Africa, W. Asia and W. Europe.

biocultural: An approach to the study of human evolution taking into account the interaction

between morphological evolution and cultural changes.

Contemporaneous: living at the same time

encephalization: the relationship between brain size and overall body size

mandible: jaw bone

morphology: refers to the form or shape of anatomical structures or an entire organism

Nariokotome: also known as WT 15,000. Refers to an almost complete skeleton of a 12 year old boy from West Lake Turkana in Kenya classified as *Homo erectus*.

Nuchal torus: large muscle attachment at the base of the skull

Pleistocene: the epoch of the Cenozoic dating from 1.8 m.y.a. to 10,000 y.a. characterized by

continental glaciations of the northern latitudes. Frequently referred to as the "Age

of Glaciers" or the "Ice Age."

Postcranial: refers to the skeleton. Anything except the cranium.

Sagittal ridge: a ridge of bone running along the center of the skull (like parting the hair down

the middle) where chewing muscles attach.

Supraorbital torus: heavy browridge

Taxonomy: the science of classifying organisms based on evolutionary relationship

Temporal: refers to either time or a cranial bone.

Zhoukoudian: A village near Peking famous for a cave that has yielded rich fossil remains of *Homo erectus*.

FILL-IN QUESTIONS

1. Prior to World War II a variety of _____ were proposed for fossils that were later lumped under the classification of *Homo erectus*.

2. Reclassifying fossils and shifting away from taxonomic splitting was a benefit to paleoanthropology because it refocused the research away from arguments regarding classification to broader _____, _____ and _____ considerations.

3. We now have growing evidence of the early dispersal of hominids out of _____.

4. Evidence of *Homo erectus* has been found in the Republic of _____ that are as old as those in East Africa and Java.

5. The Boxgrove site in _____ dates to _____.

6. The _____ site in northern Spain dates to 780,000. If the dating can be further corroborated these finds would be _____ years older than any other Western European hominid finds.

7. The "Age of Glaciers" or the "Ice Age" refers to the epoch of the Cenozoic known as the _____ which dates from _____ to _____.

8. The Pleistocene was characterized by 15 major cold periods and 50 minor advances. This computes out to approximately one major cold period every _____ years.

9. By the end of the Pleistocene _____ had appeared.

10. We begin to see considerable brain _____ in *Homo erectus*.

11. Many scholars believe that there were more than _____ species of *Homo* in Africa 2 m.y.a.

12. The relationship of brain size to overall body size is referred to as _____.

13. The Nariokotome skeleton indicates a dramatic increase in _____ for *Homo erectus.*.

14. A robust body build is typical of hominid evolution until the appearance of _____ _____ when a more gracile skeleton appears.

15. *Homo erectus* is said to have a distinctive cranial shape. The characteristics that give *erectus* this distinct shape include _____, _____, _____, _____, and _____.

16. *H. erectus* dentition is similar to that of *Homo sapiens* however early *erectus* finds exhibit somewhat _____ teeth.

17. The incisors of *H. erectus* exhibit a unique characteristic which is _____.

18. Eugene Dubois left Holland for Sumatra in 1887 in search of "_____".

19. After Dubois published his findings from Java he was criticized. How did he combat this criticism and what was the result? _____
_____.

20. The similarities between Dubois' Java fossils and those of Beijing were obvious. How did Dubois respond to these similarities? _____.

21. Java has a complex geology making accurate dating difficult. However, it is generally accepted that the approximate dates for the majority of fossils from Java date to less than _____.

22. Modjokerto, a site in Java, has been dated to _____ m.y.a.

23. Sangiran, another site in Java, has been dated to _____ m.y.a. and has yielded the remains of at least _____ individuals.

24. After Japan invaded China in 1933 _____ attempted to ship the Peking fossils to the United States to keep them from falling into the hands of the Japanese. The bones _____ reached the U.S.

25. The Zhoukoudian Cave has yielded the remains of _____ individuals and over _____ artifacts have been found.

26. The Zhoukoudian Cave has been divided into three cultural stages. The Earliest Stage dates from _____ to _____ and its tools are _____ and made of _____.

27. The Middle Stage of the Zhoukoudian Cave dates from _____ to _____ and its tools are _____ than those from the Earliest Stage.

28. The Final Stage of the Zhoukoudian Cave dates from _____ to _____ and its tools are _____ and made of _____.

29. Peking Man (the term often used when referring to the Zhoukoudian Cave fossils) exploited various sources in the environment for subsistence including _____, _____, _____, _____, and _____.

30. *Homo erectus* from Zhoukoudian probably did/did not have articulated speech.

31. Although the life span of *H. erectus* is unknown, nearly 40% of the bones found at Zhoukoudian Cave belonged to individuals _____ years or younger and only 2.6% belonged to individuals in the _____ age range.

32. A partial cranium discovered at _____ may be the oldest known Chinese *erectus* find.

33. In 1960 Louis Leakey found the largest African *H. erectus* specimen at _____.

34. ER 3733 is a skull without a mandible that has a cranial capacity of 848cm3 which is at the _____ end of the range for *erectus* cranial capacity.

35. _____ has a reputation as an outstanding fossil hunter.

36. WT 15,000 from Nariokotome, Kenya is_____
_____.

37. The Acheulian stone tools found in Ethiopia were primarily bifaces and picks and were made of _____, _____, _____, _____, _____, _____, _____.

38. Bernard Wood proposes that African and Chinese *erectus* finds are _____ species.

39. There is _____ about how to classify the mandible found in Swartkrans in South Africa.

40. The earliest evidence for *Homo erectus* dates to 1.8-1.6 m.y.a. and comes from _____ and _____. Around a million years later, evidence appears in _____.
41. Classification of European fossils is _____ and _____.
42. The biface, an Acheulian stone tool became the all-purpose *erectus* tool for more than _____ years.
43. At the Olorgesailie site in Kenya, dated at around 800,000 y.a. thousands of _____ _____ have been recovered associated with large animal remains.

44. *Homo erectus* loved to travel. In a million years they dispersed to north and south Africa as well as into _____.
45. Tools found east of Java suggest that *Homo erectus* may have had the ability to construct _____-_____ vessels.

46. A summary of the physical and behavioral achievements of *Homo erectus* would include increased _____, more efficient _____, _____ as an adaptive strategy and whose _____ was reshaped and increased in size. They became a more efficient _____, likely _____, with increased dependence on _____, permanent bases, perhaps could build vessels to cross water and they probably used _____.

MULTIPLE CHOICE QUESTIONS
1. New dates from two sites in Java indicate that
   A. *Homo erectus* may have originated in Asia
   B. The Java finds are as old as the East African finds
   C. The Java finds are much more recent than the East African finds
   D. *Homo erectus* arrived in Java one million years later than previously thought

2. Currently, it is believed that the first hominids left Africa
   A. Between 1.5 and 2 m.y.a.
   B. Due to a geologic catastrophe
   C. Around 500,000 y.a.
   D. And went first to Western Europe

3. At the Ubeidiya site in Israel _____ are dated to 1.4-1.3 m.y.a.
   A. stone tools
   B. crania
   C. floral remains
   D. fauna remains

4. Mandibles found in the Republic of Georgia are dated to 1.8 to 1.6 m.y.a. If these dates are confirmed it would prove that

   A. these finds are as old as the Java finds

   B. these finds are about as old as East African finds

   C. these finds predate either the Java or East African finds
   D. A & B only

5. The find at the Ceprano site in central Italy
    A. shows that *erectus* never migrated to Europe
    B. is the oldest concrete evidence of *erectus* in Europe
    C. may be the best evidence we have of *erectus* in Europe
    D. provided extensive evidence of tool use among *erectus*

6. Fossil remains from the Atapuerca region of northern Spain
    A. may be the oldest hominids in Western Europe
    B. are confirmed as *Homo erectus*
    C. are the oldest fossils of *Homo sapiens*
    D. are very recent evidence of *Homo sapiens*

7. The dispersal of *Homo erectus* from Africa was influenced by all BUT
    A. continental drift
    B. climate
    C. water boundaries
    D. food

8. During much of the Pleistocene enormous masses of ice
    A. advanced
    B. melted
    C. retreated
    D. A & C only

9. Oscillations of cold and warm temperatures during the Pleistocene affected
    A. tides
    B. plants
    C. animals
    D. temperatures
    E. B & C only

10. The Pleistocene lasted
    A. approximately 100,000 years
    B. approximately 800,000 years
    C. more than 1.75 million years
    D. more than 2.25 million years

11. Compared to earlier members of the genus *Homo*, *Homo erectus* was
    A. smaller overall
    B. larger overall
    C. more or less the same size
    D. varied

12. Compared with Homo sapiens, Homo erectus was
    A. less encephalized
    B. more encephalized
    C. equally encephalized
    D. large footed

13. If the Nariokotome find had survived to adulthood he would have
    A. been obese
    B. been around 5'8"
    C. been over 6 feet tall
    D. had longer arms relative to his legs

14. A physical characteristic distinct to *H. erectus* compared with other hominids is
    A. cranial height
    B. alveolar prognathism
    C. large teeth
    D. the cranial breadth is below the ear

15.   Shovel-shaped incisors are

    A. found among Chinese *erectus* specimens
    B. a primitive feature of *Homo erectus*
    C. are found on the Nariokotome specimen
    D. all of the above

16. Eugene Dubois was the first scientist to
    A. see the significance of cranial size
    B. design a research plan to take him out of the lab and into the field
    C. dissect specimens
    D. apply dating techniques to fossils

17. In 1894 Dubois published a paper based on his discoveries in Java. This paper was
    A. embraced by the scientific community
    B. strongly criticized
    C. immediately followed up with similar findings to support it
    D. rejected outright

18. With regard to his analysis of the skullcap from Java, Dubois was
    A. correct in identifying it as a previously undescribed species
    B. incorrect in identifying it as a previously undescribed species
    C. correct in his classification as *australopithecus*
    D. correct in his classification as early *Homo*

19. All BUT which of the following is true of the *Homo erectus* finds from Java?
    A. Six sites have yielded all the fossils found to date
    B. Dating is difficult due to complex geology
    C. Most of the fossils are older than 1.2 million years
    D. Most fossils are less than 800,000 years old

20. If the date range of 50,000 to 25,000 from Java is confirmed it would show that
    A. *Homo erectus* lived contemporaneously with *Homo sapiens*
    B. Homo erectus had art
    C. *Homo erectus* died immediately before the appearance of modern *H. sapiens*
    D. *Homo erectus* exhibited complex tool use

21. All BUT which of the following is true of the skull uncovered in 1929 and cleaned by Davidson Black?

    A. It was a juvenile
    B. The shape was thick and low
    C. It was relatively large
    D. It was an early hominid

22. Which of the following traits is NOT characteristic of *Homo erectus*?
    A. supraorbital torus
    B. shovel-shaped incisors
    C. gracile muscle attachments
    D. pentagonal contour to the cranium

23. Zoukoudian Cave
    A. was discovered after Europeans had heard about "dragon bones"
    B. shows evidence of a bear cult
    C. has firm evidence of cannibalism
    D. was inhabited intermittently for almost 250,000 years
    E. A & D

24. The cultural remains at Zoukoudian Cave
    A. Are minimal
    B. Are limited to hearths
    C. Consist of over 100,000 artifacts
    D. Enable archaeologists to easily reconstruct a day in the life of *H. erectus*

25. It appears that *erectus* exploited
    A. primarily meat sources
    B. primarily fruits
    C. meat, fruit, eggs and seeds
    D. marine life

26. Of the fossil remains at Zhoukoudian
    A. 40% belonged to individuals 14 years old and younger
    B. 2.6% belonged to individuals 50-60 years old
    C. nuclear families were clearly represented
    D. All of the above
    E. A & B

27. Which of the following advanced characteristics was/were found on the cranium
    From Lontandong Cave which dates to 250,000 y.a.?

    A. reduced postorbital constriction
    B. temporal characteristics
    C. occipital characteristics
    D. All of the above

28. OH9 found in 1960 by Louis Leakey at Olduvai
    A. is dated at 1.4 m.y.a.
    B. has a massive cranium
    C. is gracile
    D. A & B

29. WT 15,000 from Nariokotome, Kenya
    A. is the most complete *erectus* skeleton ever found
    B. exhibits very primitive characteristics
    C. has a huge cranial capacity
    D. dates to 1.6 m.y.a.
    E. A & D

30. The importance of WT 15,000, found t Nariokotome on the west side of Lake Turkana, is
    A. the remarkable age of the specimen at death
    B. the completeness of the skeleton
    C. the estimated stature of a 12 year-old boy
    D. B & C

31. North African remains of *Homo erectus* have been found in all BUT which of the following
    places?
    A. Algeria
    B. Egypt
    C. Morocco
    D. Ternifine

32. European *Homo erectus* finds are
    A. clearly similar to ancient *erectus* finds
    B. fragmentary
    C. controversial
    D. all of the above
    E. B & C only

33. The Acheulian stone biface was a standard tool for *Homo erectus* for over a million years and was
    A. never found in Africa
    B. never found in West Asia
    C. never found in East Asia
    D. found in abundance in eastern Europe

34. Wood and bone allowed toolmakers to
    A. have more control
    B. leave shallower scars
    C. create sharper edges
    D. all of the above
    E. A & B only

35. Homo erectus was
    A. sedentary
    B. nomadic
    C. not very successful
    D. none of the above

ANSWERS TO FILL-IN OUTLINE

I. INTRODUCTION
    A. Biocultural interaction
    B. Behavioral, morphological

II. HOMO ERECTUS - TERMINOLOGY AND GEOGRAPHICAL DISTRIBUTION
    A. *Pithecanthropus*
    B. World War II
    C. 1.8 m.y.a.
    D. Java
    E. 1 m.y.a.
    F. To South and North Africa, southern and northeaster Asia and perhaps Europe
    G. 780,000 y.a.

III. THE PLEISTOCENE (1.8 m.y.a. - 10,000 y.a.)
    A. Age of Glaciers, Ice Age
    B. Northern Hemisphere
    C. 15, 50
    D. Appeared, disappeared

IV. THE MORPHOLOGY OF HOMO ERECTUS
    A. Brain Size
        1. 750 to 1250 cm3
        2. 1000 cm3
        3. Body size
        4. less encephalized
    B. Body Size
        1. Increase

2. Over 100 pounds
3. 5'6"
4. sexually dimorphic
C. Cranial Shape
1. Shape
2. Asian
3. Large browridges
4. Receding with little development
5. Below the ear opening
D. Dentition
1. Shovel-shaped
2. Chinese, Nariokotome

V. HISTORICAL OVERVIEW OF <u>HOMO</u> <u>ERECTUS</u> DISCOVERIES
A. Java
1. Eugene Dubois
2. Skullcap and femur
3. *Pithecanthropus erectus*
4. Bipedalism
B. *Homo erectus* from Java
1. Six
2. Dating
3. 1.8 m.y.a., 1.6 m.y.a
4. 50,000 to 25,000 y.a.
5. contemporary
6. Artifacts
C. Peking
1. Dragon bones
2. Zhoukoudian
3. Never been found (lost or stolen)
D. Zhoukoudian *Homo erectus*
1. 40
2. supraorbital torus, nuchal torus
3. Sagittal ridge
4. protrudes, shoveled
5. bottom
6. Cultural Remains
a. 100,000
b. 250,000
c. Three
d. Crude, shapeless
e. Stone, bone, horn
f. Deer skulls
g. Deer, horse, fruits, berries, eggs, seeds, herbs, tubers
h. Unlikely
i. long
j. 40

        k. 2.6
E. Other Chinese Sites
    1. Lantian
    2. Hexian
    3. 650,000 y.a.
    4. 1.15 m.y.a.
    5. Cranium, advanced
    6. 350,000 y.a.
    7. Modern Asians
F. East Africa
    1. Olduvai
        a. Louis Leakey
        b. 1.4 m.y.a.
        c. 1,067 cm3
        d. largest
    2. East Turkana
        a. Skull
        b. 1.8 m.y.a.
        c. Tools
    3. West Turkana
        a. Nariokotome
        b. Skeleton
        c. 1.6 m.y.a.
        d. 12
        e. More than 6 ft.
        f. 909 cm3
    4. Ethiopia
        a. Acheulian
        b. 1.3 m.y.a.
    5. Summary of East African *Homo erectus*
        a. Differences
        b. Asian representatives
        c. Separate species
        d. one million year
    6. South Africa
        a. mandible
    7. North Africa
        a. mandibles and mandible fragments
        b. robust
        c. 700,000 y.a.
        d. robust
    8. Europe
       a. 700,000
       b. fragmentary, recently
       debated

VI. TECHNOLOGICAL AND POPULATION TRENDS IN THE MIDDLE PLEISTOCENE

A. Technological Trends
   1. Dispute
   2. Moderate position
   3. Biface, hand axes, cleavers
   4. Biface, an Acheulian, Africa, parts of Asia, western Europe, eastern Europe, East Asia
   5. Stone
   6. Wood, bone, control
   7. Butchering, remains of large animals
   8. Hunter, scavenger

B. Population Trends
   1. Travel
   2. Nomadic
   3. Ocean-going
   4. cultural

ANSWERS & REFERENCES TO FILL IN QUESTIONS

1. splitting, p. 211
2. Populational, behavioral, ecological, p. 211
3. Africa, p. 212
4. Africa, *Homo erectus*, p. 212
5. Southern England, 500,000 y.a., p. 212
6. Gran Dolina, at least 250,000, pp. 212
7. Pleistocene, 1.8 m.y.a.-10,000 y.a., p. 213
8. 100,000, p. 213
9. Modern humans, p. 213
10. Enlargement, p. 213
11. One, p. 216
12. Encephalization, p. 216
13. Body size, p. 216
14. anatomically modern *Homo sapiens*, p. 216
15. Supraorbital tori, nuchal torus, long and low vault, receding forehead, maximum breadth below the ear opening, p. 216
16. larger, p. 218
17. shovel-shaped, p. 218
18. the missing link, p. 218
19. He elaborated on certain points and showed the actual fossil material. Many opponents became sympathetic (started to change their minds), p. 219
20. He refused to recognize the connection referring to them as "degenerate Neanderthaler," p. 219
21. 800,000 y.a., p. 219
22. 1.8 m.y.a., p. 219
23. 1.6, five individuals, p. 219
24. Franz Weidenreich, never, p. 220

25. 40, 100,000, pp. 221-222
26. 460,000, 420,000 y.a., large, soft stone, p. 222
27. 370,000-350,000 y.a., smaller and lighter, p. 222
28. 300,000-230,000 y.a., small finer quartz and flint, p. 222
29. Deer, horses, fruits, berries, eggs, seeds, herbs, tubers, p. 223
30. did not, p. 223
31. 14, 50-60, p. 223
32. Gongwangling, p. 224
33. Olduvai, p. 225
34. lower, p. 225
35. Kamoya Kimeu, p. 225
36. The almost complete skeleton of a 12 year old boy classified as H. *erectus*, dated to1.6 m.y.a., who was 5'3" and had a cranial capacity of 880cm3 at death. It is estimated that his adult height would have been over 6' and his cranial capacity would have been approximately 909cm3, pp. 225-226.
37. Quartz, quartzite, volcanic rock, p. 226.
38. Separate, p. 226
39. disagreement, p. 226
40. East Africa, Java, China, p. 227
41. tentative, controversial, p. 227
42. a million, p. 229
43. Acheulian hand axes, p. 229
44. Asia, Europe, p. 230
45. Ocean-going, p. 231
46. body size, bipedalism, culture, brain, scavenger, hunter, meat, fire, p. 231

ANSWERS & REFERENCES TO MULTIPLE CHOICE QUESTIONS
1. B, p. 211
2. A, p. 212
3. A, p. 212
4. D, p. 212
5. C, p. 212
6. A, p. 212
7. A, p. 212
8. D, p. 213
9. E, p. 213
10. C, p. 213
11. B, p. 216
12. A, p. 216
13. C, p. 216
14. D, p. 218
15. D, p. 218
16. B, p. 218
17. B, p. 219
18. A, p. 219
19. C, p. 219

20. A, p. 220
21. C, p. 220
22. C, pp. 216-218
23. E, pp. 220-222
24. C, p. 222
25. C, p. 223
26. E, p. 309
27. D, p. 224
28. D, p. 225
29. E, p. 225
30. D, p. 225
31. B, p. 227
32. E, p. 227
33. C, p. 229
34. D, p. 229
35. B, p. 230

CHAPTER 10
NEANDERTALS AND OTHER ARCHAIC <u>HOMO</u> <u>SAPIENS</u>

LEARNING OBJECTIVES

After reading this chapter you should be able to

- See the morphological changes between *Homo erectus* and archaic *Homo sapiens* (pp. 240-241)
- Know the geographic distribution of archaic *Homo sapiens*. (p. 241)
- Discuss specific fossils of archaic *sapiens* and their distinguishing characteristics (pp. 241-245)
- Compare the tool technology of archaic *sapiens* to that of *H. erectus* and early modern *Homo sapiens* (pp. 246-249)
- Discuss the physical characteristics of classic Neandertals (pp. 249-256)
- Discuss specific Neandertal finds and their distinguishing characteristics (pp. 253-259)
- Describe Neandertal shelters, subsistence strategies and burials. (pp. 259-264)
- Be familiar with the three major transitions in the evolution of *Homo sapiens*. (pp. 264-266)
- Have an understanding of the confusion surrounding the origins and disappearance of Neandertal (pp. 262-263)
- Understand the debate regarding how to classify the early *Homo* fossil material. (pp. 266-267)

FILL-IN OUTLINE

Introduction

In the previous chapter we examined *Homo erectus*, believed by most to be the ancestor of modern *Homo sapiens*. In this chapter we take a look at archaic *Homo sapiens* from Europe, Africa, China and Java who display both *H. erectus* and *H. sapiens* characteristics. We then take a look at Neandertals including their physical characteristics, culture, technology, settlements, subsistence patterns and burials. We include a discussion on the confusion surrounding Neandertal origins as well as their disappearance.

I. INTRODUCTION
    A. Some fossils from Europe, Africa, China and Java display both *Homo erectus* and _____ characteristics.
    B. They are referred to as _____ *Homo sapiens* because they exhibit certain _____ traits.
    C. Some populations of *Homo erectus* continued to evolve and emerge as _____ forms between *Homo erectus* and *Homo sapiens sapiens*.

II. EARLY ARCHAIC *HOMO SAPIENS*
    A. exhibit _____ characteristics like brain expansion.
    B. It is difficult to _____ the Middle Pleistocene material.
    C. have been found on _____ continents including _____,

_____ and _____.

D. The most well-known from Europe are the _____.

E. Africa

    1. The Broken Hill cranium has a very heavy _____.

    2. In Africa the archaic *H. sapiens* are morphologically similar which may signify a close _____ relationship.

F. Asia

    1. Certain *erectus* features can be found in modern Chinese such as a _____ and flattened _____ bone.

    2. This could indicate that modern Chinese evolved from a separate _____ lineage in _____.

G. Europe

    1. Early archaic *sapiens* from Europe show *erectus* characteristics like a _____ mandible.

    2. Later archaics from Europe show derived characteristics like a _____ occipital area and reduced _____ size.

    3. The later group of European archaics may have given rise to _____.

    4. The largest sample of archaic *sapiens* comes from a site called Sima de los Huesos in northern _____.

III. **A REVIEW OF MIDDLE PLEISTOCENE EVOLUTION (CIRCA 400,000-125,000 Y.A.)**

A. Fossils from Europe, Africa and China exhibit a _____ of traits from both *erectus* and *sapiens*.

B. The earlier European forms are more _____.

C. The later European forms are more like _____.

D. African and Asian forms begin exhibiting a more _____ pattern.

IV. **MIDDLE PLEISTOCENE CULTURE**

A. The basic tools are _____ and _____.

B. African and European archaics invented the _____ technique for tool making.

C. This technique indicates an increased _____ ability.

D. Acheulian tools are associated with _____.

E. We see _____ tool traditions co-existing in some areas.

F. Archaic *sapiens* lived in _____ and _____ sites.

G. Chinese archaeologists insist that humans _____ (did/did not) control fire.

H. The Lazaret Cave shelter was supported by _____ and large _____.

    1. Inside were two _____.

    2. The people exploited _____ fish.

I. At Terra Amata we have found evidence of short-term, _____ visits.

J. To hunt large prey early *H. sapiens* probably drove the animals _____.

K. In Schoningen, Germany three well preserved wooden _____ were found.

    1. These implements are provisionally dated to _____-_____y.a.

V. **NEANDERTALS: LATE ARCHAIC *HOMO SAPIENS* (130,000-35,000 Y.A.)**

A. Neandertals are _____.

B. _____ Neandertals dated from around 75,000 y.a. to 35,000 y.a. and are from _____ Europe.

C. Modern *H. sapien* brain size is around _____.

D. Neandertal brain size was around _____.
   1. This may be associated with _____ in cold weather.

E. The Neandertal cranium is large _____, _____ and bulging at the sides.
   1. The forehead begins to _____ more vertically.
   2. Over the orbits we see _____ instead of a supraorbital torus.

F. Postcranially Neandertals are very _____.

G. Neandertals lived in Europe and Western Asia for around _____ years.

H. France and Spain
   1. In La Chapelle-aux-Saints in S.W. France a nearly complete skeleton was found _____.
      a.   It was turned over to _____ for analysis.
      b.   He depicted this find as a _____, bent-kneed, not fully erect _____.
      c. This resulted in a general misunderstanding that Neandertals were highly _____.
      d. In fact, the skeleton was of an older male suffering from _____ _____.
      e. This individual is not a _____ Neandertal.
      f. He is unusally _____.
   2. If the date for the Zafarraya Cave in southern Spain is correct it would make this the most _____ of Neandertal fossils.
   3. It appears that Neandertals and modern *sapiens* _____ _____ _____ _____for several thousand years.

I. Central Europe
   1. Krapina, Croatia
      a. has remains of up to _____ individuals.
      b. has 1,000 _____ tools
      c. dates to _____-_____ y.a.
      d. has one of the oldest intentional _____ on record.

J. Western Asia
   1. Israel
      a. Tabun
         1. yielded a female skeleton dated at about _____y.a.
         2. if the dating is correct it indicates that Neandertal and modern _____ _____ lived contemporaneously.
      b. Kabara
         1. the most complete Neandertal _____ was found here.
         2. yielded the first ever _____ bone.
            a. important to reconstruct _____ capabilities.
   2. Iraq
      a. Shanidar

1. yielded the remains of _____ individuals.
   a._____ of them were deliberately buried.
2. Shanidar 1 was a _____to_____ year old male.
   a. his stature is estimated at _____.
   b. he exhibited extreme injuries that he_____.

K. Central Asia
   1. Uzbekistan
      a. is the _____ Neandertal discovery.
      b. is a _____ year old _____.

VI. **CULTURE OF NEANDERTALS**
   A. The stone tool industry associated with Neandertals is the _____.
      1. which extended geographically into _____, _____,
         _____, _____, _____,
         _____ and perhaps even _____.
   B. Technology
      1. Neandertals improved on the previous _____ techniques.
      2. We see some indication of _____ of tools.
   C. Settlements
      1. Neandertals lived in _____, _____, _____and
         _____.
      2. On the tundra there is some evidence of _____.
      3. Archeologists found traces of an oval ring of _____ bones.
      4. Inside the ring they found traces of a number of _____.
      5. _____ was in general use by this time.
   D. Subsistence
      1. Neandertals were successful _____.
      2. After the beginning of the Upper Paleolithic (around 40 k.y.a.) the
         _____ or _____ was invented.
      3. The pattern of trauma found among Neandertals is similar to modern day
         _____.
      4. Besides meat, Neandertals also ate _____, _____ and other_____.
      5. Since it was so cold we assume that Neandertals _____.
   E. Symbolic Behavior
      1. We believe that Neandertals _____(were/were not) capable of speech.
      2. The hypoglossal canal may be significant for _____ production.
      3. Neandertals are being viewed as an _____ dead end.
      4. Tentative interpretations of DNA comparisions of Neandertals and modern
         humans estimate the divergence between them at _____-
         _____y.a.
   F. Burials
      1. Some form of deliberate and consistent disposal of the dead dates back to
         _____ from the Atapuerca, Spain site.
         a. this is seen in Western Europe long before it appears in either
            _____ or _____.

2. After 35,000 y.a. with <u>H</u>. sapiens sapiens we see deliberate burials containing grave goods like _____ and _____.

3. In Neandertal burials the bodies were put in a _____ position.

VII. EVOLUTIONARY TRENDS IN THE GENUS *HOMO*

A. At least _____ major transitions have taken place.

B. The first transition was from early _____ to _____.

    1. was geographically limited to _____.

    2. occurred quite _____.

C. The second transition was _____ grading into _____.

    1. It _____(was/was not) geographically limited.

    2. occurred slowly and _____.

    3. interpretations are _____

    4. many populations could have been _____ and small.

D. The third transition was from _____ to _____.

    1. It was _____ than the second transition.

E. Taxonomic Issues

    1. In this text the *Homo* fossil materials have been classified into _____ recognized species.

       a. This is a _____ interpretation.

    2. The major issues relating to interpretations of what we have termed archaic *Homo sapiens* are:

       a. The classification is viewed as _____.

       b. Several early archaic specimens from Africa and Europe show derived characteristics different from *Homo sapiens*. They have been classified as *Homo* _____.

       c. Neandertals are also viewed by numerous researchers as representing a _____ _____.

KEY TERMS

archaic *Homo sapiens*:: earlier forms of *Homo sapiens*, including but not limited to Neandertals, that come after *Homo erectus* but before modern humans.

Chatelperronian: a tool industry created from Neandertals modifying technology borrowed from anatomically modern humans

Flexed: the position in which bodies were found in Neandertal burials. The arms and legs are drawn up to the chest

Hearth: floor of a fireplace

Levallois: a technique for the manufacture of tools by striking flakes from a flat flint nodule

Mousterian: the stone tool technology associated with Neandertals and some modern *Homo sapiens* groups

Transitional forms: fossils that have both primitive and derived characteristics. They are not fully one form but rather exhibit traits from two different species, i.e., *erectus/sapiens* or Neandertal/moderns.

FILL-IN QUESTIONS

1. The earliest members of our species that date from around 400,000 to 130,000 y.a. are called _____ _____ ___ ___.

2. These early human forms exhibited both derived characteristics like those found in modern humans as well as primitive characteristics typical of either *Homo erectus* or Neandertal. They presence of both the primitive and derived characteristics suggest that these are _____ forms.

3. Early archaic humans exhibit morphological changes more derived than ____ _____.

4. Some of the derived characteristics present in archaic *sapiens* include _____, _____, _____ and a general decrease in cranial and post cranial _____.

5. In this text we take a conservative taxonomic approach and classify all of the specimens within the species _____ _____.

6. The Broken Hill skull exhibits both primitive and derived characteristics. The cranial base is _____ _____ although it dates from 150,000 to 125,000 y.a.

7. No _____ have been found in Africa or the far east.

8. Chinese paleoanthropologists interpret the presence of _____ _____ and _____ _____ _____ in both modern Chinese people and Chinese *erectus* populations to be evidence that modern Chinese evolved from a specific lineage of *erectus* in China.

9. The skeletal remains from Jinniushan in N.E. China dates to around 200,000 y.a. and exhibits a fairly large _____ _____ for an individual this old.

10. In 1982 a partial skull was found in the Narmada Valley of _____.

11. It is difficult to acurately interpret European archaic *sapiens* because definite_____ and/or adequate_____ are lacking.

12. Archaic *sapiens* from Europe exhibit *erectus* characteristics such as _____ cranial bones and heavy _____ torus but they also exhibit *H. sapiens* characteristic like reduced tooth size or a more rounded _____ area.

13. At Atapuerca, in northern Spain, the site dates to 300,000 y.a. yet the morphological characteristics are similar to Neandertal. Specifically, these fossils exhibit arching _____ and a _____ midface.

14. The mosaic Chinese fossils are/are not similar to the African or European mosaic finds.

15. In China the _____ is rare in the Middle Pleistocene.

16. Although bone is a very useful material from which to make tools _____ did not seem to use it.

17. The Levallois technique for manufacturing tools required several _____ suggesting an increase in cognitive abilities among archaic *sapiens*.

18. Although the Acheulian tool assemblages have been found in a wide geographical range it is important to consider the intraregional _____ of the tools.

19. At the Lazaret Cave in southern France the hearth charcoal indicates that the occupants burned oak and boxwood. The advantages of these woods are that they are _____ _____ and _____.

20. At the Channel Island of Jersey off the west coast of France remains of large _____ and _____ have been found associated with stone flakes.

21. In the text the bulk of information on Neandertals comes from Western Europe and date from 75,000 to around 30,000 y.a. These specimens are usually referred to as "_____" Neandertals.

22. The climate in Eastern Europe and western Asia was not as cold as Western Europe during the last glaciation which may explain why Neandertal skeletons from there are _____ _____ as their W. European relatives.

23. Neandertals are well-known for their large brain. Among modern populations we find this same characteristic as an adaptation to _____ climates.

24. Neandertals lived in _____ and _____ for about 100,000 years.

25. Neandertal gets its name from the Neander Valley in _____ where the first fossil was found in 1856.

26. The first Neandertal skeleton was a-typical as to its size and the health of the individual. It was very large exhibiting a cranial capacity of _____ and immense _____.

27. It appears that Neandertals and modern *sapiens* lived near each other for several thousand years. The _____ tool tradition is the result of the blending of their technologies.

28. The Krapina fossils are similar to the classic Neandertals of Western Europe although they are less _____.

29. In Israel, although the overall pattern of the fossils is Neandertal, they display _____ features and are _____ than classic Neandertals of Europe.

30. One of the most impressive Neandertal finds is the Shanidar 1 male who was between 30-45 years old, 5'7" tall and had terrible injuries that he had survived for years. His injuries were numerous including _____, _____, _____, _____, _____ and _____.

31. In order for Shanidar 1 to survive his injuries _____.

32. A 9 year old boy who was deliberately buried is the easternmost Neandertal discovery in _____.

33. Evidence exists that Neandertal developed specialized tools for skin and meat preparation, _____, _____ and _____.

34. In the cold tundra evidence suggests that Neandertal _____.

35. Because of the level of their tool technology, it appears that Neandertal was still required to get up close when hunting large animals. An analysis of the pattern of _____ (particularly _____) in Neandertals and found that they were most like contemporary rodeo performers.

36. One of the greatest mysteries is "What happened to Neandertals?" Paleoanthropologists are suggesting that _____ differences between Neandertals and anatomically modern *sapiens* must account for our survival and the demise of Neandertal.

37. Neandertal speech capabilities _____ (would/would not) have been hampered by anatomical structures.

38. It appears that _____ burial was practiced among Neandertals.

39. Some form of deliberate and consistent disposal of the dead dates back to _____y.a. From Atapuerca, Spain.

40. In Neandertal burials, the bodies were put in a _____ position.

41. Three major transitions have taken place in human evolution over the last 2 million years. They are (1) from _____ to _____; (2) _____ to _____; and (3) _____ to _____.

42. Paleoanthropologits suggest _____ and _____ in the evolution of our genus.

43. At every major stage of the evolution of *Homo* over the last 2 million years, some professional opinion has argued for more than one _____.

MULTIPLE CHOICE QUESTIONS

1. Archaic *sapiens* refer to
   A. Neandertals
   B. Broken Hill
   C. *H. erectus*
   D. All of the above
   E. A & b

2. Derived morphological changes found in archaic *sapiens* include all but which of the following?
   A. Brain expansion
   B. Increase in molar size
   C. Increased parietal breadth
   D. Decreased robusticity

3. The archaic *sapiens* finds from South and East Africa
   A. Are similar to Broken Hill
   B. Very different from Broken Hill
   C. Indicate a lot of genetic variation
   D. Exhibit Neandertal characteristics

4. Neandertals are found in
   A. Africa
   B. Eastern Asia
   C. Europe
   D. Java
   E. A & c

5. Modern Chinese populations exhibit certain archaic *sapiens* traits including
   A. A sagittal ridge
   B. Flattened nasal bones
   C. Post orbital constriction
   D. All of the above
   E. A & b

6. European archaic *sapiens* fossils
   A. Contain strong evidence that *erectus* inhabited Europe around 250,000 y.a.
   B. Have problems with dating
   C. Are sketchy
   D. All of the above
   E. B & c

7. The earliest archaic *sapiens* from Europe
   A. Exhibit Neandertal characteristics
   B. Exhibit primarily *sapiens* characteristics
   C. Exhibit both *erectus* and *sapiens* traits
   D. Have a more gracile cranium

8. Many archaic *sapiens* finds
   A. Exhibit mosaic traits
   B. Appear to be transitional forms from *erectus* to modern *sapiens*
   C. Exhibit Neandertal and modern *sapiens* traits
   D. All of the above
   E. A & b

9. Mosaic forms from China
   A. Are surprisingly similar to those from W. Europe
   B. Are not the same as those from Europe and Africa
   C. Exhibit many Neandertal characteristics
   D. All of the above

10. The Levallois technique for tool manufacturing
    A. Arose in both Africa and Europe
    B. Enabled the toolmaker to control flake size and shape
    C. Required coordinated steps
    D. All of the above

11. The stone tool tradition referred to as Acheulian
    A. Exhibits considerable intra-regional diversity
    B. Has been found in E. Asia
    C. Is uniform throughout Europe and Africa
    D. Is associated with Neandertals

12. All but which of the following was found in or around the Lazaret Cave in southern France?
    A. A lot of stone waste
    B. Rock and large bone supports
    C. Two hearths
    D. Evidence of a framework of poles

13. All <u>but</u> which of the following is true of the spears found in Schoningen, Germany?
    A. They did not require considerable planning to manufacture.
    B. They were about 6 feet long
    C. They were made out of hard spruce wood
    D. They were expertly balanced

14. The majority of Neandertal fossils have been found in
    A. Africa
    B. Israel
    C. Europe
    D. Asia

15. Average brain size among Neandertals
    A. Is larger than modern humans
    B. May be related to metabolic efficiency in cold climates
    C. Is close to that of modern Inuit (Eskimo) brain size
    D. All of the above
    E. A & b

16. All but which of the following is typical of a Neandertal cranium?
    A. Long and low
    B. Arched browridges
    C. Sharply angled occipital bone
    D. Forehead begins to appear

17. The LaChapelle-aux-Saints burial in southwest France was buried with
    A. Nonhuman long bones over the head
    B. A bison leg
    C. Food
    D. Flowers
    E. A & b

18. The skeleton from the LaChapelle-aux-Saints burial
    A. Was a gracile, adult female
    B. Was an arthritic older male
    C. Was larger than the "typical" Neandertal
    D. Showed evidence of trauma
    E. B & c

19. If the date is accurate, the most recent Neandertal find comes from
    A. Southwestern France
    B. Spain
    C. Iran
    D. Croatia

20. The Krapina, Croatia Neandertal finds
    A. Include fragments of up to 70 individuals
    B. Date to around 30,000 y.a.
    C. Are particularly robust
    D. Have very few tools associated with them
    E. All of the above

21. The Tabun Neandertal finds
    A. Are less robust than the classic finds from Europe
    B. Date to around 110,000
    C. Were contemporarneous with modern <u>H</u>. <u>sapiens</u>
    D. All of the above
    E. A & c

22. The Shanidar 1 male
    A. Was obviously high ranking
    B. Was unusually large and robust
    C. Exhibited evidence of extreme trauma
    D. Was around 25 years old when he died

23. The tool industry associated with Neandertals is
    A. Mousterian
    B. Levallois
    C. Chatelperronian
    D. All of the above

24. Neandertal hunting
    A. Included spears
    B. Included bows and arrows
    C. Probably required close contact with the prey
    D. Was not very successful

25. DNA from a Neandertal fossil was compared with samples of contemporary human DNA. Tentative interpretations show that
    A. Neandertals contributed genetically to modern humans
    B. Neandertals did not contribute genetically to modern humans
    C. Neandertals are more closely related to modern humans than to chimpanzees
    D. Neandertals are more closely related to chimpanzees than to modern humans
    E. B & D only

26. The evolution of the genus *Homo* over the last 2 million years
    A. Can be divided into at least three major transitions
    B. Has been fairly steady
    C. Has been uniform over the different geographic regions
    D. Can be clearly interpreted

27. Deliberate burial of the dead
    A. Is seen among Neandertals
    B. Is seen in Africa prior to 120,000 y.a.
    C. Appears in Europe before eastern Asia
    D. Appears in Europe before Africa
    E. All except B

ANSWERS TO FILL-IN OUTLINE

I. INTRODUCTION
    A. *Homo sapiens*
    B. archaic, derived
    C. Transitional
II. EARLY ARCHAIC <u>HOMO</u> <u>SAPIENS</u>
    A. Derived
    B. Classify
    C. Three, Africa, Asia, Europe
    D. Neandertals
    E. Africa
        1. Supraorbital torus
        2. Genetic
    F. Asia
        1. Sagittal ridge, nasal
        2. *Homo erectus*, China
    G. Europe
        1. Robust
        2. Rounded, tooth
        3. Neandertals
        4. Spain
III. A REVIEW OF MIDDLE PLEISTOCENE EVOLUTION (CIRCA 400,000-125,000 Y.A.)
    A. Mosaic
    B. Robust
    C. Neandertal
    D. Modern *Homo sapiens*
IV. MIDDLE PLEISTOCENE CULTURE
    A. Choppers, flake
    B. Levallois
    C. Cognitive
    D. Hand axes
    E. Different
    F. Caves, open-air
    G. Did
    H. Rocks, bones
        1. Hearths

      2. freshwater
I. Seasonal
J. Off cliffs
K. Spears
      1. 380,000, 400,000

V. NEANDERTALS: LATE ARCHAIC <u>H.</u> <u>SAPIENS</u> (130,000-35,000 Y.A.)

A. Misfits
B. Classic, western
C. 1400 cm3
D. 1520 cm3
      1. metabolic efficiency
E. Large, long, low
      1. rise
      2. Arched browridges
F. Robust
G. 100,000
H. France and Spain
      1. Buried
            a. Marcellin Boule
            b. brutish, biped
            c. primitive
            d. spinal osteoarthritis
            e. Typical
            f. robust
      2. Recent
      3. Lived in close proximity
I. Central Europe
      1. Krapina, Croatia
            a. 70
            b. stone
            c. 130,000-110,000
            d. burial site
J. Western Asia
      1. Israel
            a. Tabun
                  1. 110,000
                  2. *Homo sapiens*
            b. Kabara
                  1. Pelvis
                  2. hyoid
                       a. language
      2. Iraq
            a. Shanidar
                  1. Nine
                     a. four

2. 30, 45
    a. 5'7"
    b. survived

  K. Central Asia
    1. Uzbekistan
      a. easternmost
      b. nine, boy

VI. CULTURE OF NEANDERTALS

  A. Mousterian
    1. Europe, North Africa, former Soviet Union, Israel, Iran, Uzbekistan, China
  B. Technology
    1. Levallois
    2. Specialization
  C. Settlements
    1. Open sites, caves, rock shelters
    2. Building of structures
    3. Mammoth
    4. Hearths
    5. Fire
  D. Subsistence
    1. Hunters
    2. Spearthrower, atlatl
    3. Rodeo performers
    4. Berries, nuts, plants
    5. Wore clothing
  E. Symbolic Behavior
    1. Were
    2. Speech
    4. Evolutionary
    5. 690,000-550,000
  F. Burials
    1. 300,000
      a. Africa, eastern Asia
    2. Bone, stone tools
    3. Flexed

VII. EVOLUTIONARY TRENDS IN THE GENUS HOMO

  A. Three
  B. *Homo, H. erectus*
    1. Africa
    2. rapidly
  C. *H. erectus*, early *H. sapiens*
    1. was not
    2. unevenly

3. ambiguous
4. isolated
D. Archaic *H. sapiens*, modern *H. sapiens*
1. faster
E. Taxonomic Issues
1. Three
a. Conservative
2. a. Imprecise
b. *heidelbergensis*
c. Distinct species

ANSWERS & REFERENCES TO FILL IN QUESTIONS

1. Archaic *H. sapiens*, p. 240
2. Transitional, p. 240
3. *H. erectus*, p. 240
4. Brain expansion, increased parietal breadth, decrease in the size of the molars, decreased skeletal robusticity, p. 240
5. *Homo sapiens*, p. 241
6. Essentially modern, p. 241
7. Neandertals, p. 241
8. Sagittal ridge, flattened nasal bones, pp. 241-244
9. Cranial capacity, p. 244
10. India, p. 244
11. dates, remains, p. 244
12. Thick, supraorbital, occipital, pp. 244-245
13. Browridges, projecting, p. 245
14. Are not, p. 246
15. Hand ax, p. 246
16. Archaic *H. sapiens*, p. 247
17. Coordinated steps, p. 247
18. Diversity, p. 247
19. Slow burning, easy to rekindle, p. 247
20. Mammoth, woolly rhinoceros, p. 248
21. Classic, p. 250
22. Less robust, p. 250
23. Cold, p. 250
24. Europe, western Asia, p. 250
25. Germany, p. 251
26. 1620cm3, supraorbital ridges, p. 253
27. Chatelperronian, p. 256
28. Robust, p. 257
29. Modern, less, p. 257

30. Blow to the left side of the head, probably blind in the left eye, blow to the right side of the body leaving a withered right arm (probably amputated later), atrophied shoulder blade, color bone and upper right arm, damged lower right leg, pathology in the right knee and left leg, p. 259
31. He must have been helped by others, p. 259
32. Uzbekistan, p. 259
33. Hunting, woodworking, hafting, p. 260
34. Built structures, p. 260
35. Trauma, fractures, p. 261
36. Behavioral, p. 261
37. Would not, p. 262
38. Deliberate, p. 263
39. 300,000, p. 264
40. Flexed, p. 264
41. Early *Homo, H. erectus, H. erectus* to archaic *H. sapiens*, archaic *H. sapiens*, modern *H. sapiens*, pp. 265-266
42. Diversity, complexity, p. 266
43. Species, p. 267

ANSWERS & REFERENCES TO MULTIPLE CHOICE QUESTIONS

1.   E, p. 240
2.   B, pp. 240-241
3.   A, p. 241
4.   C, p. 241
5.   E, pp. 241-244
6.   E, p. 244
7.   C, p. 244
8.   D, pp. 244-245
9.   B, p. 246
10.   D, p. 247
11.   A, p. 247
12.   A, p. 247
13.   A, p. 249
14.   C, p. 250
15.   D, p. 250
16.   C, p. 250
17.   E, p. 253
18.   E, p. 253
19.   B, p. 256
20.   A, p. 257
21.   D, p. 258
22.   C, p. 258
23.   D, pp. 256 & 259-260
24.   C, p. 260
25.   E, p. 262

26. A, p. 264
27. E, pp. 263-264

CHAPTER 11

HOMO SAPIENS SAPIENS

LEARNING OBJECTIVES

After reading this chapter you should be able to:

- Compare the three basic hypotheses for the origin and dispersal of anatomically modern humans (pp. 272-276)

- Discuss the earliest evidence of modern *Homo sapiens sapiens* including geographic distribution, technology and art (pp. 276-293)

- Distinguish between the cultural periods of the Upper Paleolithic (p. 285)
- Describe early art from Europe and Africa (pp. 284-293)
- Evaluate the various hypotheses attempting to interpret Upper Paleolithic art (pp. 291-292)

FILL-IN OUTLINE

Introduction

In the previous chapter we looked at archaic *Homo sapiens* including Neandertals. In this chapter we arrive at anatomically modern humans. We discuss the problems in attempting to determine when, where and how modern *H. sapiens* first appeared and look at the two basic hypotheses that attempt to answer these questions. We then examine modern *H. sapiens* fossils, technological artifacts and art in a wide range of geographic locations.

I. **INTRODUCTION**
   A. It is difficult to say when modern *H. sapiens* first appeared due to ongoing
   _____ in dating.

   B. It appears that the dispersal of modern humans in the Old World was _____.

II. **THE ORIGIN AND DISPERSAL OF HOMO SAPIENS SAPIENS (ANATOMICALLY MODERN HUMAN BEINGS)**
   A. The Complete Replacement Model (Recent African Evolution)

   1. This hypothesis was developed by _____ and_____ (1988).

   2. According to this theory, moderns originate in _____ within the last _____ years.

   3. Moderns then migrate out of _____ and into _____ and _____.
       a. Where they _____ the existing populations.

   4. This theory does not explain the transition from _____ to modern *H. sapiens* anywhere except Africa.

   5. The appearance of moderns is seen as a biological _____ event.
       a. Which means that no _____ could have occurred between

moderns and any of the local populations.

      6.   The evidence used to support this theory comes from _____

           _____ obtained from living peoples.

         a.   Specifically, DNA found in the cytoplasm, called_____
            DNA (mtDNA).
         b.   Which is only inherited through the _____.

      7.   Using the mtDNA scientists at Berkeley have constructed "trees" and concluded that the world's population descended from a_____ African _____.

      8.   Other scientists, using the same mtDNA material, have constructed different "trees" and found that some of them have no _____ _____.

  B. The Partial Replacement Model (African-European *H. sapiens* Hypothesis)

      1.   Modern *H. sapiens* populations first evolved in _____.

      2.   The earliest dates for African modern *Homo sapiens* is over_____ y.a.

      3.   This theory is proposed by _____ _____ from University of Hamburg.

      4.   The initial dispersal out of _____ was a _____ process.

      5.   Moderns then moved into _____ where they_____ with local

         archaic *H. sapiens* populations.

         a.   Eventually moderns _____ archaic populations.

  C. The Regional Continuity Model (Multiregional Evolution)

      1.   This model is proposed by _____ _____ and his associates.

      2.   They propose that some local archaic populations in _____, _____ and _____ continued on their indigenous evolutionary paths.

         a.   Some of these archaic populations evolved into _____
            _____.

      3.   Moderns are not considered to be a separate species because some _____ _____ (migration) occurred between archaic populations.

III. THE EARLIEST <u>HOMO</u> <u>SAPIENS</u> <u>SAPIENS</u> DISCOVERIES

  A. Africa

      1.   Fully anatomically modern forms date to about_____-_____ y.a.

      2.   Problems exist with dating, provenience and _____ _____ of the evidence.

  B. Near East

      1.   In Israel at least 10 individuals have been found in the _____
         _____ at Mt. Carmel.

         a.   This site is close to the _____ site of Tabun.
         b.   It has been dated to about _____ y.a.

      2.   The Qafzeh Cave in Israel has yielded the remains of at least _____ individuals.

      a.   Some exhibit certain archaic (_____) features.

      b.   it has been dated at around _____ y.a.

  3. It seems that modern *H. sapiens* and Neandertals _____
In the Near East.

C. Central Europe

  1. At many sites the fossils display both Neandertal and _____

features.

      a.   This would support the _____ _____ hypothesis.

  2. From Mladec, in the Czech Republic moderns have been found that date
to_____.

      a.   They exhibit a great deal of _____.

      b.   Although modern, all but one crania exhibit a prominent_____

          _____.

D. Western Europe

  1. Previously, theories on human evolution were based almost exclusively on
_____ _____ material.

  2. The best known of the W. European modern fossil finds is from the
_____ site.

      a.   Discovered in _____.

      b.   In a _____ shelter in southern France.

      c.   The tool industry is known as _____.

      d.   The site dates to _____ y.a.

      e.   A child's skeleton from Portugal gives evidence of possible
_____ between Neandertal and anatomically

         modern Homo sapiens.

        1. This provides support for the _____ _____

           Model.

E. Asia

  1. Ordos (from Dagouwan, Inner Mongolia) is probably the oldest

anatomically modern find in _____ dating to at least

_____ y.a.

  2. Chinese paleoanthropologists see a continuous evolution in their

geographic area from _____ to _____ to

anatomically modern humans.

F. Australia

  1. _____ refers to the area including New Guinea and Australia.

2. Some archeological sites in Australia date to at least_____y.a.
3. Human fossils date to _____ and at least _____y.a.
4. The Kow Swamp people date to _____ and _____ y.a. and exhibit certain _____traits such as a receding forehead.

G. The New World
   1. Humans entered the New World over the _____ _____ _____.
   2. Although debates continue, at present, the only direct evidence we have of hominids in the New World date to about _____y.a.

IV. TECHNOLOGY AND ART IN THE UPPER PALEOLITHIC
A. Europe
   1. The Upper Paleolithic began approximately _____ y.a. in western Europe.
     a. It has been divided into _____ cultural periods based on _____ _____ technologies.

   2. A warming trend lasting _____ _____ years began around _____ y.a.
     a. which resulted in the growth of _____ plants and other kinds of _____.
     b. _____ animals lived off of the new vegetation.
       1. and _____ animals lived off of them.
     c. It became a hunter's _____.
     d. For the first time humans also began to regularly eat _____ and _____.

   3. Clothing is better fitting now because it is _____.
   4. Around 20,000 y.a. the weather became _____ in Europe and Asia.
   5. Around 20,000 y.a. the weather became _____ in Africa.
   6. Humans had an advantage to changing conditions due to _____.
   7. Humans began inventing new and _____ tools.
   8. _____ tools were the finest stone tools known.
   9. The _____ is the last stage of the Upper Paleolithic stone tool industry.
  10. To catch fish a _____ _____ was used.
  11. We begin to see a reduction in _____ size.
  12. The lower face of moderns is less _____ compared to archaics.
  13. We begin to see the distinctive characteristic of modern humans, the _____.
  14. For the first time we begin to see "symbolic representation" in the form of ____ _____.

15. Paleolithic art covered _____ years and is found in Europe, _____, North and South _____ and _____.

16. Bone and ivory _____ and _____ was improved with the use of specialized tools.

17. The first use of ceramics dates to _____ y.a.

18. The majority of cave art comes from _____ and _____.

19. In 1994 the _____ cave in France was disovered.
    a. It dates to the Aurignacian perior, more than _____y.a.
    b. It contains images of _____, _____ and _____ which have never been seen in cave art before.
    c. On the floor there are footprints of _____ and _____.

20. A common motif in cave art is _____.

21. The partial sculpting of a rock face is termed _____.
    a. which were found in areas thought to be _____ _____.
    b. the subjects of this type of art include _____ _____ and onehuman.

22. The themes in portable art are _____ and _____.

23. In caves the themes are _____ and _____.

24. Women are always painted in _____.

25. Most of the cave art in southwestern France and northern Spain was created around _____-_____ y.a.

B. Africa
    1. Rock art is found in southern Africa dating to between _____ and _____ y.a.
    2. Personal adornment dates back to _____ y.a. in the form of _____ made from _____.

    3. In central Africa _____ and _____ were used to make tools.
    4. Harpoons from Katanda of eastern Zaire are made from _____ or long bone _____ of large _____.

    5. The Katanda sites date between _____ and _____ y.a.

V. SUMMARY OF UPPER PALEOLITHIC CULTURE
    A. For most of the Pleistocene change was very _____.
    B. In Europe and central Africa cultural innovations were dramatic including big game hunting, new _____, body _____ and _____ clothing.

KEY TERMS

Aurignacian: an Upper Paleolithic stone tool assemblage dating to around 30,000 y.a. and associated with Cro-Magnon

Chatelperronian: an Upper Paleolithic stone tool assemblage dating to around 35,000 y.a. and associated with Neandertals. It appears that Neandertals modified technology borrowed from anatomically modern humans thus creating a new tool technology.

Cro-Magnon: A term commonly used when referring to early modern humans from Europe. It comes from a specific find in southern France which dates to around 30,000 y.a. where eight skeletons were found in 1868. The skeletons included three adult males, one adult female and four young children.

Gravettian: An Upper Paleolithic stone tool assemblage dating to around 27,000 y.a.

Magdalenian: The final stage of the Upper Paleolithic stone tool assemblage dating to around 17,000 y.a.

Salutrean: An Upper Paleolithic stone tool assemblage dating to around 21,000 y.a. Considered to be the most highly developed stone tool industry.

Upper Paleolithic: refers to a cultural period of early modern humans distinguished by innovative stone tool technologies. Dates from around 40,000 to 10,000 y.a.
It is further divided into five different cultural periods associated with stone tool technology. These five cultural periods (from the oldest to the most recent) are Chatelperronian, Aurignacian, Gravettian, Solutrean and Magdalenian.

FILL IN QUESTIONS

1. Taxonomically, anatomically modern humans are known as _____.
2. Early *H. sapiens sapiens* are our _____ kin.
3. Two major hypotheses have been proposed to explain the origins of modern humans. They are the _____ model (recent African evolution), and the _____ (Multiregional Evolution).
4. The Complete Replacement Model holds that modern humans originated in _____, migrated out and later completely _____ populations in Europe and Asia.
5. One of the problems with the Complete Replacement Model is that it does not take into account any transitions from _____ to _____ anywhere except _____.
6. An important aspect of this theory is that _____ are a different species.
7. Mitochondrial DNA (mtDNA) are _____ found in the cytoplasm (not the nucleus) and genetically passed on only by the _____.
8.. To test their theory scientists from Berkeley took mtDNA from different populations and constructed _____ (something like a family tree). Based on this research they concluded that the world's population descended from a single _____ _____.

9. Other scientists, using the same mtDNA and the same methodology have constructed different _____ that show _____.

10. Recent investigation of the Y chromosome found much _____ variation in humans than in other primates.

11. The use of mtDNA as evidence for proving genetic relatedness among contemporary populations remains controversial. Many paleoanthropologists are _____ of the conclusions drawn from such data.

12. The Partial Replacement Model has been proposed by Gunter Brauer of the University of _____.

13. The Partial Replacement Model holds that modern *Homo sapiens* first evolved in _____ over _____ y.a.

14. Brauer's theory is that early modern *sapiens* gradually migrated out of South Africa as the result of _____ _____ conditions.

15. The Partial Replacement Model explains the disappearance of archaic *sapiens* as being partly due to _____ (moderns breeding with archaics) and _____.

16. The Regional Continuity Model holds that some local populations of archaic *sapiens* in Europe, Asia and Africa continued on independent _____ paths and developed into _____.

17. This model holds that archaic *sapiens* did not evolve exclusively in _____.

18. This model further holds that since a certain amount of breeding (gene flow /migration) probably took place between archaic populations, modern *sapiens* would not be considered a separate _____.

19. This genetic mixing would result in humans being a single _____ species.

20. Although there is some dispute as to dates, it appears that the earliest modern *H. sapiens* evidence comes from _____.

21. Three sites in Africa have yielded very old fossils of early modern *sapiens*. These sites are_____, _____ and _____ which date to between _____ y.a.

22. The Skhul Cave at Mt. Carmel in Israel is very near the Neandertal site of Tabun. The fossil remains from this site, although fully modern, exhibit certain _____ characteristics.

23. The dating at Tabun indicates that Neandertals and modern *H. sapiens*_____ in their occupation of this area.

24. At Mladec, in the Czech Republic, the modern *H. sapiens* remains date to around _____y.a. and although fully modern, exhibit prominent _____, an archaic trait.

25. Most of our evidence for early modern *H. sapiens* comes from western Europe for two reasons:
    (1) _____; and
    (2) _____.

26. Until recently, most of our theories on human evolution have been based on the fossils and evidence from _____.

27. The Cro-Magnon site in southern France includes _____ skeletons and dates to _____.

28. Cro-Magnon is associated with the _____ tool assemblage.

29. The most modern looking of the crania discovered at the Cro-Magnon site is that of the
_____. Her more gracile features may be the result of _____.

30. A four-year-old child's skeleton was recently found in _____ exhibiting a
blending of Neandertal and modern *H. sapiens* characteristics.

31. The two most important sites in China for early modern *sapiens* are the Upper Cave at
_____ and _____ at Dagouwan, _____ _____.

32. _____ may be the oldest site with modern fossils, dating to _____
y.a. or more.

33. Chinese paleoanthropologists contend that in China evolution of the genus *Homo* has been
continuous from Chinese *erectus* to archaic *sapiens* to modern *sapiens*. They further state
that their fossils have features typical of their geographic region and these features are
definitely not _____.

34. In Sri Lanka modern *sapiens* remains have been found that date to _____ y.a.

35. Although the oldest human fossil remains from Australia only date to _____
y.a., archeological evidence dates to at least _____ y.a.

36. The oldest Australian fossils are two burials dating from _____ y.a. and
at least_____ y.a. The crania of these finds are _____.

37. The Kow Swamp people with the relatively recent date of 14,000 and 9,000 y.a. exhibit
some surprisingly archaic traits on the crania. Specifically, they have _____
foreheads, heavy _____ and _____.

38. Debates continue over when modern humans first entered the New World. Although
some claims date prior to 15,000 y.a. and geographically they range from the Yukon to
Pennsylvania and Peru, the first direct evidence for modern humans in the New World
dates to about _____ y.a.

39. Modern humans entered the New World through the _____
_____.

40. The Upper Paleolithic in Europe began around 40,000 y.a. It has been divided into five
cultural periods based on _____ technologies.

41. Due to the warming trend that occurred around 30,000 y.a. and lasted several thousand
years the food chain underwent dramatic changes. Vegetation became more diverse and
abundant therefore the numbers and variety of herbivores increased which in turn gave rise
to the number of carnivores that could eat the herbivores. It became a _____
paradise.

42. During this time humans _____ new and specialized _____.

43. Perhaps because of the increased use of tools in processing food, selective pressures were
relaxed for large front (anterior) _____ resulting in reduced prognathism and
the appearance of the _____.

44. During this warming trend we also begin to see _____

45. Art takes many forms including _____ paintings, _____ on tools and tool
handles, our first evidence of _____ dating back to 27,000 y.a. and
_____ figurines.

46. Cave art is found in France and Spain. The themes in cave art include _____,
stylized _____ and human _____.

47. We also begin to see bas-relief art which is a partial _____ of a rock face. These are generally found in close association with _____. (first interior decorators?)
48. Many attempts have been made to _____ ancient art.
49. In Africa the first evidence of personal _____ is found in the form of beads made from ostrich egg shells.

MULTIPLE CHOICE QUESTIONS

1. The dispersal of anatomically modern *H. sapiens*
   A. Was a relatively rapid event
   B. Was a relatively slow event
   C. Is agreed upon by scientists to have occurred 175,000 y.a.
   D. Is agreed upon by scientists to have occurred from Africa into Europe

2. Regarding the evolution of anatomically modern humans
   A. Scientists agree that it took place in Africa
   B. Scientists agree that it took place in China
   C. Scientists debate regarding both geography and dates.
   D. Scientists debate regarding dates but not necessariy geography.

3. The two hypotheses explaining the origins and dispersal of anatomically modern humans include all but which of the following?
   A. The Partial Replacement Model
   B. The Regional Continuity Model
   C. The Regional Replacement Model
   D. The Complete Replacement Model

4. The model also known as the "Recent African Evolution" is
   A. Based on the origin of modern humans in Africa and their interbreeding with local African populations
   B. Based on the origin of modern humans in Africa and their replacement of local populations in Europe and Asia.
   C. Based on the origin of modern humans in China and their relatively recent evolution in Africa.
   D. Based on the origin of modern human simultaneously in Africa and China.

5. According to the theory proposed by Gunter Brauer of University of Hamburg
   A. Modern humans evolved in Africa and Europe at the same time
   B. Archaic <u>H.</u> <u>sapiens</u> evolved into modern <u>sapiens</u> in southern Africa
   C. The dispersal of modern humans was relatively rapid
   D. Moderns did not breed with archaics in Eurasia

6. According to the model also known as the Multiregional Evolution model
    A. Anatomically modern *H. sapiens* originated exclusively in Africa
    B. Archaic *H. sapiens* were a separate species
    C. Some local populations of archaic *H. sapiens* in Europe, Asia and Africa evolved into moderns
    D. A & B

7. Although not everyone agrees on dates, current evidence strongly indicates that
    A. Modern *H. sapiens* evolved simultaneously in Africa, Europe and Asia
    B. Modern *H. sapiens* arose from Neandertals
    C. Modern *H. sapiens* arose in western Europe
    D. Modern *H. sapiens* arose in Africa

8. Provenience refers to
    A. A geographic region in western Europe
    B. The specific location of an archeological discovery
    C. A dating technique
    D. A fossil find in western Asia

9. The Skhul Cave at Mt. Carmel, Israel
    A. Has yielded more than 20 individuals
    B. Is very near the Neandertal site of Tabun
    C. Has yielded purely modern looking fossils
    D. Has yielded purely archaic looking fossils

10. At the Vindija site in Croatia
    A. Typical Neandertals were found in early contexts
    B. No modern/Neandertal mixtures were found
    C. Late *H.erectus* is found overlapping with archaics
    D. Evidence of art is abundant

11. The area of the world from which the most early modern *H. sapiens* evidence has come is
    A. Africa
    B. Western Asia
    C. China
    D. Western Europe

12. Cro-Magnon is
    A. Typical of the European races of early modern *H. sapiens*
    B. A site from southern France
    C. A site yielding eight individuals
    D. B & C

13. Aurignacian refers to
    A. A tool assemblage associated with France's earliest anatomically modern humans
    B. A site in western Europe yielding 10 skeletons
    C. An archeologist who uncovered a rich site in northern Spain
    D. A tool tradition associated with archaic *H. sapiens* in western Asia

14. The Mladec and Vindija fossils
    A. Date to around 100,000 y.a.
    B. Are rich and numerous
    C. Indicate a combination of both modern and Neandertal characteristics
    D. Show evidence of social stratification

15. The Upper Cave at Zhoukoudian
    A. Dates to between 18,000 and 10,000 y.a.
    B. Has yielded fossils that exhibit both modern and Neandertal characteristics
    C. May be the oldest anatomically modern find
    D. Has evidence of burials

16. The oldest anatomically modern find in Asia may be
    A. Vindija
    B. Zhoukoudian
    C. Ordos
    D. Batadomba

17. In Australia
    A. The oldest fossils date to 55,000 y.a.
    B. The oldest fossils date to 30,000 y.a.
    C. Archeological sites date to 80,000 y.a.
    D. Evidence of body adornment was found

18. The Kow Swamp people
    A. Date to 14,000 to 9,000 y.a.
    B. Date to about 30,000 y.a.
    C. Exhibit archaic traits on their cranial skeleton
    D. A & C

19. Modern humans entered the New World
    A. Prior to 15,000 y.a.
    B. About 12,000 y.a.
    C. By boat
    D. On horses

20. In the former Soviet Union
    A. Storage pits have been found
    B. Evidence of social status distinctions were found
    C. The first evidence of language has been found
    D. A & B

21. Magdalenian refers to
    A. The first evidence of religion
    B. A geographic region in western Asia
    C. The final phase of the stone tool tradition in the Upper Paleolithic in Europe.
    D. A type of facial structure found among early moderns

22. Paleolithic art has been found in all but which of the following locations?
    A. Australia
    B. Siberia
    C. North America
    D. South Africa

23. Dolni Vestonice and Predmosti from the Czech Republic yielded
    A. The first documented use of ceramics
    B. The first documented use of metal
    C. The first documented use of controlled fire
    D. The first documented use of buttons

24. Solutrean refers to
    A. A cultural period of the Upper Paleolithic
    B. An archeological methodology for cleaning artifacts
    C. A famous paleoanthropologist working in Western Europe
    D. The cranial structure typical of early moderns in Western Asia

25. The partial sculpting of a rock face is called
    A. Knapping
    B. Pressure-engraving
    C. Punch technique
    D. Bas-relief

26. In Africa we find the first evidence of
    A. Ceramics
    B. Personal adornment
    C. Use of fire
    D. Cave paintings

27. In Paleolithic art
    A. Women are always depicted alone
    B. Women are always depicted in groups
    C. Women are usually depicted with animals
    D. Women are not depicted

28. During the Magdalenian
    A. European prehistoric art reached its climax
    B. We begin to see carvings on tools
    C. Ceramics are numerous
    D. We begin to see burins

29. The fossils from the Upper Cave at Zhoukoudian
    A. Share similarities with the African moderns
    B. Share similarities with the African archaics
    C. Do not share features with Africa
    D. Do not exhibit features that are regional

30. Prehistoric art
    A. Has a common theme over a vast geographic region
    B. Shows strong signs of ritual significance
    C. Ranged from 35,000 to 10,000 y.a.
    D. Was limited to cave paintings

ANSWERS TO FILL-IN OUTLINE

I. INTRODUCTION
    A. Ambiguities
    B. Rapid

II. THE ORIGIN AND DISPERSAL OF HOMO SAPIENS SAPIENS (ANATOMICALLY MODERN HUMAN BEINGS)
    A. 1. Stringer, Andrews
       2. Africa, 200,000
       3. Africa, Europe, Asia
          a. Replaced
       4. Archaic *Homo sapiens*
       5. Speciation
          a. Admixture
       6. Genetic data
          a. mitochondrial
          b. mother
       7. Single, lineage
       8. African roots
    B. The Partial Replacement Model
       1. Africa

2. 100,000
3. Gunter Brauer
4. South Africa, gradual
5. Eurasia, hybridized
   a. replaced
C. The Regional Continuity Model (Multiregional Evolution)
   1. Milford Wolpoff
   2. Europe, Asia, Africa
      a. anatomically modern humans
   3. Gene flow

III. THE EARLIEST <u>HOMO</u> <u>SAPIENS</u> <u>SAPIENS</u> DISCOVERIES
A. Africa
   1. 120,000-80,000
   2. Differing interpretations
B. Near East
   1. Skhul Cave
      a. Neandertal
      b. 115,000
   2. 20
      a. Neandertal
      b. about 100,000
   3. Overlapped
C. Central Europe
   1. Modern
      a. Regional continuity
   2. 33,000
      a. variation
      b. prominent supraorbital torus
D. Western Europe
   1. Western European
   2. Cro-Magnon
      a. 1868
      b. rock
      c. Aurignacian
      d. 30,000
E. Asia
   1. China, 50,000
   2. *Homo erectus*, archaic *H. sapiens*
F. Australia
   1. Sahul
   2. 55,000
   3. 25,000, 30,000
   4. 14,000 and 9,000, archaic
G. The New World
   1. Bering Land Bridge

2. 12,000
IV. TECHNOLOGY AND ART IN THE UPPER PALEOLITHIC
A. Europe
1. 40,000
   a. five, stone tool
2. Several thousand, 30,000
   a. flowering, vegetation
   b. herbivorous
      1. carnivorous
   c. paradise
   d. fish, fowl
3. Sewn
4. Colder
5. Wetter
6. Technology
7. Specialized
8. Solutrean
9. Magdalenian
10. Barbed harpoon
11. Tooth
12. Prognathic
13. Chin
14. Art
15. 25,000, Siberia, Africa, Australia
16. Carving, engraving
17. 27,000
18. Southwestern France, northern Spain
19. Grotte Chauvet
    a. 30,000
    b. panther, hyena, owl
    c. bears, humans
20. Human hands
21. Bas-relief
    a. living sites
    b. several animals
22. Horses, reindeer
23. Bison, horses
24. Groups
25. 20,000-18,000
B. Africa
1. 28,000-19,000
2. 38,000, beads, ostrich eggshells
3. Bone, antler
4. Ribs, splinters, mammals
5. 180,000, 75,000

V. SUMMARY OF THE UPPER PALEOLITHIC CULTURE
   A. Slow
   B. Weapons, ornaments, tailored

ANSWERS & REFERENCES TO FILL-IN QUESTIONS
1. *Homo sapiens sapiens*, p. 272
2. Direct, p. 272
3. Complete Replacement, Regional Continuity Model, p. 272
4. Africa, replacing, p. 273
5. archaic *Homo sapiens*, modern *Homo sapiens*, Africa, p. 273
6. African moderns, p. 273
7. Organelles, mother, p. 273
8. Trees, African lineage, p. 273
9. Trees, no African roots, p. 273
10. Less, p. 275
11. Skeptical, p. 275
12. Hamburg, p. 275
13. Africa, 100,000, p. 275
14. Shifting environment, p. 275
15. Hybridization, replacement, p. 275
16. Evolutionary, anatomically modern humans, p. 276
17. Africa, p. 276
18. Species, p. 276
19. Polytypic, p. 276
20. Africa, p. 276
21. Klasies River Mouth, Border Cave, Omo Kibish 1, 120-000-80,000, p. 276
22. Neandertal, p. 277
23. Overlapped, p. 277
24. 33,000, supraorbital torus, p. 279
25. Interested scholars happened to live there, it caught the curiosity and pride of the local population, p. 280
26. Western Europe, p. 280
27. Eight, 30,000, p. 281
28. Aurignacian, p. 281
29. Female, sexual dimorphism, p. 281
30. Portugal, p. 281
31. Zhoukoudian, Ordos, Inner Mongolia, p. 282
32. Ordos, 50,000, p. 282
33. African, p. 282
34. 25,500, p. 282
35. 30,000, 55,000, p. 282
36. 25,000, 30,000, gracile, p. 282
37. Receding, supraorbital tori, thick bones, p. 284
38. 12,000, p. 284
39. Bering Land Bridge, p. 284

ANSWERS & REFERENCES TO MULTIPLE CHOICE QUESTIONS

CHAPTER 12
MICROEVOLUTION IN MODERN HUMAN POPULATIONS

LEARNING OBJECTIVES
After reading this chapter you should be able to

• Define biological evolution, p. 299

• Describe the agents that are responsible for generating and distributing variation, pp. 299-303

• Discuss the role natural selection in the direction of evolution, pp. 303-306

• Discuss how evolutionary change occurs as an integrated process. Illustrate through an example, pp. 300-306

• Explain what a population is and the evolutionary dynamics that lead to populations, pp. 299-300.

• Discuss the different polymorphisms and understand why they are studied, pp. 305 & 308-311

• Discuss how human cultural activities have influenced human evolution, pp. 306-308.

▪ Distinguish between the clinal approach to human variation and the racial approach, pp. 312-313

• Discuss Lewontin's multivariate study of 17 polymorphic traits, pp. 312-313

FILL-IN OUTLINE
Introduction

In the preceding chapters we looked at human macroevolution. However, our species continues to evolve and in this chapter we look at the minute changes that occur within our species. This is called microevolution and, unlike macroevolution, does not result in the evolution of new species. In chapters three and four we learned about the genetic basis of life. We now continue to look at how these genetic principles lie at the very foundation of the evolutionary process and how these processes interact to produce evolutionary change in living human populations. We also look at another aspect of human evolution, the biocultural influences. Humans are unusual in the natural world because cultural activities has influenced our evolution.

I. **MODERN THEORY OF EVOLUTION**

    A. Darwin and Mendel each discovered essential mechanisms for how evolution worked.

        1. those who followed saw the work of these two men incompatible for explaining evolution.

        2. by the 1930's biologists realized that Darwinian selection and Mendelian genetics were complementary factors that explained evolution - the fusion of these two ideas as called the _____ _____ .

    B. The Modern Synthesis partitioned evolution into two stages:

1. small new changes in the genetic material was _____ by Mendelian principles and resulted in variation.

2. the genetic variation was acted on by _____ _____ .

II. DEFINITION OF EVOLUTION

A. The modern definition of evolution is a _____

_____ .

B. Allele frequencies are numerical indicators of the genetic makeup of a _____ .

C. _____ consists of small, short-term inherited changes that occur over a short period within a species.

D. _____ are major evolutionary changes that occur over geological time and may result in new species.

III. POPULATION GENETICS

A. A population is a group of _____ individuals.

1. populations contain a degree of relatedness and, thus, share a _____ _____ .

2. the largest population of *Homo sapiens* that could be described is the entire _

_____ .

a. all members of a species are _____ capable of interbreeding, but are incapable of fertile interbreeding with members of other species.

b. a species such as ours is a _____ _____ system.

B. Breeding isolation.

1. geography, by isolating populations through barriers such as bodies of water or mountains, causes the formation of _____ _____ .

2. however, _____ rules can also play a role by prescribing who is most appropriate among those potentially available.

a. human populations tend to mate within their own group; this is called _____ .

b. however, human populations are not completely closed and individuals may choose mates from outside of their group; this is called _____ .

C. The _____ - _____ theory of genetic equilibrium is a mathematical model that helps researchers to determine if evolution is occurring at any particular genetic locus.

D. Mutation.

1. an actual change in DNA is called _____ .

2. mutation rates for any given trait are quite _____ .

223

3. mutation is the only way to produce "new" _____; hence, mutation is the basic creative force in evolution.

E. Gene Flow.
  1. gene flow is the exchange of _____ between populations.
  2. African Americans have had considerable influx of alleles from _____ -_____populations.
  3. Significant alterations in gene frequency can be caused by long-term patterns of _____ _____.

F. Genetic Drift.
  1. is a _____ factor that is due mainly to sampling phenomena.
     a. gene drift is directly related to the _____of the population.
     b. _____ populations are more prone to randomness in evolution, i.e., gene drift.
  2. a special case of gene drift is _____ (Sewell Wright effect).
     a. in founder effect only a very small proportion of a population contributes _____ to the next generation.
     b. founder effect can result when a small group _____ and founds a new population.
     c. through founder effect an individual who carries an allele, rare in the parent population, can make a _____ genetic contribution to the next generation.
  3. genetic drift has probably played an _____ role in human evolution.
     a. nevertheless, the effects of drift have been irregular and _____.
     b. drift, along with gene flow, probably results in _____ changes within a species.
     c. however, there is some evidence that our species experienced a genetic bottleneck in the last 100,000 to 200,000 years; if this is the case genetic drift would have played a very important role in our evolution.

G. Natural Selection
  1. Natural selection Influences the _____ of evolution.
  2. The _____ - _____ allele Is the best documented case of natural selection in humans.
  3. If sickle-cell is inherited in a double dose the individual will suffer severe _____.

4. the mutation for sickle-cell occurs in all human populations, but doesn't have a high frequency most places.

    a. the sickle-cell trait allele is frequent in some populations, especially in west and central _____ ; there are also high frequencies in Greece and India.

    b. associated with higher frequencies of sickle-cell is the presence of _____ .

        1. the malaria plasmodial parasite invades red blood cells where they obtain oxygen.

    c. an experiment was done in the 1950's in which _____ and individuals homozygous for normal hemoglobin were compared in their response to infection by malaria.

        1. heterozygote _____ _____ _____ do not provide a conducive environment for the malarial parasite to reproduce.

        2. hence, the parasite often dies before infecting the body of a _____.

IV. HUMAN BIOCULTURAL EVOLUTION

A. _____ is the human strategy of adaptation.

B. Culture, evolution, and malaria.

    1. before the advent of agriculture humans rarely lived near mosquito breeding areas.

        a. about 2,000 years ago slash-and-burn agriculturists penetrated and cleared forested areas in Africa.

        b. a result of deforestation was the creation of stagnant pools of water which served as prime breeding areas for _____, the vectors for malaria.

    2. malaria has served as a powerful _____ force.

        a. sickle-cell trait is a _____ adaptation to malaria.

        b. there is an advantage for carriers of sickle-cell, but only in _____ environments.

    3. after WWII extensive spraying of DDT eliminated large numbers of mosquito breeding grounds.

        a. malaria _____, as did the sickle-cell aliele.

        b. during the intervening years, mosquitoes, also subject to natural selection, have developed DDT-resistant strains with the result that _____ is again on the rise.

    4. two other traits that may be influenced by malaria as a selective agent are G-6-PD

deficiency and _____ .

C. Lactose Intolerance

    1. _____ is a sugar found in milk which is broken down by the enzyme lactase.

        a. in adult mammals the gene coding for lactase is "switched off."

        b. in most adult _____ (including humans and cats) lactose in milk that is ingested is not broken down and ferments in the large intestine. This results in diarrhea and gastrointestinal distress.

        c. many African and Asia populations, _____ of the world's population, are intolerant of milk.

        d. this inability to digest milk is called _____ _____ .

    2. why can the majority of adults in some populations tolerate milk?

        a. peoples who ancestors were _____ (such as modern Europeans and African peoples like the Tutsi and Fulani) probably drank large quantities of milk

        b. in a cultural environment where milk was consumed strong selection pressures would act to _____ allele frequencies in the direction of more lactose tolerance.

c. some populations rely on dairying, but consume milk products as fermented dairy products such as cheese and yogurt. These populations have _____ developed a tolerance for lactose.

    3. this interaction of human cultural environments and changes in lactose tolerance is another example of _____ evolution.

V. HUMAN POLYMORPHISMS

A. Simple Polymorphisms

    1. _____ traits are those traits governed by a locus with more than one allele and found at frequencies greater than accounted for by mutation.

        a. simple Mendelian traits, linked to _____ locus, are polymorphic traits.

        b. simple Mendelian polymorphic traits are much more straight forward than the _____ traits (traits governed by more than one locus) usually associated with human variation.

    2. polymorphic traits are useful in studying the genetic differences between different _____ .

        a. genetic differences between human populations demand _____ explanations.

    b.   by comparing allele _____ evolutionary events can be reconstructed.

B. ABO blood system

    1.   the ABO system is a polymorphic trait with three different alleles, _____ , _____, and _____ .

    2.   the phenotypes associated with this system are expressed by antigens (proteins) found on_____ _____ _____.

    3.   the frequencies of the three alleles vary tremendously, with most human groups being polymorphic for all three alleles.

        a.   one exception is blood type O among South American Indians, where the allele frequency for O is 100%. This is referred to as being "_____" in the population.

C. HLA

    1.   the _____ (human lymphocyte antigen) system is an antigen system found on white blood cells (lymphocytes).

        a.   the HLA system is very complex and there is a potential of at least _____ genotypes.

D. Miscellaneous polymorphisms

    1.   PTC Tasting.

        a.   PTC is a _____ chemical which individuals can either taste, or not taste.

        b.   PTC is inherited by a simple _____ transmission.

        c.   the ability to _____ PTC by humans may have resulted from selection to taste bitter (and toxic) plants.

    2.   earwax (cerumen)

        a.   the two phenotypes are _____ and _____, and gray and dry.

        b.   this trait is also inherited as a _____ Mendelian transmission.

E. Polymorphisms at the DNA level

    1.   mitochondrial DNA (mtDNA)

        a.   mitochondria (organelles involved with energy production for the cell) have their own_____ (called mtDNA).

        b.   mtDNA is considerably _____ than nuclear DNA

c. the smaller length of mtDNA has enabled researchers to work out the mtDNA genome

    1. variation of the mtDNA genome in humans is much _____ pronounced than is the case for other species.

    2. the small degree of variation in the human mtDNA genome suggests that all modern humans have a _____ origin from a restricted ancestral population base.

2. nuclear DNA

    a. by using _____ enzymes considerable insight has been gained regarding human variation directly at the DNA level.

    b. researchers have observed great variation in the length of the DNA fragments at numerous DNA sites. These genetic differences are called _____ _____ _____ _____ (RFLPs).

VI. PATTERNS OF HUMAN POPULATION DIVERSITY

A. a _____ is a gradual change in the frequency of a single trait in populations dispersed over space.

B. utilizing single traits has _____ when we try to sort our population relationships.

C. _____ approaches consider several traits simultaneously.

    1. R. D. Lewontin analyzed human diversity using a multivariate approach.

        a. Lewontin considered 17 polymorphic traits for seven geographical areas ("races").

        b. after breaking down his seven geographical groups into subgroups, Lewontin could only account for about 15% of human genetic diversity as being due to "_____."

        c. most human genetic diversity appears to be explained in terms of _____ from one village to another, one family to another, and even between one individual to another (even within the same family!).

        d. superficially, visible traits that standout suggest that human races exist.

            1. however, those traits used to form races may produce a _____ _____ sample and not give an accurate picture of the actual pattern of genetic variation.

            2. Lewontin's final conclusion is that human racial classification, shown to have no genetic or taxonomic significance, should be_____

D. other geneticists have conducted multivariate studies.
1. Cavalli-Sforza *et al.* analyzed 44 different polymorphisms from 42 different populations
   a. this analysis led to a genetic "_____" (dendogram)
   b. this genetic tree depicted the _____ of the populations under study.
2. Stoneking analyzed populations using mitochondrial DNA.
   a. mtDNA is inherited solely through the _____ line; however, because it acts like a single large locus, it must be supplemented with other genetic data.
   b. mtDNA analysis shows that the greatest genetic diversity exists among _____ populations.
3. comparative studies from nuclear DNA suggests that the vast majority of variation occurs within populations at the _____ level.

KEY TERMS

ABO blood group system: a polymorphism based on the presence (or absence) of two antigens found in the cell membrane of red blood cells.

balanced polymorphism: the maintenance of two or more alleles in a population due to the selective advantage of the heterozygote.

breeding isolates: a population that is distinctly isolated geographically and/or socially from other breeding groups.

cline: a gradient of genotypes (usually measured as allele frequencies) over geographical space.

endogamy: mating with individuals from the same group.

exogamy: mating with individuals from other groups.

gene pool: the total complement of alleles shared by the reproductive members of a population.

Hardy-Weinberg theory of genetic equilibrium: the mathematical relationship expressing, under ideal conditions, the predicted distribution of genes in populations; the central theorem of population genetics.

Human Lymphocyte Antigen (HLA): antigens found on the surface of an individual's cell surfaces which provides a way for the immune system to identify "self." "Non-self" antigens are attacked. HLA is a very complex genetic system and provides a rich ground for anthropologists to study human genetic relationships.

inbreeding: a type of nonrandom mating in which relatives mate more often than predicted under random mating conditions.

incest taboo: the rule found in almost every human society that prohibits sexual relationships between parents with offspring and siblings with each other.

lactose intolerance: the inability to digest fresh milk products; caused by the discontinued production of lactase, the enzyme that breaks down lactose or milk sugar.

mitochondrial DNA (mtDNA): circular DNA found in the mitochondria and inherited through the maternal line.

MN blood group system: a blood polymorphism based upon the presence of the two alleles, which are codominant.

negative assortative mating: a type of nonrandom mating in which individuals of different phenotypes mate more often than predicted under random mating conditions.

non-random mating: patterns of mating in a population in which individuals choose mates preferentially.

polymorphism: genetic trait governed by a locus with more than one allele in appreciable frequencies.

population: a group of individuals of the same species that regularly interbreed with one another.

positive assortative mating: a type of nonrandom mating in which individuals of like phenotype mate more often than predicted under random mating conditions.

PTC Tasting: refers to the ability to taste, or not to taste, the chemical phenylthiocarbamide (PTC).

racial: in biology, pertaining to populations of a species that differ from other populations of the same species with regard to some aspects of outwardly expressed phenotype. Such phenotypic variation within a species is usually associated with differences in geographical location.

restriction fragment length polymorphisms (RFLPs): variation among individuals in the length of DNA fragments produced by enzymes that break the DNA at specific sites.

Rh system: a blood polymorphism with two phenotypes, Rh+ and Rh-. This system is clinically important because of its involvement with hemolytic disease of the newborn.

slash-and-burn agriculture: a traditional land-clearing practice whereby trees and vegetation are cut and burned. In many areas, fields are abandoned after a few years and clearing occurs elsewhere.

sickle-cell anemia: a severe inherited disease that results from a double dose of a mutant allele, which in turn results from a single base substitution at the DNA level.

FILL-IN QUESTIONS

1. The fusion of Darwinian selection with Mendelian genetics was termed the _____

   _____.

2. A change in allele frequencies from one generation to the next is the definition of

   _____ .

3. Everyone in your class has had their blood typed. Your lab instructor has tallied up the results and put them into the following categories: type A = .5, type B = .4, type O = .1. This proportion of each of these types represents the _____

   _____ for this population.

4. If one allele changes into another a _____ has occurred.

5. The Afro-American gene pool in the northern United States is estimated to contain around 20% European alleles. This is an example of _____ .

6. The force of evolution that is more likely to affect a small population rather than a large population is _____ .

7. When plague hit Europe in the fourteenth century large populations were reduced to small remnants. Genetically these survivors represented a _____ population.

8. Sickle-cell trait in humans is a good example of _____ .

9. A _____ is a group of interbreeding individuals.

10. In an Indian village, a marriage is arranged between two first cousins. This mating pattern is called _____ .

11. Among the Inuit, males must find a mate from a distant village. This mating pattern is called _____ .

12. An important polymorphic trait found in white blood cells is _____ .

13. HLA patterns among the Lapps, Sardinians, and Basques show deviations from other _____ populations.

14. If you were given a strip of PTC paper ,which you placed on your tongue, and you tasted a bitter taste, you would be a PTC _____ .

15. PTC tasting varies in different human populations, but in most populations the majority of individuals are _____ .

16. Cerumen is most commonly known to most people as _____ .

17. The sticky cerumen allele is _____ to the dry cerumen allele.

18. In addition to the DNA enclosed by the cell's nucleus, DNA is also found in cytoplasmic organelles, the _____ .

19. The persistence of the sickle-cell allele seems to be correlated with a human activity, _____-_____-_____ agriculture.

20. The maintenance of two or more alleles in a population due to the selective advantage of the heterozygote is called a _____ _____ .

21. The inability to digest fresh milk due to the discontinued production of the enzyme lactase is called _____ _____ .

22. Comparative data indicate that most human variation occurs _____ populations at the individual level.

23. Our biological differences should be viewed as traces of our _____ past which adapted humans to different environments as a species spread throughout the world.

MULTIPLE CHOICE QUESTIONS

1. The total complement of genes shared by reproductive members of a population, is that population's
    A. gene flow.
    B. gene drift.
    C. gene pool.
    D. bottleneck effect.

2. Which of the following is **not** a factor that influences mate choice?
    A. geography.
    B. ecology.
    C. social.
    D. genetic diversity.

3. Most human populations are polymorphic for the ABO system, but one notable exception is the fixed O allele among
    A. Australian Aborigines.
    B. the peoples of central Asia.
    C. South American Indians.
    D. Blackfeet Indians.

4. One of the results of mitochondrial DNA research has been
    A. the variation of mtDNA within *Homo sapiens* is much less than found in other species.
    B. the variation of mtDNA within *Homo sapiens* is much more than found in other species.
    C. chimpanzees have much less variation in their mtDNA than humans do.
    D. the length of the mtDNA is as long as nuclear DNA, about 3 billion nucleotides.

5. The surprising results of mtDNA analysis can be explained if
    A. the common ancestor of humans and chimps separated 3 million years ago.
    B. the last common ancestor of modern humans was in east Africa about 2 million years ago.
    C. all modern humans have a fairly recent common ancestor.
    D. the common ancestor for modern humans goes back before the first hominids.

6. DNA can actually be "cut" at particular points by
    A. lipids.
    B. restriction enzymes.
    C. phospholipids.
    D. nanosaws.

7. The sickle cell allele is maintained at relatively high frequencies in some populations by
   A. the selective advantage of the heterozygote in malarial areas .
   B. mutation
   C. positive assortative mating
   D. the susceptibility of the heterozygote to malarial infection

8. Which of the following is **not** a way that humans have adapted to living in malarial environments?
   A. sickle-cell trait.
   B. G-6-PD deficiency.
   C. thalessemia.
   D. lactose.

9. Many individuals have difficulty digesting milk because
   A. they have an Rh antigen producing an immune response to milk.
   B. they don't have enough lactose in their cardiovascular system.
   C. they cannot process the lipoproteins in the milk.
   D. as adults, they lack the enzyme, lactase.

10. The modern synthesis integrates Darwinian natural selection with
   A. paleontology
   B. embryology
   C. genetics
   D. ecology

11. The most complete definition of evolution is
   A. change
   B. a change in allele frequency from one generation to the next
   C. mutation
   D. survival of the fittest

12. The only source for new DNA for a species' gene pool is
   A. mitosis
   B. natural selection
   C. mutation
   D. recombination

13. When alleles are introduced into a population from another population it is a case of
   A. genetic drift
   B. gene flow
   C. founder effect
   D. bottleneck effect

14. An example of gene flow would be
    A. the Amerasian children of Vietnam
    B. the isolated Amish of Pennsylvania
    C. the American colonization of Antarctica
    D. a small hunting and gathering society in Siberia with little outside contact

15. The force of evolution which is significant when small human populations become isolated is
    A. gene flow
    B. mutation
    C. genetic drift
    D. random mating

16. In Tenth Century Norway, Eric the Red and his followers were banished for murders and general rowdiness (even by Viking standards). This small group, which had a higher representation of the red hair allele than the rest of the population of Norway, sailed west and established a colony on Iceland. Within several centuries the colony had a population of several thousand with a high incidence of red hair. This would BEST be explained as
    A. gene flow
    B. natural selection
    C. mutation
    D. founder effect

17. In any sexually reproducing species both parents contribute genes to the offspring. This is
    A. mutation
    B. genetic drift
    C. recombination
    D. natural selection

18. A genetic trait which gives an advantage to a heterozygote for this trait in a malarial environment is
    A. hemophilia
    B. sickle-cell trait
    C. brachydactyly
    D. albinism

19. The unit of evolutionary change is the
    A. family
    B. individual
    C. population
    D. pedigree

20. A gradual distribution of allele frequencies over space is called a
    A. race
    B. phenotypic grade
    C. cline
    D. Hardy-Weinberg equilibrium

21. Multivariate population genetics studies seek
    A. to prove races exist
    B. to study one genetic trait at a time
    C. to describe the pattern of several traits at one time
    D. to find non-adaptive traits that can be used to describe groups

22. In Lewontin's multivariate computer study of race, he concluded that
    A. There is more variation between races than is found within any one specific race
    B. The seven "geographic" races cluster independently, indicating that they are true races
    C. There is more variation within any one race than there is between races
    D. The idea of race is a valid one

23. Which of the following statements is true?
    A. many anthropologists consider groups such as the Japanese to be a race
    B. forensic anthropologists can identify the ethnicity of a skeleton to 100% accuracy
    C. many physical anthropologists see human race as a meaningless concept
    D. the five races of Blumenbach are still the standard in modern physical anthropology

ANSWERS TO OUTLINE

I. MODERN THEORY OF EVOLUTION
    A. 2. "modern synthesis"
    B. 1. transmitted
        2. natural selection

II. DEFINITION OF EVOLUTION
    A. a change in allele frequency from one generation to the next
    B. population
    C. microevolution
    D. macroevolution

III. POPULATION GENETICS
    A. interbreeding
        1. gene pool
        2. species
            a. potentially
            b. genetically closed
    B. 1. breeding isolates
        2. cultural
            a. endogamy
            b. exogamy

C. Hardy-Weinberg
D. 1. mutation
   2. low
   3. variation
E. gene flow
   1. genes
   2. non-African
   3. mate selection
F. genetic drift
   1. random
      a. size
      b. small
   2. founder effect
      a. genes
      b. migrates
      c. disproportionate
   3. important
      a. nondirectional
      b. microevolutionary
G. natural selection
   1. course
   2. sickle-cell
   3. sickle-cell anemia
   4. a. Africa
      b. malaria
      c. carriers (heterozygotes
         1. red blood cells
         2. carrier

IV. HUMAN BIOCULTURAL EVOLUTION
A. Culture
B. 1. b. mosquitoes
   2. selective
      a. biological
      b. malarial
   3. a. declined (or decreased)
      b. malaria
   4. balanced polymorphism
      a. 1. mutation
         2. natural selection.
      b. heterozygotes
   5. thalessemias

C. 1. lactose
    b. mammals
    c. most
    d. lactose intolerance
  2. a. pastoralists
    b. shift
    c. not
  3. biocultural

V. HUMAN POLYMORPHISMS
A. 1. polymorphic
    a. one
    b. polygenic
  2. populations
    a. evolutionary
    b. frequencies
B. 1. A, B, and O.
  2. red blood cells
  3. a. fixed
C. 1. HLA
    a. 30 million
D. 1. a. bitter
    b. Mendelian
    c. taste
  2. a. yellow and sticky
    b. simple
E. 1. a. DNA
    b. shorter
    c. 1. less
       2. recent
  2. a. restriction
    b. restriction fragment length polymorphisms

VI. PATTERNS OF HUMAN POPULATION DIVERSITY
A. cline
B. limitations
C. multivariate
  1. b. "race"
    c. differences
      1. highly biased
      2. discontinued
D. 1. a. "tree"
    b. relationships
  2. a. maternal
    b. African
  3. individual

ANSWERS & REFERENCES TO FILL-IN QUESTIONS

1. modern synthesis, p. 298
2. evolution, p. 299
3. evolution, p. 299
4. mutation, p. 300
5. gene flow, p. 301
6. genetic drift, p. 302
7. founding, p. 302
8. natural selection, p. 303
9. population, p. 299
10. endogamy, p. 300
11. exogamy, p. 300
12. HLA, p. 309
13. European, p. 310
14. taster, p. 310
15. tasters, p. 310
16. earwax, p. 310
17. dominant, p. 310
18. mitochondria, p. 311
19. slash-n-burn, p. 306
20. balanced polymorphism, p. 305
21. lactose intolerance, p. 307
22. within, p. 312
23. evolutionary, p. 311

ANSWERS & REFERENCES TO MULTIPLE CHOICE QUESTIONS

1. C, p. 299
2. D, p. 300
3. C, p. 309
4. A, p. 311
5. C, p. 311
6. B, p. 311
7. A, pp. 303-305
8. D, pp. 306-307
9. D, p. 307
10. C, p. 298
11. B, p. 299
12. C, p. 300
13. B, p. 301
14. A, p. 301
15. C, pp. 302-303
16. D, p. 302
17. C, p. 299
18. B, pp. 304-305
19. C, p. 299

20. C, p. 312
21. C, p. 312
22. C, pp. 312-313
23. C, p. 313

CHAPTER 13
HUMAN VARIATION AND ADAPTATION.

LEARNING OBJECTIVES

After reading this chapter you should be able to

- Understand the history of how human racial categories were established (pp. 317-319).
- Describe the concept behind biological determinism and associated philosophies (pp. 319-320).
- Understand the difference between "race" and "ethnicity" and the problems with using these terms (pp. 320-323).
- Understand what racism is and how it affects lives (pp. 323-324).
- Discuss the interaction between genetic and environmental factors on intelligence (pp. 324-325).
- Describe the reason that different human populations vary (p. 325).
- Discuss why humans vary in skin color (pp. 326-328).
- List how humans respond to the thermal environment (pp. 328-331).
- List the ways that humans respond to high altitude stress (pp. 331-332).
- Understand how infectious disease has played a role in human evolution, and vice versa (pp. 333-335).
- Discuss current culturally mediated factors that may contribute to the spread of infectious disease (pp. 336-337).

FILL-IN OUTLINE
Introduction.

In previous chapters we have focused on the patterns of inheritance from one generation to the next and the physical mechanisms (DNA) for inheritance. We also learned how evolution works and saw how Mendelian traits have been used to study evolutionary factors in human populations.

In this chapter, our focus shifts to polygenic traits, or traits that express *continuous* variation. We will see how these traits have been used as a basis for traditional racial classification and we look at some of the issues that currently surround the topic of race in physical anthropology.

After reviewing the traditional ideas of human biological diversity we look at more recent explanations of certain polygenic traits; instead of emphasizing their usefulness as "racial" markers, we will focus on their adaptive value for human populations living in specific environments. We will also examine how populations and individuals differ in their adaptive responses to the environment. Finally, we consider the role of infectious disease in human evolution and adaptation.

I.   HISTORICAL VIEWS OF HUMAN VARIATION.

A.   When Humans First Came into Contact with Other Human Groups They

_____ Them.

1. _____ _____ was one of the more noticeable traits that was used to classify people and there were attempts to explain skin color.

2. during the European "Age of Discovery," there was an increased awareness of human biological _____.

3. _____ schools of thought developed to explain human diversity.

B. Monogeny.

    1. monogenists believed that all humans were descended from a _____ _____ of humans.

        a. according to monogenists, the reason modern humans exhibited a great deal of biological diversity was due to _____ of the human phenotype in response to local environmental conditions.

        b. human races were the result of _____ to the original form.

    2. _____ was attractive because it did not contradict Genesis.

C. Polygeny.

    1. polygenists believed that all humans were descended from a number of _____ pairs of humans (i.e., different Adams and Eves).

    2. polygenists believed that, in addition to _____ differences, there were differences between humans in intelligence and morality.

    3. polygenists did not accept the idea that the environment could _____ a phenotype.

D. Racial classification.

    1. throughout the eighteenth and nineteenth centuries the primary focus regarding human variation was on description and _____.

    2. Linnaeus' classification of life also included _____.

        a. in addition to the physical features used to classify other life forms, Linnaeus also used cultural attributes to _____ humans.

        b. Linnaeus ranked humans.

            1. The _____ complimentary traits were assigned to sub-Saharan (black) Africans.

           2. Europeans were ranked highest and reflected the view that Europeans were _____.

    3. J. F. Blumenbach

        a. Blumenbach classified humans into _____ races: Caucasoid, Mongoloid, American, Ethiopian, and Malayan.

        b. Blumenbach emphasized that racial divisions based on skin color were _____.

        c. Blumenbach recognized that many traits, including skin color, were not _____ phenomena.

            1. individuals within a group that expressed traits that were intermediate would be difficult to classify.

2. furthermore, many traits showed _____ expression between groups.

4. it was thought that racial taxonomies should be based on characteristics _____ to particular groups and uniformly expressed within them.

   a. such traits were believed to be stable and not influenced by the environment.

   b. these _____ traits should exhibit only minimal within group variation.

5. in an attempt to find unique traits, Anders Retzius developed the _____ index to describe head shape.

   a. peoples, such as northern Europeans, with a long narrow head and a cephalic index under 75 were termed _____.

   b. populations with broad heads, such as southern Europeans, had a cephalic index over _____ and were termed brachycephalic.

   c. _____ were people that were intermediate, with cephalic indices between 75 and 80.

   d. the cephalic index was abandoned when it was shown that northern Europeans shared their dolichocephalic tendancies with several _____ populations.

E. Biological Determinism.

1. the idea that there is an association between physical characteristics and behavioral characteristics is called _____ _____; i.e., cultural variations are inherited.

   a. it follows from this logic that there are inherent behavioral and cognitive differences between groups. This is called _____.

   b. it also follows from this logic that there are inherent behavioral and cognitive differences between the sexes. This is called _____.

2. when biological determinism is accepted as a reasonable explanation, it is easy to _____ the persecution and enslavement of other peoples.

3. _____ was a scientific discipline which was grounded in biological determinism. Eugenics promoted the idea of "race improvement" and suggested that the government should be involved in this endeavor.

F. By the End of W. W. I Some Scientists Began Turning Away From Racial _____ in Favor of a More Evolutionary Approach.

II. THE CONCEPT OF RACE

A. All Modern Humans Belong to the Same _____ Species, *Homo sapiens*.

    1. a polytypic species consists of local populations that differ from one another in the expression of one or more _____.

    2. most species are polytypic, thus there is no species "type" to which all members conform.

B. The Traditional Concept of Race.

    1. in the past people were clumped together by various combinations of attributes and placed into categories associated with particular _____ areas.

    2. the term race is often misused and has developed various _____.

        a. race has been used synonymously with _____.

        b. since the 1600s race has been used to refer to various _____ defined groups.

            1. the perception that there is an _____ between physical traits and many cultural attributes is still widespread.

            2. "racial traits" are not the only phenotypic expressions that contribute to social identity: _____ and _____ are also critically important.

    3. in the 1950's the use of the term "race" was challenged and it was proposed that the term "_____" replace it.

    4. the biological use of the word "race."

        a. "race" refers to geographical _____ of phenotype within a species.

        b. even within modern biology there are no established _____ by which races of plants and animals are to be assessed. Even for a biologist studying nonhuman life the classification of an organism into a races is a subjective matter.

    5. prior to W. W. II, most studies of human variation focused on phenotypic variation between _____ _____ _____ populations.

C. Modern Studies of Human Variation Focus on the Examination of Allele Frequencies _____ and _____ Populations.

    1. specifically we want to know the _____ _____ of phenotypic and genotypic variation.

    2. application of _____ principles to human variation has replaced the older view that was based solely on observed phenotype.

    3. races are no longer viewed as _____ biological entities, composed of

individuals fitting a particular type, which do not change.

    4. while human variability is recognized between geographic areas, the following questions must be asked regarding this phenotypic difference.

        a. what is the _____ significance attached to observed phenotype variation?

        b. what is the _____ of underlying genetic variation that influences the observed variation?

        c. how _____ is the underlying genetic variation?

D.   Controversies and Debates About Human Variation.

    1. attempts to reach a _____ regarding "race" in humans have failed.

    2. some modern anthropologists feel there are at least _____ major human racial groups.

        a. however, no modern scholar subscribes to the pre-modern synthesis concept of races as _____ biological units.

        b. many who continue to use broad racial categories do not view them as

        _____.

        c. _____ anthropologists find the phenotypic criteria associated with race to have practical applications.

            1. these anthropologists assist in identification of human _____ remains.

            2. metrical analysis assists forensic anthropologists in identifying the sex, age, stature and "racial" or "ethnic" background of skeletal remains up to _____ percent accuracy.

        d. other modern anthropologists see race as a _____ concept when applied to humans.

    3. objections to racial taxonomies.

        a. such classificatory schemes are _____.

            1. the categories are discrete and based on _____ that comprise a specific set of traits.

            2. such typologies do not account for individuals who do not _____ to the particular type for the group.

        b. many of the characteristics used to define races are _____.

            1. polygenic traits exhibit a _____ range of variation.

            2. using polygenic traits to define a group makes it difficult, if not impossible, to draw _____ boundaries between populations.

III. **RACISM**

A. The Most Detrimental Outcome of Biological Determinism is _____.

   1. racism is based on the false belief that intellect and various cultural factors are _____ along with physical characteristics.

   2. according to this view culturally defined variables typify all members of particular populations.

   3. such beliefs commonly rest on the assumption that one own's group is _____ to other groups.

B. Racism is a Cultural, not a _____, Phenomenon, and it is Found Worldwide.

IV. **INTELLIGENCE**

A. Whether There is an _____ Between "Race" and Intelligence has been Controversial.

B. Both Genetic and Environmental Factors Contribute to _____.

   1. it is not possible to _____ accurately the percentage each factor contributes to intelligence.

   2. IQ scores are often confused with intelligence; IQ scores and intelligence are _____ the same thing.

     a. many psychologists say that IQ scores measure life experience.

     b. IQ scores can _____ within an individual's lifetime.

   3. complex cognitive abilities, no matter how measured, are influenced by _____ loci and are strikingly polygenic.

   4. Individual abilities result from complex _____ between genetic and environmental factors.

     a. one product of this interaction is _____.

     b. elucidating what proportion of the variation in test scores is due to biological factors is probably _____ possible.

C. Innate Differences in Abilities Reflect Individual Variation Within Populations, Not _____ Differences Between Groups.

D. There is No Convincing Evidence that Populations Vary with Regard to _____ abilities.

V. **THE ADAPTIVE SIGNIFICANCE OF HUMAN VARIATION**

A. Physical Anthropologists View Human Variation as the Result of Adaptations to Environmental Conditions, Both _____ and _____.

B. Physiological Response to Environmental Change is Under Genetic Control and Operates at Two Levels.

1. _____-_____ (i.e. genetic) _____ changes characterize all individuals within a population or species.

2. short-term physiological response to environmental change is called _____; such physiological change is temporary.

C. Solar Radiation, Vitamin D, and Skin Color.

   1. before 1500 skin color in populations followed a particular geographical distribution, particularly in the _____ _____.

     a. populations with the _____ amount of pigmentation are found in the tropics.

     b. populations with lighter skin color are associated with more _____ latitudes.

   2. skin color is influenced by _____ substances.

     a. _____, when it is carrying oxygen, gives a reddish tinge to the skin.

     b. _____ is a plant pigment, which the body synthesizes into vitamin A, and it provides a yellowish cast.

     c. _____ is the most important contributor to skin color.

   3. melanin has the ability to absorb _____ radiation, preventing damage to DNA to which UV radiation can cause mutations and ultimately skin cancer.

     a. melanin is produced by specialized cells in the epidermis called _____.

     b. all humans appear to have about the same _____ of melanocytes.

     c. exposure to sunlight triggers a protective mechanism which temporally _____ melanin production (i.e., a tan).

   4. natural selection appears to have favored dark skin in areas nearest the _____ where the most intense UV radiation is found.

     a. as hominids migrated to the northern latitudes, selective pressures changed.

       1. Europe had cloudy skies, a winter with fewer hours of daylight, and with the sun to the south, solar radiation was _____.

       2. the use of _____ prevented exposure of the skin to sunlight.

       3. selection favoring dark skin was _____, but there also had to be a selective pressure favoring lighter skin.

     b. _____ ____ plays a vital role in mineralization and normal bone growth during infancy and childhood.

       1. while vitamin D is available in some foods, the body's primary source comes from its own ability to synthesize vitamin D through the interaction of _____ _____ light and a

cholesterol-like substance found in the subcutaneous layer of the skin.

    2. insufficient amounts of vitamin D during childhood results in

        _____, which leads to bone deformities.

  c. the vitamin D hypothesis.

    1. reduced exposure to sunlight would have been detrimental to _____

      skinned individuals in northern latitudes who would have been deficient in

      vitamin D.

      a. the higher _____ content of their skin would have filtered out

         much of the UV radiation available.

      b. additionally, if the diet did not provide adequate amounts of vitamin D,

         selective pressures would have shifted over time to favor _____

         pigmented skin.

    2. there is substantial evidence to support this vitamin D _____.

 5. perhaps more social importance has been attached to variations in skin color than any

    other single human biological trait. However, biologically skin color is of no

    importance except in terms of its _____ _____.

D. The Thermal Environment.

 1. mammals and birds have evolved complex physiological mechanisms to maintain a

    constant body _____ .

 2. humans are found in a wide variety of _____ environments, ranging from

    120° F to -60° F.

 3. human response to heat.

  a. humans and many other mammalian species have _____ _____

    widely distributed throughout the skin.

    1. sweat on the body surface removes heat through _____

      cooling. This is a mechanism that has evolved to a high degree in humans.

    2. the capacity to dissipate heat by sweating is a feature found in all human

      populations almost _____.

      a. however, there is variation in that people not generally exposed to hot

         conditions need a period of _____ to

         warmer temperatures.

      b. the down side to heat reduction through sweating is that critical amounts

         of water and minerals can be _____.

  b. another mechanism for radiating body heat is _____.

    1. vasodilation refers to a widening (dilation) of the _____.

    2. vasodilation of the capillaries near the skin's surface permit "hot" blood from

the body's core to dissipate heat to the surrounding air.

   c. size also plays a role in temperature regulation.

      1. there is a general relationship between _____ and body size and shape in homeothermic species (although, as always in biology, there are exceptions). Two biological rules apply to body size, body proportions, and temperature.

         a. _____ rule states that body size tends to be greater in populations that live in cold environments.

            1. this is because surface area _____ relative to mass as an object increases in size. For example, for every three-fold increase in the mass of a globular animal, there is only a two-fold increase of surface area.

            2. because heat is lost from the surface, increased mass allows for greater heat _____ and reduced heat loss.

         b. Allen's rule.

            1. in colder climates, populations should have shorter _____ (arms, legs, and sometimes noses) to increase mass-to-surface ratios preventing heat loss.

            2. in warmer climates, populations should have _____ appendages with increased surface area relative to mass which promotes heat loss.

      2. according to both Bergmann's rule and Allen's rule:

         a. in _____ environments body shape should be linear with long arms and legs, such as is found among East African pastoralists.

         b. in _____ environments people should have stocky bodies with shorter arms and legs as is found among the Inuit.

      3. there is much human variability regarding body proportions and not all populations conform to Bergmann's and Allen's rules.

4. human response to cold.

   a. humans can respond to cold by increasing heat production or in ways that enhance heat retention; heat retention is _____ efficient because it requires less energy.

   b. _____ _____ human responses to cold include:

      1. increased _____ rate uses energy to produces body heat.

         a. people living in chronic cold generally have _____ metabolic rates than people living in warmer environments.

b. high metabolic rates can be maintained by larger consumptions of animal
      _____ and _____ such as is seen among the Inuit.
2. _____, uses energy to produces body heat.
3. _____ is a narrowing of the blood vessels
   which reduces blood flow to the skin
   a. vasoconstriction _____ heat loss
   b. a small amount of energy is used to constrict blood vessels, but more energy
      is saved by _____ heat and avoiding the use of more
      energetically expensive responses.
4. behavioral modifications include
   a. _____ physical activity to produce heat from
      contracting muscles.
   b. _____ food consumption, which provides more calories
      from which to produce more energy.
   c. bringing all body parts into a center, such as a _____ -____
      position, in order to reduce the amount of surface area exposed to the cold.
   c. long-term human responses to cold _____ among human groups.
E. High Altitude.
1. multiple factors produce stress on the human body at higher altitudes. These include:
   a. _____ intense solar radiation,
   b. cold,
   c. _____ humidity,
   d. _____ (which amplifies cold stress, hence the wind chill factor in winter
      weather reports),
   e. hypoxia.
      1. _____ refers to a reduction in the available oxygen.
         a. it can mean reduced oxygen in the _____, due to a
            lower barometric pressure (i.e. for every cubic meter of air there are actually
            fewer oxygen molecules at high altitude, than there is in a cubic meter of air
            at sea level).
         b. it can also refer to decreased oxygen available, or presence, in the body's
            _____.
      2. of the factors mentioned, _____ exerts the greatest amount of
         stress on human physiological systems, especially the heart, lungs, and brain.
2. people who live at higher elevations exhibit a number of manifestations of their
   hypoxic environment.

a. reproduction is affected through

    1. increased rates of infant_____,

    2. _____ ,

    3. _____ .

b. low birth weight is more common, probably because of decreased fetal _____ due to impaired maternal-fetal oxygen transport.

3. adult acclimatization to high altitude.

a. adult acclimatization occurs when people, born at lower elevations, acclimatize to the higher elevation. These are usually _____-term modifications.

b. adult acclimatization to high altitude includes

    1. _____ in respiration rate,

    2. _____ in heart rate,

    3. increased production of _____ _____ cells.

4. developmental acclimatization to high altitude.

a. developmental acclimatization occurs in people born in high altitudes in which they acquire adaptations to high altitude during their _____ and

_____ .

b. development acclimatizations to high altitude include

    1. greater _____ capacity,

    2. more efficient diffusion of _____ from blood vessels to body tissues.

c. developmental acclimatization provides a good example of physiological plasticity by illustrating how, within the limits of genetic factors, development can be influenced by _____ .

5. there is evidence that populations can _____ to high attitudes.

a. highland Tibetan populations appear to have evolved accommodations to _____ (over the last 25,000 years) and do not have reproductive problems.

b. both highland Tibetans and highland Quechua appear to utilize _____ in a way that permits more efficient use of oxygen.

    1. this implies the presence of genetic _____ in the mtDNA.

    2. this also implies that natural selection has acted to increase the _____ mutations in these groups.

VI. INFECTIOUS DISEASE.

A. _____ Disease Refers to Those Diseases Caused by Invading Organisms Such as Bacteria, Viruses, or Fungi.

1. throughout the course of human evolution, infectious disease has exerted enormous _____ _____ on human populations.

2. infectious disease influences the frequency of certain alleles that affect the _____ response.

B. _____ is the Disease that More Humans Suffer From Today than any Other.

1. there are between _____ - _____ million people, worldwide, suffering from malaria.

2. recently some of the malarial parasites have become drug _____

C. AIDS (acquired immune deficiency syndrome) is a _____ Infection that was First Reported in 1981.

1. the virus that causes AIDS is _____ (human immunodeficiency virus)

2. HIV is transmitted through the exchange of _____ _____ - it is not spread through casual contact.

3. HIV can attack a variety of cell types, but its predilection is for ____ _____ cells, one of the cell types that initiates an immune response. When a person's T cell count drops below minimum levels, "opportunistic" infections, pathogens present but not HIV, are able to mount an attack on the body.

4. some individuals test positive for HIV, but show few if any symptoms, even after 15 years; this suggests that some individuals may possess natural _____ or resistance to HIV.

   a. a receptor site is on the plasma membrane of some immune cells, including _____ cells.

   1. pathogens, including _____, attach to these receptors and invade the cells.

   2. some individuals possess a _____ allele that results in a malfunctioning receptor site to which HIV is unable to bind.

      a. homozygotes for this allele may be _____ resistant to HIV.

      b. in _____ , infection may still occur, but the progress of the disease is much slower.

   b. the mutant allele

   1. occurs mainly in people of _____ descent where the allele frequency is around 0.1

   2. is not present in Japanese and West Africa samples; however, it does occur at a frequency of around 0.02 in _____ _____, perhaps due to gene flow from Euro-Americans.

   3. may have resulted from selection for an earlier disease that occurred in Europe.

      a. this selection was _____ against HIV, but another pathogen that required the same receptor site.

      b. this earlier selective agent provided some _____

against the later HIV.

5. examples such as AIDS and sickle-cell anemia reveal new insights into the complex interactions between pathogens and _____ populations; these insights in turn provide a growing basis for understanding the adaptive responses to these diseases by both individuals and populations.

D. The Role of Infectious Disease as Selective Agents.

1. _____ _____ is the only disease considered to be eliminated as a result of modern medical technology; it provides a good example of how infectious disease can produce polymorphisms in human populations.

   a. smallpox has a _____ indicidence in individuals with type A or AB blood than in persons with type O blood.

   b. the small pox virus has an _____ that is similar to the A antigen.

      1. this means that the immune systems of individuals with type A antigen may not _____ the small pox antigen as a threat.

      2. thus, individuals with type ___ antigen were selected against in those areas where small pox was prevalent in the past.

2. _____ plague may have had a major selective role; one-third of the population of Europe died when the plagues first appeared in the thirteenth century.

3. in the 20th century the influenza _____ of 1918 killed over 21 million

4. there is no clear evidence that bubonic plague or influenza shaped human populations, but the mortality resulting from these diseases suggests that they may have influenced human _____ responses in ways that we do not know.

E. The Effects of Human Infectious Disease are Due to Both _____ and Biological Factors.

1. until the advent of agriculture and sedentary living sites, infectious disease was _____ a major problem to human populations.

2. eventually human settlements became large, crowded, unsanitary cities where the opportunity for _____ was great.

3. humans also domesticated _____ that carried diseases that affected humans.

VII. THE CONTINUING IMPACT OF INFECTIOUS DISEASE.

A. Before the 20th Century, _____ _____ was the Number One Limiting Factor to Human Populations.

1. since the 1940s the use of _____ coupled with improved public health measures has reduced the mortality resulting from infectious disease.

2. in the late 1960s the Surgeon General declaredthe war against infectious disease won,

but this was an overly optimistic pronoucement; between 1980 and 1992 deaths from infectious disease increased by _____ percent.

B. Humans are Currently Speeding Up Microbe Evolution.

1. increases in the prevalence of infectious disease may be due to overuse of

_____.

2. antibiotics have exerted selective pressures on bacteria and some species have developed drug _____ strains.

C. Some Diseases are Making "Comebacks."

1. _____ is now the world's leading killer of adults and this disease, once controlled by antibiotics, has developed drug-resistant strains.

2. cholera has also developed antibiotic-resistant strains; recent cholera outbreaks have been partly attributed to rising ocean temperatures, lack of sanitation, and

_____.

D. Environmental Factors.

1. a concern regarding the reemergence of infectious disease is _____ _____ which may expand the range of tropical diseases.

2. a factor associated with the _____ spread of disease is the widespread encountering of peoples everyday; this includes the crossing of borders and penetration into remote areas.

a. fundamental to the spread of disease is the increasingly large human _

_____ -_____.

b. overcrowding leads to _____ conditions and the spread of communicable disease.

KEY TERMS

acclimatization: short-term physiological response by an individual to changes in the environment. The capacity for acclimatization may also typify the entire population or species. This capacity is under genetic influence and is subject to evolutionary factors such as natural selection.

AIDS: acquired immune deficiency syndrome. A condition caused by suppression of the immune system due to the human immunodeficiency virus (HIV). The syndrome includes any number of "opportunistic" infections which are able to attack the body due to an inefficient immune response.

biological determinism: the concept that phenomena, including various aspects of behavior, are governed by genetic factors.

brachycephalic: having a broad head in which the width measures more than 80 percent of the length.

coevolution: evolution of two or more species in which they are exerting reciprocal selective pressures on one another.

dolichocephalic: having a long, narrow head in which the width measures less than 75 percent of the length.

endemic: in regards to disease, a population in which there is always some individuals that are infected.

ethnocentrism: viewing other cultures from one own's cultural perspective. This often leads to thinking of other cultures as odd and inferior.

eugenics: a former scientific discipline, now largely discredited, that promoted the improvement of the human species through controlled breedings and sterilizations of "undesirables."

hypoxia: a lack of oxygen, either in the body's tissues or in the atmosphere (at higher altitudes).

intelligence: mental capacity: the ability to learn, reason, or comprehend and interpret information, facts, relationships, meanings, etc.

monogeny: a theory that all living humans are descended from one original pair of humans (Adam and Eve) and that all subsequent human biological variation is due to environment.

pandemic: an extensive outbreak of disease affecting large numbers of people over a wide area wide; potentially, a world-wide phenomenon.

pathogen: any organism or substance that causes disease.

plasticity: physiological change in response to the environment.

polygeny: the theory that living humans are descended from many different pairs of humans (other Adams and Eves) that has led to different human races.

polytypic: referring to species composed of populations that differ with regard to the expression of one or more traits.

races: populations of a species that differ from one another in some aspect of the visible phenotype. Biological (AKA geographic)races are taxonomic expressed as subspecies.

vasoconstriction: narrowing of blood vessels by decreasing their diameter permitting reduced blood flow to the skin. Vasoconstriction is an involuntary response to cold and reduces heat loss at the skin's surface.

vasodilation: an involuntary expansion of blood vessels by increasing their diameter, permitting increased blood flow to the skin. Vasodilation permits warming of the skin and also facilitates radiation of warmth as a means of cooling.

vector: an agent that serves to transmit disease from one carrier to another.

FILL-IN QUESTIONS

1. The first step toward understanding natural phenomena is the ordering of variation into _____ that can be named, discussed, and perhaps studied.

2. As early as 1350 B. C., the ancient Egyptians had classified humans on the basis of _____ _____.

3. A school of thought, popular in the 18th and 19th centuries, that posited that the different varieties of humans were descended from <u>different</u> Adams and Eves was _____.

4. The idea that behavior, including intelligence and morals, is innate due to an individual's (or peoples') genetics is called _____ _____.

5. The scientific discipline founded in the 19th century by Francis Galton that advocated "race improvement," including government intervention to reach this goal, was _____.

6. When physical anthropologists have tried to define the word "race," they have _____

to reach a consensus.

7. _____ traits exhibit a continuous range of variation.

8. The most detrimental outcome of _____ _____ is racism.

9. Ultraviolet Radiation stimulates the production of _____ ___.

10. Insufficient vitamin D synthesis can cause rickets. The most likely cause to this situation is lack of exposure to _____ .

11. A hypothesis which attempts to explain why more northern populations have more lightly pigmented skin is the _____ ___ hypothesis.

12. The ability to maintain a constant _____ body temperature, as found in mammals and birds, is called homeothermy.

13. In regards to thermal conditions, humans tend to cope better physiologically with _____ than they do with _____ .

14. Allen's rule involves the length of _____ .

15. Bergmann's rule concerns the relationship between body mass (or volume) to _____ _____ .

16. Integrated with sweating, reduced amounts of body _____ on humans exposes more body surface to allow more efficient evaporation to occur.

17. The most serious stress that the human body is exposed to at high altitudes is _____ .

18. A trait that is genetically determined can be influenced by the environment. This is called _____ _____ .

19. Lifelong residents of high altitudes show slower growth and maturation, larger chest size, greater lung volume, and larger _____ .

20. A tremendous selective factor during the course of human evolution has been _____ _____ .

21. AIDS is the acronym for _____ _____ _____ _____ .

22. The ultimate cause of AIDS is _____ .

23. HIV is the acronym for _____ _____ _____ .

24. Many _____ factors, such as architectural styles, subsistence techniques, and even religious practices, all affect how infectious disease develops and persists.

25. Disease was probably not a major selective factor on humans prior to _____ years ago.

MULTIPLE CHOICE QUESTIONS

1. Some polygenists looked for traits that they could use to define races. These traits would not be affected by the environment, would exhibit only minimal in-group variation, and were
    A. non-adaptive traits.
    B. convergencies.
    C. parallelisms.
    D. monogenic traits.

2. Anthropometrists were able to classify European populations into
    A. western and eastern Europeans.
    B. Caucasoids and Mongoloids.
    C. northern and southern Europeans.
    D. brachycephalics and dolichocephalics.

3. A local sheriff believes that the people of a town in his district, who have high arrest and conviction rates, are born thieves because of their genetic constitution. Which of the following would this sheriff's attitudes **best** fit into?
    A. relativism.
    B. ethnocentrism.
    C. biological determinism.
    D. post-modernism.

4. The scientific discipline that provided scientific justification for purging Nazi Germany of its "unfit" was
    A. anthropometry.
    B. eugenics.
    C. genetics.
    D. monogeny.

5. Within *Ammodramus maritimus* , the seaside sparrow, there are four distinct populations that differ from one another in at least one trait. This species is a
    A. monotypic species.
    B. polytypic species.
    C. chronospecies.
    D. syngamic species.

6. The criteria for describing a biological race is
    A. at least 50 per-cent of the member of one population of a species must be distinguishable from another population.
    B. two populations of the same species are located in two different geographical area.
    C. two populations have different vocalizations or, in humans, languages.
    D. there are no established criteria by which organisms are assessed.

7. An objection to the use of racial taxonomies is that they are
    A. typological in nature.
    B. based on polygenic traits.
    C. based on continuous traits.
    D. evolutionary in nature.

8. Which of the following statements is true?
    A. many anthropologists consider groups such as the Japanese to be as race.
    B. forensic anthropologists can identify the ethnicity of a skeleton to 100 per-cent accuracy.
    C. many physical anthropologists see human race as a meaningless concept.
    D. the five races of Blumenbach are still the standard in modern physical anthropology.

9. Which of the following is a true statement?
    A. individual abilities are due only to an individual's genetic inheritance.
    B. IQ can change within an individual's lifetime.
    C. IQ scores are essentially the same thing as innate intelligence.
    D. IQ scores are discrete between populations.

10. Black children adopted by advantaged white families score better on IQ tests. This suggests
     A. IQ is correlated with race
     B. IQ is not correlated with race
     C. the social environment plays a dominant role in determining the average IQ level of black children
     D. both B and C are correct.

11. If an Illinoian leaves the 300 foot elevation of Urbana-Champaign and flies to Quito, Ecuador, elevation 8,000 feet, this person's body will begin to produce more red blood cells to compensate for lower oxygen levels. This type of short-term physiological change is called
     A. acclimation.
     B. homeothermy.
     C. acclimatization.
     D. remodeling.

12. The pigment which helps protect against ultraviolet radiation by absorbing it is
    A. carotene
    B. melanin
    C. lactose
    D. hemoglobin

13. When insufficient ultraviolet radiation is absorbed during childhood the condition resulting from a Vitamin D deficiency is
    A. cancer
    B. gastroenteritis
    C. rickets
    D. trisomy 21

14. It has been suggested that Neanderthal populations, which inhabited a cloud covered Europe 100,000 years ago, were the last dark skin population of Europe. Which of the following would be support for this suggestion?
    A. the use of caves for shelters.
    B. deaths that appear to have resulted from cutaneous carcinomas (skin cancer).
    C. Neanderthals appear to have been wearing clothing.
    D. the prevalence of rickets in these populations.

15. Inuits have a large "globular" body, while the body structure of the Kalahari !Kung is thin and linear. This is explained by
    A. Bergmann's rule
    B. Allen's rule
    C. Gloger's rule
    D. Kleiber's Rule

16. The long arms and legs of the East African Masai, and the short arms and legs of the Inuit conform to
    A. Bergmann's rule
    B. Allen's rule
    C. Gloger's rule
    D. Cope's rule

17. Which of the following processes is most associated with human acclimatization to cold?
    A. sweating.
    B. vasodilation.
    C. vasoconstriction.
    D. evaporative cooling.

18. Which of the following is **not** a short-term response to cold?
    A. increased metabolic rate.
    B. shivering.
    C. increased food consumption.
    D. vasodilation.

19. The people with the highest metabolic rates in the world are the
    A. inland Inuit.
    B. Arctic Inuit.
    C. Australian Aboriginals.
    D. Choctaw of Oklahoma.

20. Which of the following is **not** a way that the Inuit adapt to the cold?
    A. clothing
    B. high fat diet
    C. dark skin
    D. a short "stocky" body build

21. A problem associated with high altitude stress is
    A. kidney failure.
    B. low birth weights.
    C. high red blood cell counts.
    D. high white blood cell counts.

22. There is some evidence that highland Tibetans
    A. do not need to breathe oxygen.
    B. have made genetic adaptations to hypoxia.
    C. have evolved more efficient kidneys.
    D. need to go down to lower elevations in order to reproduce.

23. A disease that currently infects 300-500 million people worldwide and has had tremendous effect on the course of human evolution, as evidence by blood adaptations against it, is
    A. rickets.
    B. malaria.
    C. bubonic plague.
    D. influenza.

24. A serious concern of medical workers is that
    A. disease causing microbes are evolving resistance against antibiotics.
    B. insect vectors have developed resistance against pesticides.
    C. HIV is going into a dormant stage in which it will be difficult to detect.
    D. both A and B are correct.

25. Which of the following statements is true?
    A. HIV can be transmitted through casual contact.
    B. HIV can be carried by an insect vector.
    C. HIV is transmitted through exchange of body fluids.
    D. HIV is the immediate cause of death for a victim.

ANSWERS TO OUTLINE

I. **HISTORICAL VIEWS OF HUMAN VARIATION.**
   A. categorized
      1. skin color
      2. diversity or variation
      3. two
   B. 1. single pair
         a. plasticity
         b. modification
      2. monogeny
   C. 1. different
      2. physical
      3. modify
   D. 1. classification
      2. humans
         a. classify
         b. 1. least
            2. superior
      3. a. five
         b. arbitrary
         c. discrete
            2. overlapping
      4. unique
         b. nonadaptive
      5. cephalic
         a. dolichocephalic
         b. 80
         c. mesocephalic
         d. African
   E. 1. biological determinism
         a. racism
         b. sexism
      2. justify
      3. eugenics
   F. typologies

II. **THE CONCEPT OF RACE.**
   A. polytypic
      1. traits
   B. 1. geographical
      2. definitions
         a. species
         b. culturally
            1. association
            2. sex, age
      3. ethnicity
      4. a. variation

                    b. criteria
              5. large geographically defined
       C. within, between
              1. adaptive significance
              2. evolutionary
              3. fixed
              4. a. adaptive
                    b. degree
                    c. important
       D. 1. consensus
              2. three
                    a. fixed
                    b. important
                    c. forensic
                           1. skeletal
                           2. 80
                    d. meaningless
              3. a. typological
                           1. stereotypes
                           2. conform
                    b. polygenic
                           1. continuous
                           2. discrete

III. RACISM
       A. racism
              1. inherited
              2. typify
              3. superior
       B. biological

IV. INTELLIGENCE
       A. association
       B. intelligence
              1. measure
              2. not
                    b. change
              3. multiple
              4. interactions
                    a. learning
                    b. not
       C. inherent
       D. cognitive

V. THE ADAPTIVE SIGNIFICANCE OF HUMAN VARIATION
       A. past. present
       B. 1. long-term evolutionary
              2. acclimatization
       C. 1. Old World
                    a. greatest
                    b. northern
              2. three
                    a. hemoglobin
                    b. carotene

       c. melanin
   3. ultraviolet (UV)
       a. melanocytes
       b. number
       c. increases
   4. equator
       a. 1. indirect
           2. clothing
           3. relaxed
       b. vitamin D
           1. ultraviolet radiation
           2. rickets
       c. 1. darker
               a. melanin
               b. lighter
           2. hypothesis
   5. a. adaptive significance
D. 1. temperature
   2. thermal
   3. a. sweat glands
          1. evaporative
          2. equally
             a. acclimatization
             b. lost
       b. vasodilation
          1. capillaries
       c. body
          1. climate
             a. Bergmann's
               1. decreases
               2. retention
             b. 1. appendages
               2. longer
          2. a. warmer
             b. cold
   4. a. more
       b. short-term
          1. metabolic
             a. higher
             b. protein, fat
          2. shivering
          3. vasoconstriction
             a. restricts
             b. retaining
          4. a. increased
             b. increased
             c. curled-up
       c. vary
E. 1. a. more
       c. low
       d. wind
       e. 1. hypoxia
             a. atmosphere
             b. tissues

                2. hypoxia
    2. a. 1. mortality
            2. miscarriage
            3. prematurity
        b. growth
    3. a. short
        b. 1. increase
            2. increase
            3. red blood
    4. a. growth, development
        b. 1. lung
            2. oxygen
        c. environment
    5. adapt
        a. hypoxia
        b. glucose
            1. mutations
            2. advantageous

VI. INFECTIOUS DISEASE
A. infectious
    1. selective pressures
    2. immune
B. malaria
    1. 300-500
    2. resistant
C. viral
    1. HIV
    2. body fluids
    3. T4 helper
    4. immunity
        a. T4
            1. HIV
            2. mutant
                a. completely
                b. heterozygotes
        b. 1. European
            2. African Americans
            3. a. not
                b. resistance
    5. host
D. 1. small pox
        a. higher
        b. antigen
            1. recognize
            2. A
    2. bubonic
    3. pandemic
    4. adaptive
E. cultural
    1. not
    2. disease
    3. animals

VII THE CONTINUOUS IMPACT OF INFECTIOUS DISEASE.
    A. infectious disease
        1. antibiotics
        2. 58
    B. 1. antibiotics
        2. resistant
    C. 1. tuberculosis
        2. overcrowding
    D. 1. global warming
        2. rapid
            a. population size
            b. unsanitary

ANSWERS & REFERENCES TO FILL-IN QUESTIONS

1. categories, p. 317
2. skin color, p. 317
3. polygeny, p. 318
4. biological determinism, p. 319
5. eugenics, p. 320
6. failed, p. 322
7. polygenic, p. 323
8. biological determinism, p. 323
9. vitamin D, p. 327
10. ultraviolet (solar) radiation or, simply, sunlight, p. 327
11. vitamin D, p. 327
12. internal, p. 328
13. heat, cold, p. 328
14. appendages, p. 329
15. surface area, p. 329
16. hair, p. 328
17. hypoxia, p. 331
18. developmental acclimatization, p. 332
19. hearts, p. 332
20. infectious disease , p. 333
21. Acquired Immune Deficiency Syndrome, p. 333
22. HIV, p. 333
23. Human Immunodeficiency Virus, p. 333
24. cultural, p. 335
25. 10-12,000, p. 335

ANSWERS & REFERENCES TO MULTIPLE CHOICE QUESTIONS

1. A, p. 319
2. D, p. 319
3. C, p. 319-320. This sheriff believes that the people of this town are <u>biological</u> <u>determined</u> to be thieves because of genetic inheritance. If you answered B, you were assuming more information than we gave - we did not provide enough information to know whether he is judging another ethnic group by his standards. The inhabitants of the town may be from the same ethnic group that the sheriff belongs to.
4. B, p. 320
5. B, p. 320
6. D, p. 321
7. A, p. 323
8. C, p. 322-323
9. B, p. 324
10. D, p. 324. The fact that higher IQs correlate with a change in the social environment should suggest to you that the social environment also plays a role in IQ.
11. C, p. 325
12. B, p. 326
13. C, p. 327
14. D, p. 327. Modern light-skinned European populations use shelters, fire, and clothing so whether Neanderthals were dark-skinned or not would not bear on these use of these things (choices A and C). Dark-skinned populations would be unlikely to die from skin cancers (choice B). Rickets, on the other hand, would suggest that the melanin content of Neanderthal skin was heavier than would be optimum for the environment and would result in the lack of vitamin D synthesis.

15. A, p. 329
16. B, p. 329
17. C, p. 329
18. D, pp. 328-329
19 A, p. 330
20. C, p. 330
21. B, p. 332
22. B, pp. 332
23. B, p. 333
24. D, pp. 333, 336
25. C, p. 333

CHAPTER 14
THE ANTHROPOLOGICAL PERSPECTIVE ON THE HUMAN LIFE COURSE

LEARNING OBJECTIVES

After reading this chapter you should be able to
*   Discuss examples of the interaction of biology and culture in human growth and development, p. 347
*   Define growth and development, p. 348
*   Discuss human growth in stature, pp. 348-349
*   List the five basic nutrients and give a function for each, pp. 350-351
*   Explain how evolution has molded our current dietary needs, pp. 351-353
*   Discuss the diet of pre-agricultural humans and how their diet has influence the physiology of modern humans, pp. 353-354
*   Give examples of what happens when humans have some deficiency in their diet, pp. 354-356
*   Summarize the effects of genetics, hormones, and other environmental factors on growth and development, pp. 356-358
*   Discuss the human life cycle, pp. 358-365

FILL-IN OUTLINE
Introduction.

As we have noted throughout the text, modern humans are the result of evolution in which there was a strong interaction between biology and culture. In this chapter we look at this interaction in human growth and development. Some genetic characteristics are expressed no matter what the cultural environment is. However, many genetic traits reflect their interaction with the environment. In this chapter we explore this interaction of biology and culture as it affects the human life cycle.

I.   **FUNDAMENTALS OF GROWTH AND DEVELOPMENT**
    A. The terms growth and development are often used interchangeably, but they are

        _____ processes.

        1. _____ refers to an increase in mass or number of cells

            a. an increase in cell number is referred to as _____.

            b. an increase in cell mass is referred to as _____

        2. _____ refers to differentiation of cells into different types

            of tissues and their maturation.

    B. Stature

        1. increased stature is a common indicator of _____ status in children.

        2. growth spurts

            a. growth spurts can be seen in early _____, encompassing the first

                six months of fetal growth and the first four years of childhood growth.

b. at puberty another pronounced increase in growth occurs, the

_____ _____ _____. After the

adolescent growth spurt development declines gradually until adult stature is

reached.

3. growth curves for boys and girls are significantly _____.

  a. at birth, there is a slight _____ _____ in many

  body measures, but the major divergence comes at puberty.

  b. males are _____ than females, particularly at age 18.

  c. females have more _____ _____ than males at all ages.

4. stature is influenced by _____ , health and nutrition.

  a. children with good health and adequate nutrition are more likely to reach their

  _____ potential for height.

  b. children who are malnourished or experience prolong periods of poor health

  may not reach that _____.

  c. in general, members of _____ socioeconomic groups tend to

  be taller than members of lower socioeconomic classes, reflecting the impact

  of culture and economic status on the processes of growth and development.

C. Brain Growth

1. the head is a relatively _____ part of the body at birth.

  a. the growth rate of the brain after birth is far _____ than any other

  part of the body.

    1. at birth the brain is about ____ per-cent of its adult size.

    2. by six months after birth it has reach ____ percent of its adult size.

    3. by age _____ the brain has reached 90 percent of its adult size.

    4. by age _____ the brain is at 95 percent of its adult size.

  b. there is only a very small growth spurt at adolescence making the brain an

  _____ to the growth curve characteristic of the rest of the

  body.

2. the pattern of human brain growth is _____ among primates and other

mammals.

  a. the brain of most mammals is _____ percent of the adult size at birth.

  b. the narrow human female pelvis, necessary for bipedal walking, puts a

  _____ on the size of the fetal head.

II. NUTRITIONAL EFFECTS ON GROWTH AND DEVELOPMENT.

A. _____ has an impact on human growth and development at every

stage of the life cycle.

B. Basic nutrients for growth and development.
   1. there are _____ basic nutrients for growth and development.
   2. proteins are composed of _____ _____ and are the major structural components of the body.
   3. carbohydrates are an important source of _____ for the body.
      a. carbohydrate digestion.
         1. _____ digestion begins in the mouth and continues in the small intestine.
         2. in the liver the products of carbohydrate digestion are converted into _____ .
            a. glucose is the _____ carbohydrate source of energy for the body. This occurs because glucose is converted into ATP by mitochondria.
            b. glucose is the _____ source of energy utilized by the brain.
   4. lipids.
      a. _____ include fats and oils.
      b. one of the products of lipid breakdown is _____ _____. They are further broken down and stored until they are needed for energy.
   5. vitamins.
      a. vitamins serve as _____, substances that speed up the chemical reactions necessary for running the body.
      b. there are _____ categories of vitamins
         1. _____ soluble vitamins are the B vitamins and vitamin C.
            a. these vitamins are _____ in the urine.
            b. because these vitamins are not _____ they must be consumed almost daily.
         2. fat _____ vitamins (vitamins A, D, E, and K).
            a. these vitamins _____ be stored in the liver and a few other organs.
            b. because they can be stored, deficiencies are _____ to develop.
   6. minerals.
      a. unlike the previous four nutrients, _____ are not organic.
      b. the mineral needed in greatest quality is _____ (important in such actions as nerve conductions and muscle contractions and a major component of the skeleton and teeth).
C. Evolution of Nutritional requirements.

1. our nutritional needs have _____ with the types of foods that were available to our evolutionary ancestors.
   a. we have inherited the ability to digest _____ protein from our mammalian forebears.
   b. early _____ also evolved the ability to digest plant matter.
   c. our more immediate ape-like ancestors were primarily fruit-eaters and passed on their ability to process _____ to us.
   d. in addition, human needs for specific vitamins and minerals reflect ancestral _____ adaptations.
2. vitamin C and evolution.
   a. _____ _____ is crucial in metabolism and energy production.
   b. most animals are able to _____ vitamin C.
   c. early _____ probably were capable of synthesizing vitamin C.
      1. as monkeys evolved they ate more _____ and _____ and vitamin C was plentiful in their diet.
      2. at some point in primate evolution the ancestors of higher primates _____ the ability to produce vitamin C, probably through a genetic mutation.
         a. there would have been no disadvantage as long as there was sufficient vitamin C in the _____.
         b. actually, this may have been selectively advantageous because it would _____ the energy require to produce vitamin C.
   d. a deficiency of vitamin C can result in _____ .
      1. this disease was probably rare or absent in _____--_____ populations.
      2. scurvy was _____ a problem in the past except in extreme northern areas where, during the winter, there were not fresh fruits and vegetables.
      3. essential amino acids.
         a. there are _____ amino acids that are required for growth and maintenance.
         b. humans lack the ability to synthesize _____ of the amino acids.
            1. these amino acids must be obtained from the _____.
            2. these eight amino acids are referred to as _____ amino acids.

3. the amounts of each of the essential amino acids parallel the amounts present in animal _____. suggesting that food from animal sources may have

been an important component of ancestral hominid diets.

    a. _____ consumption is expensive, both ecologically and economically.

    b. most modern populations meet their protein needs by _____ a variety of vegetables.

4. the traditional methods for processing corn into tortillas or hominy provide an example of the interaction of biology and culture in meeting nutritional requirements.

    a. wherever corn is a major component of the diet there is often a high incidence of the nutritional disease _____. This disease is due to a deficiency of niacin (vitamin B3).

    b. pellagra is not common in the Americas where lime or ashes are _____ to the cornmeal. These additives appear to increase the availability of niacin in the corn.

5. despite the fact that humans use cultural responses to adapt to environmental challenges, we still appear to be _____ by our evolved nutritional needs.

    a. our evolution reflects a food base that includes great _____ .

D. Diets of Humans Before Agriculture.

1. the pre-agricultural diet was high in protein, but low in _____.

    a. the diet was high in complex _____, including fiber.

    b. the diet was low in salt and high in calcium.

2. many of our biological and behavioral characteristics contributed to our ancestors' adaptation, but may be _____ in our modern industrialized societies. An example of this is our ability to store _____.

    a. this was an advantage in the past when food availability alternated between abundance and _____.

    b. today there is a relative _____ of foods in western nations. The formerly positive ability to store extra fat has now turned into a liability which leads to degenerative diseases..

3. the _____ food base brought upon by agriculture is not the only factor that has caused problems for human health.

a. the human population began to increase when people began to live in permanent settlements.

    1. living in permanent settlements permitted _____ children to be born

    2. an increase in children can not happen in hunting and gathering societies because the group constantly moves. One child every 4-to-6 years is the rule. (Because the group moves vast distances, small children must be carried much of the time and carrying more than one is difficult for the parents).

b. we now see billions of people completing for cereal _____ and the attendant health problems that this narrow food base has generated.

E. Undernutrition and Malnutrition.

    1. undernutrition means an _____ quantity of food.

      a. i.e., not enough _____ are consumed to support normal health.

      b. it is estimated that between _____ and _____ percent of the world's population is undernourished.

    2. malnutrition refers to an inadequate amount of some _____ _____ in the diet.

      a. in underdeveloped countries, _____ malnutrition is the most common type of malnutrition.

        1. _____ is one type of protein malnutrition, characterized by a "swollen belly."

      b. malnutrition greatly affects reproduction and infant survival.

        1. _____ mothers have more difficulties in producing healthy and surviving children.

        2. children born of malnourished mothers are smaller and behind in most aspects of _____ _____.

          a. _____ processes often slow down greatly when post-natal environment insults are severe.

          b. post-natal growth in children of malnourished mothers.

            1. _____--____ growth can make up some of the deficit in these children.

            2. however, there are _____ periods when certain tissues grow very rapidly.

            3. if a severe interruption occurs during one of these periods, the individual may _____ catch up completely.

III. OTHER FACTORS INFLUENCING GROWTH AND DEVELOPMENT.

A. Genetics.

    1. even though environmental factors can influence growth and development, an individual still can not exceed their _____ _____.

        a. _____ sets the underlying limitations and potentials for growth and development.

        b. the _____ determines how the body grows within the genetic parameters.

    2. studies of _____ have yielded information regarding the effects of genes and the environment on growth.

        a. monozygotic twins.

            1. _____ twins come from the union of a single sperm and a single ovum.

            2. they share _____ percent of their genes.

        b. dizygotic twins.

            1. _____ twins are the result of the fertilization of two separate ova by two different sperm.

            2. dizygotic twins share _____ percent of their genes.

        c. if monozygotic twins are raised apart, yet have, for example, the same stature, we can conclude that genes are the _____ determinant of that trait.

            1. twin studies have revealed that _____ is under strong genetic control.

            2. _____, on the other hand, appears to be more strongly influence by diet and environment than by the genes.

B. Hormones.

    1. one of the primary ways by which genes have an effect on growth and development is by their production of _____.

        a. hormones are substances produced in one cell that have an effect on

    2. the hypothalamus is a region of the brain that is involved with _____hormonal action.

        a. the hypothalamus secretes its own hormones which either _____ or stimulate release of hormones in other cells.

    3. _____ is produced by the thyroid gland.

        a. thyroxine _____ metabolism and is involved with heat production.

  b. when thyroxine levels in the blood fall too _____ for normal metabolism a series of events occur.

    1. the brain detects this and sends a message to the _____ to release thyrotropin-releasing hormone (TRH).

    2. TRH goes to the anterior pituitary where it stimulates the _____ of thyroid-stimulating hormone (TSH).

    3. TSH goes to the thyroid and stimulates the release of _____.

    4. when the brain detects an increase in the circulating levels of thyroxine it sends signals to _____ further release of TRH, and by this, TSH.

    5. this homeostatic process works by a negative feedback loop in which hormone levels are kept within a constant level and any great change is inhibited.

C. Environmental Factors

  1. as we have seen in chapter 6, environmental factors such as altitude and climate have effects on _____ and _____.

  2. perhaps the primary influence of such external factors comes from their effects on _____.

    a. infant birth weight is _____ at high altitude, regardless of such factors as nutrition, smoking, or socioeconomic status.

    b. in general, cold climate populations tend to be _____ and have longer trunks and shorter appendages than populations in tropical areas.

    c. exposure to _____ also appears to have an affect on growth, probably because of its effects on melatonin and vitamin D synthesis.

IV. **THE HUMAN LIFE CYCLE.**

A. Humans have five phases to their _____ _____.

  1. _____ begins with conception and ends with birth.

  2. _____ is the period in which the baby nurses.

  3. _____ (juvenile phase) is the period from weaning to puberty.

  4. _____ is the period from puberty to the end of growth.

  5. _____ is marked by the completion of growth.

  6. an extra period in females is _____, recognized as one year after the last menstrual cycle.

B. Human life cycles also have the added complexity in that they occur in _____ contexts.

1. collective and individual attitudes toward these life cycle transitions have an effect on _____ and _____.

C. Pregnancy, Birth and Infancy
   1. the biology of conception and pregnancy.
      a. a sperm _____ an egg and this union produces a zygote.
      b. the _____ travels through the fallopian (uterine) tube to become implanted in the wall of the uterus.
      c. the embryo becomes a fetus and it develops until it is _____ enough to survive outside the womb.
      d. birth occurs.
   2. food restrictions and food aversions.
      a. almost every culture imposes dietary _____ on pregnant women.
      b. many of these food restrictions appear to keep women from ingesting _____(that plants contain for defensive purposes) that could harm the fetus.
      c. woman often find certain foods nauseating during pregnancy and will not eat those foods. This is called _____ _____.
         1. such foods as coffee, alcohol and other bitter substances contain toxins and other substances that may _____ the developing embryo.
         2. food aversions may also have _____ to protect the embryo and fetus from toxins.

3. Brain Growth
   a. an undeveloped brain may also adaptive for other reasons.
      1. most of our brain growth takes place in the presence of _____ stimuli.
      2. the language centers of the brain develop during the first _____ years of life.
         a. this is when the brain is undergoing _____ expansion.

4. Infancy.
   a. infancy is the period during which _____ takes place
   b. nursing typically lasts _____ years.
      (1) _____ years is the norm for the great apes.
      (2) four years is also the norm for women in _____ societies.
      (3) this, with other evidence, has led anthropologists to _____that four years was the norm in the evolutionary past.

c. nursing and breastmilk.

    (1) human milk is extremely low in fats and protein. This is _____ for a species in which mothers are seldom separated from their infants.

    (2) prolonged and frequent nursing suppresses _____, which helps maintain a four-year birth interval.

    (3) breastmilk also provides _____ that contribute to infant survival.

5. Childhood.

  a. humans have an unusually _____ childhood.

    (1) this reflects the importance of _____ for our species.

    (2) during childhood the brain is competing its _____.

    (3) childhood is when the child is also acquiring technical and social _____.

  b. humans may be unique in _____ food for children or juveniles.

  c. during childhood, besides the role of the mother, the roles of _____ and older_____ are also significant.

6. Adolescence.

  a. a number of biological events mark the transition from childhood to adolescence.

    (1) _____ body size and _____ in body shape.

    (2) development of _____ and _____ in boys.

    (3) development of _____ in girls.

    (4) _____ changes are the driving force behind these changes

    (5) _____ is a clear sign of puberty in girls and is usually the marker of the from childhood in cultures where this event is ritually celebrated

7. Adulthood.

  a.. pregnancy and child care occupy much of a woman's adult life in most cultures.

    (1) when adult women are not pregnant or nursing they have monthly _____, which have two phases.

      a. a woman who never becomes pregnant may have as many as _____ cycles between menarche and menopause.

      b. this high number of menstrual cycles probably _____ _____ occur before the advent of reliable contraceptives

      c. during the course of human evolution women may have had as few as _____menstrual cycles over the course of their lives.

    (2) in addition to caring for children, women in the majority of world cultures also participate in economic activities.

a. for women, _____ is a sign of entry into a new phases of the life cycle.

   (1) estrogen and progesterone production begin to _____ until ovulation and menstruation cease altogether.

   (2) throughout the course of human evolution, the majority of humans did not survive to age _____; therefore, few women lived much past menopause.

b. Why do human females have such a long nonreproductive period? There are several ideas.

   (1) child-rearing theory.
   -it takes children from 12 to 15 years to become _____.
   -it is suggested that women are biologically "programmed" to live 12 to 15 years beyond the _____ of their last children.

   (2) nonselection theory.
   -another suggestion is that menopause itself is not the subject of _____ _____.
   -menopause is an artifact of the extension of the human _____ _____.

8. Aging.
   a. "Old age" is an ambiguous concept.
      (1) it is often associated with physical ailments and decreased activity.
      (2) while "old age" tends to be regarded negatively in the United States, it means wealth, higher status, and new freedoms in other cultures.
   b. one of the major reasons that people are living longer today is because they are not dying from _____ _____.
   c. compared to most mammals, humans have a _____ life span.
      (1) maximum life span in humans is around _____ years (see Table 16-7).
      (2) while life span is unlikely to increase, human _____ _____at birth (the average length of life) has increased significantly in the last 100 years.

9. the final "phase" of the human life cycle is _____.

KEY TERMS
adolescent growth spurt: the period during adolescent
anovulatory: menstrual cycle during which ovulation does not occur.
beriberi: disease resulting from a dietary deficiency of thiamine (vitamin B_1).

catch-up period: a period of time during which a child who has experienced delayed growth because of malnutrition, undernutrition, or disease can increase in height to the point of his or her genetic potential.

cretinism: mental and growth retardation in infants resulting from iodine deficiency in the mother during pregnancy.

development: differentiation of cells into different types of tissues and their maturation.

diaphysis: the shaft of a long bone.

distal: towards the end of a structure.

essential amino acids: the eight (nine in infants) amino acids that must be obtained by humans from the diet.

fertility: production of offspring; distinguished from fecundity, which is the ability to produce children.

goiter: enlargement of the thyroid gland resulting from a dietary deficiency of iodine.

growth: increase in the mass or number of cells.

homeobox (HOX) genes: a group of genes found in vertebrates that plays a major role in the embryonic development of such structures as the vertebral column, limbs, and gut.

epiphysis (pl., -es): the end of a long bone.

lactation: production of milk in mammals.

malnutrition: a diet insufficient in quality (i. e., lacking some essential component) to support normal health.

ossification: process by which cartilage cells are broken down and replaced by bone cells.

pellagra: disease resulting from a dietary deficiency of niacin (Vitamin B3).

proximal: the part of a structure that is closest to the point at which the structure attaches to the body.

scurvy: a disease resulting from a dietary deficiency of vitamin C.

sexual dimorphism: differences in physical characteristics between males and females.

undernutrition: a diet insufficient in quantity (calories) to support normal health.

FILL-IN QUESTIONS

1. Growth refers to an _____ in the mass or number of cells.

2. The differentiation of cells into different types of tissues, and their maturation, is the process

   of _____.

3. The very pronounced increase in growth that occurs in humans at puberty is called the

   _____ _____ _____.

4. Males and females often differ in certain traits. For example, adult males tend to be larger, have beards and deeper voices. Adult females have breasts. These structural differences between the sexes is called _____ _____.

5. The brain of a newborn human infant is limited in size because of _____

   _____.

6. _____ has an impact on human growth at every stage of the life cycle.

7. A woman's own supply of eggs develop while she is ____ _____.

8. _____ are composed of amino acids.

9. The nutrient that is the main source of energy for the body is _____.

10. It is rare that a person develops a deficiency of any of the fat-soluble vitamins. This is because these vitamins can be _____.

11 Higher primates are not able to synthesize vitamin ___.

12. Most humans can **best** meet their protein needs from _____ products.

13. Insufficient calories, i.e. an inadequate amount of food, is called _____.

14. Insufficient protein in the diet would fall into the category of _____.

15. The question of whether "nature or nurture" contributes to certain traits is one that scientists have attempted to answer for centuries. One insight to this question, however, is by studying _____ _____ that have been raised in different environments.

16. The structure in the brain, sometimes referred to as a" control center" that is involved with integrating and controlling hormonal action is the _____.

17. The hormone that regulates metabolism is _____.

18. Children tend to grow rapidly in times of _____ sunlight concentration.

19. Monkeys, apes, and humans have an added life cycle phase not found in other mammals, namely the _____ period.

20. The _____ of early pregnancy may function to limit the intake of foods potentially harmful to the embryo at a critical stage of development.

21. The time between weaning and puberty in the human life cycle is _____.

22. Humans may be unique in providing food for _____.

23. The end of menstruation in women is called _____.

MULTIPLE CHOICE QUESTIONS

1. An example of a cultural factor that has a strong influence on growth is
   A. an individual's skill as an artisan.
   B. marriage status.
   C. socioeconomic status.
   D. religious beliefs that require an individual to eat a particular species of animal.

2. An increase in cell mass, such as when a body builder increases the size of individual muscle fibers (cells), is called
   A. neotoma.
   B. sarcoplasm.
   C. hyperplasia.
   D. hypertrophy.

3. At all ages, girls generally
   A. are taller than boys.
   B. grow later than boys.
   C. have more body fat than boys.
   D. have more hair than boys.

4. At birth the human brain is only _____ percent of its adult size.
   A. 25
   B. 50
   C. 90
   D. 95

5. enzymes are?
   A. carbohydrates.
   B. proteins.
   C. lipids.
   D. fats.

6. The only source of energy that is utilized by the brain is
   A. sucrose.
   B. sucrase.
   C. fructose.
   D. glucose.

7. Why are essential amino acids called "essential?"
   A. because these are the only proteins that the human body produces.
   B. because they must be produced when we are infants.
   C. because they must be obtained from the diet.
   D. because they can not be absorbed in the gut.

8. Scurvy is a disease that is the result of insufficient amounts of
   A. vitamin C.
   B. calcium.
   C. iodine.
   D. vitamin D.

9. Which of the following illustrates how cultural processes interact with biological processes to produce successful adaptations in obtaining the complete complement of proteins?
   A. the habit of consuming black-eyed peas with cornbread in the southern United States.
   B. the preference for eating cabbage with potatoes among some Irish populations.
   C. consumption of rice among Vietnamese populations.
   D. the avoidance of eating swine among Jewish and Muslim populations.

10. The disease pellagra, whose symptoms include skin lesions and gastrointestinal disturbances, is caused by a deficiency of niacin. It is common where corn is a major part of the diet. The exception is in the Americas. Why?
    A. vitamin C in the fruits of the Americas serves as a substitute for niacin.
    B. the habit of adding lime or ashes to cornmeal when cooking it increases the availability of niacin in the corn.
    C. the soil of the Americas is rich in niacin which is taken up through the roots of the corn plants. Soil in the rest of the world is poor in niacin.
    D. the people have adapted genetically to lower amounts of niacin in their diet.

11. Which of the following is **not** correct regarding the pre-agriculture human diet?
    A. high in protein.
    B. high in complex carbohydrates.
    C. high in fat.
    D. high in fiber.

12. A child born to a malnourished mother is normally smaller and behind in most aspects of their physical development. This can be made up in accelerated growth during
    A. the adolescent growth spurt.
    B. velocity growth curve.
    C. lactation.
    D. the catch-up period.

13. The life cycle phase that ends with birth is
    A. prenatal.
    B. infancy.
    C. weaning.
    D. childhood.

14. The language centers of the brain
    A. are difficult to find on the human brain.
    B. are well developed at birth.
    C. develop in the first three years of life.
    D. do not develop until puberty.

15. Human breastmilk
    A. has the same ratio of fat to protein as in all other mammals.
    B. has a nutrient content similar to that found in mammals that have to be separated from their infants while the mother forages.
    C. is almost identical to cow's milk.
    D. contains some of the mother's antibodies which help to protect the infant from some diseases.

16. There is some evidence that frequent nursing
    A. enables a woman to conceive more quickly after giving birth.
    B. suppresses ovulation.
    C. inhibits gestation.
    D. conserves the mother's energy.

17. A clear sign of puberty in girls is
    A. menarche.
    B. pregnancy.
    C. menopause.
    D. senescence.

18. Which of the following statements is **not** correct?
    A. a woman who never becomes pregnant may have as many as 400 menstrual cycles.
    B. during the course of human evolution, women may have had as few as 60 menstrual cycles during their lives.
    C. one theory regarding menopause is that menopause is simply not the subject of natural selection and is simply an artifact of the increase in human life span.
    D. if, in a particular month, the egg is not fertilized it is resorbed into the uterine lining and menstruation does not occur.

ANSWERS TO OUTLINE

I. FUNDAMENTALS OF GROWTH AND DEVELOPMENT
    A. different
        1. growth
            a. hyperplasia
            b. hypertrophy
        2. development
    B. 1. health
        2. a. infancy
            b.. adolescent growth spurt
        3. different
            a. sexual dimorphism
            b. larger
            c. body fat
        4. genetics
            a. Genetic
            b. potential
            c. higher
    C. 1. large
            a. greater
                1. 25
                2. 50
                3. five
                4. ten

        b.   exception
    2.   unusual
        a.   50
        b.   limit

II. NUTRITIONAL EFFECTS ON GROWTH AND DEVELOPMENT

A. Nutrition
B. 1. five
    2. amino acids
    3. energy
        a. 1. carbohydrate
            2. glucose
               a. primary
               b. only
    4. a. lipids
        b. fatty acids
    5. a. enzymes
        b. two
            1. water
               a. excreted
               b. stored
            2. soluble
               a. can
               b. slow
    6. a. minerals
        b. calcium
C. 1. coevolved
        a. animal
        b. primates
        c. fruit
        d. nutritional
    2. a. vitamin C
        b. synthesize (or manufacture or produce)
        c. primates
            1. leaves, fruit
            2. lost
               a. diet
               b. conserve
        d. scurvy
            1. pre-agricultural
            2. not
    3. a. 20
        b. eight
            1. foods
            2. essential
            3. protein
               a. meat
               b. combining

4. a. pellagra
   b. added
5. constrained
   a. variety
D. 1. fats
   a. carbohydrates
   2. maladaptive, fat
   a. scarcity
   b. abundance
   3. narrow
   a. 1. more
   b. grains
E. 1. inadequate
   a. calories
   b. 16, 63
   2. key element
   a. protein
      1. kwashiorkor
   b. 1. malnourished
      2. physical development
         a. growth
         b. 1. catch-up
            2. critical
            3. never

III. OTHER FACTORS INFLUENCING GROWTH AND DEVELOPMENT
A. 1. genetic potential
   a. genetics
   b. environment
   2. twins
   a. 1. monozygotic
      2. 100
   b. 1. dizygotic
      2. 50
   c. primary
      1. stature
      2. weight
B. 1. hormones
   a. another cell
   2. stimulating
   a. inhibit
   3. thyroxine
   a. regulates
   b. low
      1. hypothalamus
      2. release
      3. thyroxine
      4. inhibit

C. 1.   growth, development
    2.   nutrition
           a.   lower
           b.   heavier
           c.   sunlight

IV. THE HUMAN LIFE CYCLE.

A. life cycle
    1.   prenatal
    2.   infancy
    3.   childhood
    4.   adolescence
    5.   adulthood
    6.   menopause
B. cultural
    1.   growth, development
C. Pregnancy, Birth & Infancy
    1.   a.   fertilizes
           b.   zygote
           c.   mature
    2.   a.   restrictions
           b.   toxins
           c.   food aversion
                  1.   harm
                  2.   evolved
    3.   Brain growth
           a.   1.   environmental
                  2.   three
                         a.   Rapid
    4.   Infancy
           a. nursing
           b. four
                  1.   four or five
                  2.   foraging
                  3.   conclude
           c. nursing and breastmilk
                  1.   typical
                  2.   ovulation
                  3.   antibiotics
    5.   Childhood
           a.   long
                  1.   learning
                  2.   growth
                  3.   skills
           b.   providing
           c.   fathers, siblings
    6.   Adolescence
           a.   increased, change
           b.   testes, penes

        c.   breasts

        d.   hormonal

        e.   menarche

   7.   Adulthood

        (1) menstruations

            a.   400

            b.   did not

            c.   60

        (2) b.   menopause

            (1) decline

            (2) 50

           c.. (1) -independent

                    -birth

               (2) -natural selection

                    -life span

  8. Aging

       b.   infectious diseases

       c.   long

         (1) 120

         (2) life expectancy

  9. death

ANSWERS & REFERENCES TO FILL-IN QUESTIONS

1. increase, p. 348
2. development, p. 348
3. adolescence growth spurt, p. 348
4. sexual dimorphism, p. 348
5. narrow pelvis, p. 349
6. nutrition, p. 350
7. in utero, p. 350
8. proteins, p. 350
9. carbohydrates, p. 350
10. stored, p. 351
11. C, p. 351
12. Animal, p. 352
13. Undernutrition, p. 354
14. Malnutrition, p. 355
15. Monozygotic twins, p.356
16. Hypothalamus, p. 357
17. Thyroxine, p. 357
18. High, p. 358
19. Adolescent, p. 359
20. Nausea, 359
21. Childhood, p. 362
22. Children, p., 362
23. Menopause, p. 364

ANSWERS & REFERENCES TO MULTIPLE CHOICE QUESTIONS

1. C, p. 347
2. D, p. 348
3. C, p. 349
4. A, p. 349
5. B, p. 350
6. D, p. 350
7. C, p. 352
8. a, p. 351
9. A, p. 352
10. B, p. 353
11. C, p. 353
12. D, p. 355
13. A, p. 358
14. C, p. 360
15. D, p. 361
16. B, p. 361
17. A, p. 362
18. D, p. 363

CHAPTER 15

LESSONS FROM THE PAST, LESSONS FOR THE FUTURE

Learning Objectives

After reading this chapter you should be able to:
* Put the success of *Homo sapiens* in perspective relative to other life forms, pp. 369-370
* See both the adaptive and destructive aspects of culture, pp. 370-374
* Appreciate the magnitude of loss of biodiversity due to human practices, pp. 374-376
* Understand the urgent need for conservation and population control if we are to survive as a species, pp. 377-379
* Comprehend the dangers of global warming and depletion of the ozone layer, pp. 379-381
* Identify solutions and understand the difficulties of implementing them, pp. 381-383

Introduction

In previous chapters we have traced the diversity of evolutionary history of humanity. We have emphasized the importance of culture as an adaptive strategy for humanity. In this chapter we look at the problems that have developed as a result of our abuse of the environment, overexploitation of resources and overpopulation. We look at some of the damage that has been done to our environment and address the question, "Could the human species become extinct?" We end the chapter by emphasizing the need for immediate action and self-sacrifice.

Fill-in Outline

I. **INTRODUCTION**
   A. *Homo sapiens* are one of _____ million species known to science.
   B. All of these various species share the same _____ material.
   C. The future of _____ as we know it will be decided in the next few decades.
   D. The decisions we make in the next few years will be _____.

II. **HOW SUCCESSFUL ARE WE?**
   A. Human beings are part of a _____ of related biological species.
   B. Humans regard themselves as the _____ of the planet. Nature is seen to exist for the _____ of humankind.
   C. Currently there are more than _____ billion people on this planet.
   D. Bacteria could be viewed as the _____ form of life on the earth.
   E. There are around _____ species of mammal, less than _____ are primates.
   F. Over 750,000 _____ species have been identified.
   G. Some _____ and _____ have survived unchanged for 400 million years.

III. **HUMANS AND THE IMPACT OF CULTURE**
   A. For most of human history, the rate of culture change has been _____.
   B. Domestication of plants and animals occurred around _____ y.a. It is seen as one of the most _____ events in human history.

C. A more reliable food source gave rise to _____ growth.
D. Compared to humans living in early settlements, the health of _____ _____ was good.
E. There were probably only a few million early _____ worldwide.
F. Before people began living in permanent settlements _____ and _____ Europe were blanketed with forests and woodlands. By _____ y.a. many of England's forests had disappeared.
G. Humans began to exploit and depend on _____ _____ resources.
H. Only about _____ of the earth's original forests remain intact today.
I. The human experience would not have been possible without the _____ of woodlands and forests.
J. The Old Testament tells of _____ _____'s temple being built of cedar from Lebanon. This wood became so desirable that it resulted in the _____ of the mountains of Lebanon.
K. The 1990 typhoon and flood in Bangladesh killed over _____ people partly because of previously deforested areas.
L. The _____ had one of the largest and best-organized empires in the world around 500 years ago. Their success was due in great part to agricultural _____ and _____.

IV. THE LOSS OF BIODIVERSITY
A. The totality of all living things is _____.
B. In the last 570 million years there have been at least _____ mass extinctions. _____ of these altered the earth's ecosystems.
C. A third major extinction is _____ _____.
D. Massive _____ by early populations probably caused several large mammalian species to become extinct.
E. The Moa, a large flightless bird from New Zealand, was _____ once humans colonized the island.
F. Some early hunter-gatherers believed overhunting would _____ _____ so they were more conservative in hunting.
G. Early hunting techniques were frequently _____ with conservation.
  1. Game drives into blind canyons, over cliffs or into arroyos led to unavoidable _____.
  2. Repeated _____ _____ over many centuries probably contributed to the extinction of many large-bodied species in the New World.
H. Today, species are disappearing at an _____ rate. _____ _____ is the primary cause of extinction today. The _____ human population is the primary cause of habitat destruction.
I. It is estimated that over _____ of all plants and animals on earth live in rain forests.
J. By the year _____ half of the world's remaining rain forests will be gone.

V. COULD THE HUMAN SPECIES BECOME EXTINCT?
A. The obvious answer is _____.
B. We are the only species with the ability to envision our possible _____. We are the only species with the _____ to do anything about it.

C. The only way we will survive is through _____ and _____ means.
D. The process of natural selection acts on an _____'s ability to _____.
E. By _____ an individual's reproductive success _____ occurs.
F. We are part of an integrated _____ system.
G. All _____ _____ can become extinct.
H. Australopithecines endured for at least _____ million years but in the end they _____.

VI. THE PRESENT CRISIS: OUR CULTURAL HERITAGE?
A. Few people are aware of how _____ our current environmental problems are.
B. Overpopulation
   1. The number one problem facing humanity is _____ growth.
   2. _____ people die in childhood.
   3. If unchecked the human population will increase _____.
   4. The length of time for the population to double is called _____ _____.
   5. In the 37 years from 1950 to 1987 the world's population doubled from _____ to _____.
   6. The current population of the world is _____.
   7. Every year we add _____ to _____ million people. That averages out to around _____ every day.
   8. The majority of the population explosion occurs in _____ countries.
   9. The United Nations International Conference on Population and Development has a goal to _____ the world's population by _____.
   10. In _____ nations the birth rate ha declined since 1955.
   11. Approximately one-half of the people living in the developing world are under the age of _____. They have not yet _____.
   12. Is there enough _____ or _____ to support the increasing demands for housing, cultivation and grazing?

VII. THE GREENHOUSE EFFECT AND GLOBAL WARMING
A. _____ _____ is released into the atmosphere by the burning of fossil fuels. This _____ heat.
B. Greenhouse gases, such as methane and _____ (CFCs), are expected to cause "_____ _____."
C. Trees absorb _____ _____ and _____ reduces the number of trees.
   1. Burning trees _____ the carbon dioxide contained in the trees into the atmosphere.
   2. It is estimated that 20% of all carbon dioxide emissions are from the burning of the _____ _____ _____.
D. If global warming continues and the annual temperature rises by _____ degrees, it could result in the melting of the _____ _____.

VIII. DEPLETION OF THE OZONE LAYER
    A. The _____ layer is a form of oxygen that filters out _____
        _____.

    B. There is a hole in the ozone layer above _____, caused primarily by
        _____'s found in propellants, _____, _____ and components
        of _____.

    C. _____ _____ rates will increase as a result of the ozone depletion.

IX. LOOKING FOR SOLUTIONS
    A. Auto manufacturers are looking for _____-_____ automobiles.

    B. In 1987 an international _____ was signed to protect the ozone layer.

    C. _____ has become the environment in which we live, and it has become
        _____.

    D. Any assessment of the future offers little _____.

    E. In 30 years the world's population will be over _____.

    F. In order to _____ current trends, every individual will have to make
        _____.

    G. The average American uses _____ times the resources that an individual
        from Bangladesh uses.

    H. The United States produces _____ to _____ percent of all carbon dioxide
        emissions into the atmosphere.

    I. Many of today's problems are the fault of the _____ _____.

    J. Developed nations need to get by with fewer _____.

    K. _____ sacrifice is required or we are _____.

KEY TERMS

anthropocentric: being concerned with humans rather than the world's biodiversity. Human beings seem to think that they are the most important life form and everything else (plants and animals) are here for their benefit or use.

arable: land that is fit for cultivation by plowing or tilling or that has already been cultivated by plowing or tilling.

DNA: deoxyribonucleic acid is the double-stranded molecule that contains the genetic code. It is the main component of chromosomes.

global warming: the increase in the mean annual temperature worldwide due to the "greenhouse effect."

greenhouse effect: heat is trapped in the air with the increase of carbon dioxide and other "greenhouse gases" such as methane and chlorofluorocarbons (CFCs) being released into the atmosphere. With the increase of trapped heat the result could be "global warming" which could have serious environmental effects.

Holocene: the most present epoch of the Cenozoic Era. The Holocene began around 10 k.y.a.

Mesolithic: a transitional period of the Stone Age between the Paleolithic and the Neolithic in which humans exploited smaller animals, increased their variety of tools and became less nomadic. The dates vary for different geographic regions depending upon when the Neolithic began in that area.

Neolithic: the period after the Mesolithic when humans began domesticating plants and animals and living in permanent settlements. The dates vary for different geographic regions depending upon when domestication occurred.

non-renewable resources: natural resources such as oil and coal (fossil fuels) of which there is a finite amount. Other natural resources can become non-renewable if they are over-used and not allowed to replenish themselves. Trees, forests, plants and water are examples of natural resources that due to over-exploitation are becoming non-renewable.

ozone layer: a form of oxygen surrounding the earth that filters out ultraviolet radiation.

sedentism: staying in one place.

Fill-In Questions

1. Human beings have become the dominant species on the planet through _____ innovation and ever-expanding _____.

2. To explain human behavior it is important to consider the interplay between _____ and _____.

3. Since the domestication of plants and animals, human beings have altered the face of the planet. In the process we have shaped the _____ of ourselves as well as thousands of other species.

4. Because of the dramatic changes human beings have made to the planet the future of life as we know it will be decided in the next few _____.

5. From a biological perspective, human beings are _____.

6. Since all life forms share the same basic genetic foundation, it is reasonably argued that life evolved from a _____ _____.

7. Even though human beings are mammals, specifically primates, and share the same basic genetic foundation as other life forms, we have the selfish and arrogant idea that we are the _____ of the planet.

8. In Western cultures, the idea of human beings having dominion over other animals is reinforced in the _____ _____.

9. The idea of human superiority and that nature is here for the betterment of humanity is extremely _____.

10. Each individual on earth is comprised of approximately ____ _____ cells.

11. The vast majority of _____ on the planet are bacteria.

12. Three possible ways to measure the evolutionary success of life forms are:
    1) sheer numbers of the _____ among reproducing organisms.
    2) the number of _____ (as an indicator of biological diversity), and
    3) species _____.

13. In the first method of measuring species success _____ would be the winner.

14. In the second method of measuring species success _____ would be the winner.

15. In the third method of measuring species success _____ and _____ could be the winners.
16. Cultural innovations that enabled early *Homo sapiens* to expand and exploit previously unavailable areas include stone _____, temporary _____, _____ products and _____.
17. For most of human history we had a comfortable relationship with our adaptive strategy (culture) because our technology was _____.
18. Our comfortable relationship with culture and technology became complicated and less comfortable with an _____ lifestyle.
19. Humans first began a more sedentary lifestyle around _____ years ago.
20. With sedentism people could keep _____ animals and could _____ vegetable crops. For the first time people had food supplies that were _____ and _____.
21. One of the most significant events in human history is the _____ of plants and animals.
22. To accommodate the demands of a more reliable food source in the form of domesticated plants and animals, people had to become progressively more _____.
23. One of the drawbacks to a settled lifestyle as opposed to the nomadic lifestyle of hunter-gatherers is the increased exposure to _____ _____.
24. Infectious disease is a powerful _____ force among humans.
25. When people began living in _____ settlements their impact on the environment increased.
26. People began to live in permanent settlements during the _____.
27. In Britian today the _____ and _____ are the result of the deforestation that began over _____ years ago.
28. In Britian, deforestation _____ around 5,000 years ago when people began _____.
29. As people became more sedentary they began to _____ and _____ on non-renewable resources.
30. Normally, forests would be considered renewable resources. Unfortunately, in many areas, they were not allowed the opportunity to _____.
31. In areas where forests were not given enough time for regrowth _____ erosion occurred, along with overgrazing and overcultivation which led to further _____ erosion. In these areas trees became a _____ resource.
32. To accommodate a sedentary lifestyle and the various cultural requirements that accompany it, human beings have "waged war" on _____.
33. _____ ago much of the earth's original forests were cleared so that today only one-fifth of its original forests remain.
34. Some of the reasons behind cutting trees down include clearing land for _____ and grazing, _____ and _____.
35. Over 3,000 years ago the _____ of Lebanon were highly valued. As a result they only exist now in small patches.

36. The _____ in the Middle East and the _____ _____ in Africa are the result of overgrazing in the past.
37. Over 100,000 people were killed in Bangladesh in 1990 because of severe _____ which, in part, was due to _____ in the Himalayas of northern India.
38. By reconstructing ancient cultures, archaeologists have found examples of things humans have done _____ as well as some positive _____ techniques like the Inca terracing and irrigation systems in South America.
39. Archaeologist Craig Erickson introduced some of the ancient Incan techniques to modern farmers resulting in improved _____ yields, less environmental _____ and it cost _____ than before.
40. Biodiversity refers to species, individuals, ecosystems and the various _____ combinations that are present.
41. We are currently losing _____. In fact, we are now in the midst of the third major _____ that has occurred in the last 570 million years.
42. The major extinction we are now experiencing is due to the activities of _____.
43. Many scientists believe that toward the end of the Pleistocene (around 10,000 years ago) many _____ mammalian species were overhunted. At least 57 mammalian species became extinct including _____, _____, giant ground _____, _____-_____ cat, some large _____ and numerous _____ (grazing animals).
44. Humans were firmly established in the New World by _____ y.a.
45. After humans arrived in _____ the Moa was exterminated.
46. On Madagascar, ____ species of lemur became extinct after humans settled there.
47. Hunter-gatherers had differing views on conservation of _____ species.
48. Some hunter-gatherers were afraid to overhunt for fear their _____ would become angry. Others would kill large numbers but allow time for them to _____ their numbers.
49. Some of the early hunting techniques were particularly wasteful of animals. The game drives included stampeding animals into blind _____ or human-made _____ or over _____.
50. 10,000 years ago at Olsen-Chubbuck in Colorado 190 _____ were killed. Of those _____ complete skeletons were found that had been untouched.
51. The primary cause of the mass extinction of species we see today is _____ _____.
52. The growing human population puts a tremendous strain on the environment in its need for _____ materials, _____, _____ land and living areas.
53. It is estimated that over half of all plants and animals on earth live in the _____ _____.
54. If destruction of the rain forest continues at its present rate, by the year 2022 _____ of the world's existing rain forest will be gone.
55. Can the human species become extinct? _____
56. An individual organism's ability to reproduce is a measure of their success in the process of _____ _____.
57. In humans the individual's reproductive success has resulted in _____.

58. As the human population continues to increase, more crops, pasture and shelter are needed placing tremendous demands on _____.
59. The human population _____ from 1950 to 1987.
60. At present, the world's population is _____ billion.
61. The population explosion is worse among _____ nations.
62. India adds _____ people per month to their population.
63. Approximately _____ of the people in developing nations are under 15 years old and have yet to _____.
64. Carbon dioxide, methane and chlorofluorocarbons (CFCs) are examples of _____ "gases."
65. Scientists fear that the greenhouse effect will cause the global temperature to rise which could cause the melting of the polar caps and result in _____, _____ of agricultural land, changes in _____ patterns and _____ of plants and animals.
66. The ozone layer is a form of _____ that _____ out ultraviolet radiation from the sun. Ultraviolet radiation causes _____ cancers.
67. In an attempt to limit the damage to the environment, alternate fuels are being explored. For cars _____ and _____ are being experimented with.
68. When looking at the future, it is difficult to be optimistic. We have poor _____ quality, depletion of the _____ layer, possible _____ effect and reduced amounts of _____ land.
69. In order to save our environment, people are going to have to _____ now. In developing nations family planning is needed immediately. In developed nations, particularly the U.S., we must alter our consumption and get by with fewer _____.

Multiple Choice Questions

1. The 1.4 million species known to science
   A. have undergone different evolutionary processes
   B. are the result of the same basic evolutionary processes
   C. share the same DNA material
   D. both B & C

2. The successful development of the species *Homo sapiens* is due to
   A. our superior physical stamina
   B. bipedalism
   C. culture
   D. sedentism

3. According to the text, the success of a life form can be measured by
   A. the number of cells contributed to the planet
   B. the number of species
   C. species longevity
   D. All of the above

4. *Homo sapiens* have been on earth
   A. for at least 200,000 years
   B. perhaps as long as 400,000 years
   C. for around 100,000 years
   D. both A & B

5. The adaptive strategy of humans has always been
   A. fight or flight
   B. culture
   C. aggression
   D. expansion

6. Which of the following is NOT something that allowed humans to expand from the tropics into previously unavailable areas?
   A. gathering
   B. temporary shelters
   C. fire
   D. tools

7. A sedentary lifestyle enabled early humans to
   A. hunt
   B. have domesticated animals
   C. trade
   D. build temporary shelters

8. _____ provided early humans with an abundant and reliable food source.
   A. agriculture
   B. fishing
   C. hunting
   D. gathering

9. Early agriculturalists
   A. were subject to infectious disease
   B. were in better health than hunter-gatherers
   C. were first seen around 10,000 years ago
   D. both A & C

10. The moorlands and peat bogs of Britian
    A. provided a safe place away from animals for early agriculturalists
    B. were the site of the first settlements
    C. are the result of deforestation
    D. were rich in nutrients for early agriculturalists

11. Since adopting a sedentary lifestyle, human beings have usually
    A. been conscious of the delicate balance in nature
    B. exploited nonrenewable resources
    C. over-exploited renewable resources to the point that they have
        become nonrenewable
    D. Both B & C

12. Probably the thing in nature that has suffered the most from human sedentism
    would be the
    A. ocean
    B. trees
    C. air
    D. earth (land)

13. Examples of deforestation given in the book that took place thousands of years
    ago include all BUT which of the following?
    A. the Middle Eastern desert
    B. the Saharan Desert in Africa
    C. the Mojave Desert
    D. Lebanon

14. Which of the following is one of the "innovative techniques" employed by the Inca
    empire 500 years ago?
    A. irrigation
    B. tilling
    C. large amounts of fertilizer
    D. a make-shift tractor

15. In the past 570 million years there have been _____ mass extinctions.
    A. 4
    B. 10
    C. 15
    D. 21

16. The mass extinction that is occurring now
    A. follows a similar pattern to the previous ones
    B. has been caused by the continuous shifting of the continents
    C. is due to the activities of human beings
    D. is the result of subtle climatic shifts (the beginning of the greenhouse effect)

17. Overhunting
    A. is a contemporary problem
    B. began at the end of the Pleistocene (around 10,000 years ago)
    C. is not as bad as people say it is
    D. is the result of better technology

18. For the hunter-gatherers for whom we have evidence, it seems that
    A. they were uniform in their cultural practices that balanced nature with humanity.
    B. they were uniform in their lack of concern for nature.
    C. nature was there to serve them.
    D. they had differing views regarding conservation

19. "Game drives" refers to
    A. pastoralists moving their herds
    B. using the first animals as transportation
    C. the early practice of stampeding animals into canyons or over cliffs
    D. the movement among contemporary conservationists to save species

20. It is estimated that over ½ of all plants and animals on earth live in
    A. the rain forest
    B. the African plains
    C. the Rocky Mountains
    D. the Himalayas

21. The only way that human beings will survive is
    A. to continue as we are
    B. through cultural/technological means
    C. if a portion of the population is eliminated
    D. through biological means

22. The problem that is linked to all other life forms and is therefore the most important problem facing human beings is
    A. population increase
    B. competition for resources
    C. polluted air
    D. loss of biodiversity

23. It is estimated that around 10,000 years ago the population of the world was
    A. 5 million
    B. 10 million
    C. 20 million
    D. 25 million

24. In the 37 years from 1950 to 1987 the population of the world went from
    A. 1 billion to 2 billion
    B. 800 million to 1 billion
    C. 2 billion to 4 billion
    D. 4 billion to 5 billion

25. The population of the world today is around
    A. 2 billion
    B. 3 billion
    C. 6 billion
    D. 10 billion

26. How many children are born every day in Latin America?
    A. 10,000
    B. 36,000
    C. 20,000
    D. 54,000

27. The greenhouse effect
    A. is overdramatized
    B. is caused by gases that trap heat
    C. could cause dramatic climatic changes
    D. both B & C

28. One of the primary causes of carbon dioxide emissions is
    A. automobile exhaust
    B. burning of the Amazon rainforest
    C. industry
    D. disposable diapers

29. The CFCs that have led to the hole in the ozone layer over Antarctica were caused primarily by
    A. aerosol propellants
    B. solvents
    C. components of styrofoam products
    D. all of the above

30. Solutions to our environmental problems would
    A. have to be immediate
    B. require sacrifice on everybody's part, particularly the industrialized West
    C. include family planning, particularly in developing nations
    D. all of the above

Answers to Fill-In Outline

I. **INTRODUCTION**
    A. 1.4
    B. DNA
    C. life
    D. irrevocable

II. **HOW SUCCESSFUL ARE WE?**
    A. continuum

B. masters, betterment
C. 6
D. dominant
E. 4,000, 200
F. insect
G. sharks, turtles

III. HUMANS AND THE IMPACT OF CULTURE
A. slow
B. 10,000, significant
C. population
D. hunter-gatherers
E. agriculturalists
F. Britian, continental, 2,500
G. non-renewable
H. one-fifth
I. exploitation
J. King Solomon, deforestation
K. 100,000
L. Incas, terracing, irrigation

IV. THE LOSS OF BIODIVERSITY
A. biodiversity
B. 15, 2
C. occurring now
D. overhunting
E. exterminated
F. anger deities
G. incompatible
   1. waste
   2. game drives
H. unprecedented, habitat reduction, burgeoning
I. half
J. 2022

V. COULD THE HUMAN SPECIES BECOME EXTINCT?
A. yes
B. fate, capacity
C. cultural/technological
D. individual, reproduce
E. maximizing, overpopulation
F. ecological
G. life forms
H. 1.5 vanished

VI. THE PRESENT CRISIS: OUR CULTURAL HERITAGE?
A. serious
B. overpopulation
   1. population
   2. fewer

3. exponentially
4. doubling time
5. 2 billion, 4 billion
6. 6 billion
7. 90, 95, 250,000 (quarter million)
8. developing
   a. India
   b. Latin America
9. contain, 2015
10. developing
11. 15, reproduced
12. land, water

VII. THE GREENHOUSE EFFECT AND GLOBAL WARMING
A. carbon dioxide, traps
B. chlorofluorocarbons, global warming
C. carbon dioxide, deforestation
   1. releases
   2. Amazon rainforest
D. 1 to 2, polarcaps

VIII. DEPLETION OF THE OZONE LAYER
A. ozone, ultraviolet radiation
B. Antarctica, CFC, aerosol, solvents, styrofoam
C. skin cancer

IX. LOOKING FOR SOLUTIONS
A. fuel-efficient
B. international agreement
C. culture, hostile
D. optimism
E. 8 billion
F. reverse, sacrifices
G. 400
H. 25-30
I. industrialized West
J. resources
K. personal, doomed

ANSWERS & REFERENCES TO FILL-IN QUESTIONS

9. anthropocentric, p. 370
10. 20 trillion, p. 370
11. cells, p. 370
12. 1) competition, 2) species, 3) longevity, p. 370
13. bacteria, p. 370
14. insects, p. 370
15. sharks, turtles, p. 370
16. tools, shelters, animals, fire, p. 370
17. simple, p. 370
18. agricultural, p. 370
19. 15,000, p. 371
20. domestic, grow, abundant, reliable, p. 371
21. domestication, p. 371
22. sedentary, p. 371
23. infectious disease, p. 371
24. selective, p. 371
25. permanent, p. 371
26. Neolithic, p. 371
27. moorlands, peat bogs, 5,000, p. 371
28. accelerated, farming, p. 371
29. exploit, depend, p. 372
30. regrow, p. 372
31. soil, soil, non-renewable, p. 372
32. trees, p. 372
33. centuries, p. 372
34. cultivation, firewood, lumber, p. 373
35. cedars, p. 373
36. deserts, Saharan Desert, p. 373
37. flooding deforestation, p. 373
38. wrong, innovative, p. 374
39. crop, damage, less, p. 374
40. genetic, p. 374
41. biodiversity, extinction, p. 374
42. *Homo sapiens*, p. 374
43. large, mammoth, mastodon, sloth, saber-toothed, rodents, ungulates, p. 374
44. 12,000, p. 375
45. New Zealand, p. 375
46. 14, p. 375
47. prey, p. 375
48. dieties, replenish, p. 375
49. canyons, corrals, cliffs, p. 375
50. bison, 20, p. 375
51. habitat reduction, p. 376
52. building, grazing, agricultural, p. 376
53. rain forest, p. 376
54. half, p. 376

55. yes, p. 377
56. natural selection, p. 377
57. overpopulation, p. 377
58. land, p. 378
59. doubled, p. 378
60. 6, p. 378
61. developing, p. 378
62. 1 million, p. 378
63. half, reproduce, p. 379
64. greenhouse, p. 380
65. flooding, loss, weather, extinction, p. 380
66. oxygen, filters, skin, p. 381
67. alcohol, electricity, p. 381
68. air, ozone, greenhouse, arable, p. 382
69. sacrifice, resources, p. 382

ANSWERS & REFERENCES TO MULTIPLE CHOICE QUESTIONS

1. D, p. 369
2. C, p. 369
3. D, p. 370
4. D, p. 370
5. B, p. 370
6. A, p. 370
7. B, p. 371
8. A, p. 371
9. D, p. 371
10. C, p. 371
11. D, p. 372
12. B, p. 372
13. C, p. 373
14. A, p. 374
15. C, p. 374
16. C, p. 374
17. B, p. 374
18. D, p. 375
19. C, p. 375
20. A, p. 376
21. B, p. 377
22. A, p. 378
23. A, p. 378
24. C, p. 378
25. D, p. 378
26. B, p. 378
27. D, p. 380
28. B, p. 380

29. D, p. 381
30. D, p. 381

Notes